Trafficking in humans

Trafficking in humans: Social, cultural and political dimensions

Edited by Sally Cameron and Edward Newman

**United Nations
University Press**

TOKYO · NEW YORK · PARIS

The views expressed in this publication are those of the authors and do not necessarily reflect the views of the United Nations University.

United Nations University Press
United Nations University, 53-70, Jingumae 5-chome,
Shibuya-ku, Tokyo 150-8925, Japan
Tel: +81-3-5467-1212   Fax: +81-3-3406-7345
E-mail: sales@hq.unu.edu   general enquiries: press@hq.unu.edu
http://www.unu.edu

United Nations University Office at the United Nations, New York
2 United Nations Plaza, Room DC2-2062, New York, NY 10017, USA
Tel: +1-212-963-6387   Fax: +1-212-371-9454
E-mail: unuona@ony.unu.edu

United Nations University Press is the publishing division of the United Nations University.

Cover design by Joyce C. Weston

Cover photograph by Teun Voeten / Panos Pictures

Printed in the United States of America

ISBN 978-92-808-1146-9

Library of Congress Cataloging-in-Publication Data
Trafficking in humans : social, cultural and political dimensions / edited by Sally Cameron and Edward Newman.
   p.   cm.
 Includes bibliographical references and index.
 ISBN 978-9280811469 (pbk.)
 1. Human trafficking. 2. Transnational crime. I. Cameron, Sally. II. Newman, Edward, 1970–
HQ281.T717   2008
364.15—dc22   2007037004

Contents

Tables and figures

Contributors

Maruja M. B. Asis is director of research and publications at the Scalabrini Migration Center in Manila, the Philippines.

Sally Cameron works as a consultant on gender and governance issues, based in Sydney, Australia, and is a former policy analyst at the Australian Federation of AIDS Organisations.

Kinsey Alden Dinan is a consultant based in New York, and a research associate at Colombia University.

Ratna Kapur is a director of the Centre for Feminist Legal Research in New Delhi.

Helga Konrad is an international consultant on combating human trafficking and former OSCE (Organization for Security and Cooperation in Europe) special representative on trafficking in human beings.

Edward Newman is a senior lecturer in the Department of Political Science and International Studies at the University of Birmingham, UK. Prior to that, he was director of studies on Conflict and Security in the Peace and Governance Programme of the United Nations University.

Renu Rajbhandari is the chairperson of the Women's Rehabilitation Centre (WOREC), Nepal.

Gabriela Rodríguez Pizarro is a representative of IOM Chile, and former UN special rapporteur for human rights of migrants (1999–2005).

Gulnara Shahinian is on the board of trustees of the UN Voluntary Trust Fund of Contemporary Forms of Slavery, and a board member and founder of the NGO Democracy Today.

Phil Williams is director of the University of Pittsburgh's Ridgway Center for International Security Studies and professor at the Graduate School of Public and International Affairs.

Acknowledgements

This volume is the principal result of a project on human trafficking organized by the Peace and Governance Programme of the United Nations University. The editors would like to express their thanks to the contributors for their commitment and perseverance during a rather protracted publication process. In addition, we would like to thank Jyoti Sanghera, who gave a great deal of support to the project, including a valuable input into the research workshop held in Geneva and help in identifying participants.

Acronyms

ABACEELI	American Bar Association Central and Eastern European Law Initiative
AFL-CIO	American Federation of Labor-Congress of Industrial Organizations
ARIAT	Asian Regional Initiative against Trafficking
BKA	Bundes-Kriminalamt
CAHTEH	Council of Europe Ad Hoc Committee on Actions against Trafficking in Humans
CATW	Coalition against Trafficking in Women
CEDAW	Convention on the Elimination of All Forms of Discrimination against Women
CIS	Commonwealth of Independent States
DRC	Democratic Republic of Congo
ECPAT	End Child Prostitution in Asian Tourism
ESCAP	Economic and Social Council for Asia and the Pacific
EU	European Union
FSU	former Soviet Union
GAATW	Global Alliance against Traffic in Women
HDI	Human Development Index
IDP	internally displaced person
ILO	International Labour Organization
IMADR	International Movement against All Forms of Discrimination and Racism
IMF	International Monetary Fund
IOM	International Organization for Migration
IPEC	International Programme on the Elimination of Child Labour

IPTF	International Police Task Force (Bosnia)
KFOR	Kosovo Force
MCW	Migrant Workers Convention
NATO	North Atlantic Treaty Organization
NGO	non-governmental organization
NIS	newly independent states
OECD	Organisation for Economic Co-operation and Development
OPA	overseas performing artist
OSCE	Organization for Security and Cooperation in Europe
RICO	racketeering-influenced corrupt organization
SAARC	South Asian Alliance for Regional Cooperation
STV	Foundation against Trafficking in Women (Netherlands)
UMCOR	United Methodist Committee on Relief
UNDP	UN Development Programme
UNESCO	UN Economic, Social and Cultural Organization
UNHCR	Office of the UN High Commissioner for Refugees
UNICEF	UN Children's Fund
UNIFEM	United Nations Development Fund for Women
WOREC	Women's Rehabilitation Centre (Nepal)

1

Introduction: Understanding human trafficking

Edward Newman and Sally Cameron

This volume aims to deepen understanding of the social, economic and political contexts of human trafficking: the recruitment and transportation of human beings through deception and coercion for the purposes of exploitation. Upon this basis, the book considers whether an understanding of the underlying explanatory ("structural") factors can inform policy discussion and point to strategic interventions which strengthen the fight against trafficking.

There is significant – although still insufficient – knowledge about the activities of human traffickers, and a range of policy options exist at the national and international levels to address this problem. However, instead of focusing upon these operational issues, this volume takes a different approach. It begins with the assumption that it is important to understand human trafficking in its broad social, economic and political context (structural factors), and seeks to relate this to policy and governance issues (proximate factors). The overarching argument is that the interaction between structural factors or variables (such as economic deprivation and market downturns, social inequality, attitudes to gender, demand for prostitutes) and proximate factors (such as lax national and international legal regimes, poor law enforcement, corruption, organized criminal entrepreneurship, weak education campaigns) is key to understanding why some individuals are vulnerable to trafficking through the use of deception and coercion. It is this conjunction of factors which helps to explain where and why vulnerability occurs. An understanding of the structural context – and its relationship to proximate factors – is thus vital

Trafficking in humans: Social, cultural and political dimensions, Cameron and Newman (eds), United Nations University Press, 2007, ISBN 978-92-808-1146-9

for addressing the problem at both the site of origin and destination and the international level.

This volume seeks to assess the dynamics of the trafficking business, as well as existing and possible remedial efforts, in this comprehensive context. If structural factors prove to be fundamental conditions of human trafficking, then policies must be directed towards alleviating basic problems, of which trafficking is one manifestation. Rather than being confined to the normative academic sphere, a starting point is that the structural background to trafficking may well have real relevance for policy. This volume seeks to make such integral linkages.

In particular, the volume examines the proposition that in this era of globalization, liberal economic forces have resulted in an erosion of state capacity and a weakening of the provision of public goods. Thus trafficking may be seen as a symptom of deprivation, as poverty is an important factor leading to vulnerability. Disparities in economic and social conditions provide a clear explanation for the direction and flow of trafficking. Trafficking, generally, occurs from poorer to more prosperous countries and regions. At the same time, modern forms of transportation and communication have aided the movement of people and also enabled transnational organized crime groups and trafficking rings to exploit vulnerable women and children for profit.

Socio-economic issues are clearly key explanatory factors in trafficking. Profit drives every aspect of the trafficking industry from the standpoint of the perpetrators of this crime. Economic need is the central driving force that renders potential recruits more vulnerable to deception, coercion and exploitation. Deprived individuals are also often powerless – physically, legally and politically – to extricate themselves from coercive exploitative labour, partly as a result of their social position.

At a different level, the emphasis upon the free movement of capital and deregulation may have consequences for trafficking: financial remittances are an important source of revenue for many countries, especially those with large numbers of citizens living abroad as expatriate workers. A drastic clampdown on the free movement of people – as a response to combat trafficking – could jeopardize the free flow of these remittances. This is a move that many countries of origin are reluctant to take.

Social and economic issues are not the only structural factors at work. It is argued that trafficking in women, particularly for the purpose of sexual exploitation, is a manifestation of the discrimination and disadvantages encountered by women in most contemporary societies. In addition to sexism, an analysis of the forces underlying trafficking reveals that the racism prevalent in society is also a contributing factor.

Structural factors help in understanding the causes of vulnerability that can lead to trafficking; these may not, however, constitute the entire causal paradigm of trafficking. All the structural factors reflected here apply to a significant proportion of women and children in various parts of the world, but most do not fall victim to trafficking. Moreover, it is not necessarily the case that those who are most afflicted by certain structural factors – such as poverty – are automatically most likely to become victims of trafficking. A certain alignment of factors may be the key to understanding trafficking. The principal focus of this volume is to understand the distinction and dialectical interaction between structural and proximate factors. How is the coalescence of risk factors reflected in patterns of trafficking? What specific combinations of structural and proximate factors promote trafficking? How do material and historical specificities interact with subjective realities to create a victim of trafficking who also exhibits agency? In other words, how complicated is the story of trafficking and how does one comprehend this complex reality with an adequately complicated analysis? And how may appropriate responses and interventions be developed?

Specific research questions focus on the relationship between structural and proximate factors that deepens understanding of trafficking (fig. 1.1); the socio-economic context of trafficking, including underdevelopment, poverty, sudden market fluctuations and economic downturns; trafficking

---

Structural factors

Economic factors: Globalization; poverty; deprivation and economic downturns and trends; free market economics; deregulation; migratory movements

Social factors: Social inequality; gender discrimination; discrimination and marginalization based upon age (children and minors); gender status; disadvantaged cultural, regional and linguistic status; prostitution

Ideological factors: Racism; xenophobia; gender and cultural stereotyping

Geopolitical factors: War; civil strife; violent conflict; military bases and operations

Proximate factors

Legal and policy aspects: Inadequate national and international legal regimes; poor law enforcement; immigration/migration laws and policies; inadequate and poorly enforced labour laws and standards

Rule of law: Corruption; complicity of state in criminal activities; support by state officials of underground criminal networks; organized criminal/parallel entrepreneurship including underground sex trade; smuggling; trade in arms and drugs

Inadequate partnership between civil society and state: Weak education campaigns; low awareness among vulnerable communities; apathetic civil society; poor accountability of state organizations

Note

Some structural and proximate factors apply to both source and destination countries; some apply solely to one or the other.

Figure 1.1 Examples of structural and proximate factors involved in trafficking

routes and dynamics in the context of structural factors; the relationship between trafficking and human and national security concerns, including transnational organized crime, migration management regimes, war and conflict, humanitarian imperatives and HIV/AIDS; and the explanatory value of cross-regional and geographically comparative perspectives on trafficking with regard to structural and proximate factors for identifying patterns of similarities and difference. The volume aims to raise awareness and promote recognition of trafficking as a fundamental affront to human rights and dignity. Towards this end, it brings together individuals from different institutional backgrounds to explore the political, inter-institutional and ethical dimensions of tackling these issues. The chapters also seek to offer suggestions reconciling the sometimes competing forces of globalization, free market economics and human rights.

Trafficking: Definitions

This volume applies the definition of human trafficking used in the Protocol to Prevent, Suppress and Punish Trafficking in Persons, especially Women and Children, which supplements the UN Convention against Transnational Organized Crime adopted by the UN General Assembly in November 2000:

> "Trafficking in persons" shall mean the recruitment, transportation, transfer, harbouring or receipt of persons, by means of the threat or use of force or other forms of coercion, of abduction, of fraud, of deception, of the abuse of power or of a position of vulnerability or of the giving or receiving of payments or benefits to achieve the consent of a person having control over another person, for the purpose of exploitation. Exploitation shall include, at a minimum, the exploitation of the prostitution of others or other forms of sexual exploitation, forced labour or services, slavery or practices similar to slavery, servitude or the removal of organs;
>
> The consent of a victim of trafficking in persons to the intended exploitation set forth in subparagraph (a) of this article shall be irrelevant where any of the means set forth in subparagraph (a) have been used.[1]

The selling of vulnerable people – often but not exclusively young women and girls – into sexual bondage and other exploitative activities has become one of the fastest-growing criminal enterprises in the global economy. It represents a major challenge to human rights and public security authorities. A number of different patterns are well known (fig. 1.2). Young women and men attempting to find legitimate jobs are deceived by agents who specialize in trafficking humans. Upon arrival in a

Deception
Recruitment
Transportation
Coercion
Exploitation
Forced labour
Slavery-like practices

Figure 1.2 Trafficking elements

foreign land their papers are seized and their movement confined, and, even if they have the opportunity, they are too frightened to seek help. The authorities (and sometimes even their national consular representatives) in the country into which they are trafficked can be unsympathetic. Rather than being protected and assisted as victims, people in this situation can find themselves in trouble as illegal immigrants or prostitutes. In other circumstances young adults or children are trafficked across regional borders – or sometimes within borders – as a result of familial or social acquaintances. The US Department of State has estimated that 600,000–800,000 human beings are trafficked across international borders each year; of these, approximately 80 per cent are women and girls and up to 50 per cent are minors.[2]

The trafficking of women has perhaps attracted the greatest amount of attention. Women are recruited in source countries and then subsequently forced to work for other "employers" in the destination country. Some may have some idea about what they are going to be involved in. Others will have been completely deceived into thinking that they would be working as innocent entertainers, maids or factory workers. There is evidence that recruitment operations are often well organized, large and transnational in scope. Once having entered into deceptive contractual relationships with an "employer", and upon arrival in the country, women are coerced into exploitative work, often in the sex industry.[3] Victims can be physically enslaved and imprisoned at all times, or a number of forms of leverage and coercion can be employed, including debt slavery, threats of physical violence and confiscation of travel documents. Victims are often given some of the money they generate in the sex industry. That is central to their vulnerability; they are required to pay back debts and generate something to send back to their home countries. At the same time, recourse to alternative forms of lifestyle/income and protection from abusive managers are often not available. Victims often perceive that public authorities are unsympathetic, or they are afraid of approaching these authorities for fear of being prosecuted as a prostitute or illegal immigrant. Trafficked women tend to be illegal immigrants or engaged in illegal activities – such as prostitution – and therefore are reluctant to lodge complaints with the authorities over labour issues or coercion. This increases the leverage and control that managers wield over the victims.

There are often no specific national laws that prohibit trafficking in persons as a crime that encapsulates deception, transportation, coercion and exploitation as a broad process. Trafficking issues have been and often are approached as an issue of illegal immigration and prostitution rather than illegal detention or coercion. Thus indictments for "trafficking offences" (illegal trafficking of humans for purposes of illegal exploitation, illegal detention, coercion and complicity in criminal activities) have been low. In some countries there is evidence that law enforcement units have been reluctant to investigate reports of trafficking, and that governments have not been aggressive in arresting and prosecuting suspected traffickers. Victims are often treated as criminals (prostitutes or illegal aliens) by the legal system because governments do not consider people who willingly enter for illegal work to be trafficking victims.

The UN Protocol to Prevent Trafficking in Persons is an important tool to facilitate international cooperation. Governments that sign and ratify this protocol make a commitment to criminalize trafficking and to protect its many victims. The protocol came into force in 2003, and by the end of 2006 had 117 signatories and 100 parties. Two other international instruments that address sale of and trafficking in children have also recently been adopted: International Labour Organization (ILO) Convention 182 concerning the Prohibition and Immediate Action for the Elimination of the Worst Forms of Child Labour and the Protocol to the Convention on the Rights of the Child on Sale of Children, Child Prostitution and Child Pornography.

This volume will indicate progress and obstacles towards reaching the goals of these international instruments by illuminating the wider social, economic and political picture.

Outline of volume

The chapter by Sally Cameron and Edward Newman, "Human trafficking: Structural factors", elaborates upon the themes of this introduction. The basic argument is that an understanding of human trafficking requires an analysis of the operation of, and interaction between, a range of factors that combine to make individuals vulnerable to trafficking.

The chapter considers if the intersection between these factors helps to understand why and where trafficking is more likely. These factors are divided into two categories: structural and proximate. An understanding of this broad context is vital for addressing the problem at both the site of origin and the destination, as well as at the international level. Any assessment of the dynamics of the trafficking business, as well as existing and possible remedial efforts, must be made in this comprehensive context. If structural factors prove to be fundamental conditions of human trafficking, then policy-makers must allow for them, for example by taking into account that policies which are restrictive to labour migration provide opportunities to organized crime.

Economic factors are central to an understanding of the structural context of human trafficking. Kinsey Alden Dinan's chapter, "Globalization and national sovereignty: From migration to trafficking", explores the interaction between globalization and national sovereignty as a root cause of trafficking in persons. Dinan argues that the selective resistance of states towards globalization and assertion of national sovereignty in certain sectors are important to understanding trafficking. Specifically, the insistence of governments on the right to determine who crosses national borders and the conditions under which they cross provides a market for the "services" of traffickers and facilitates their ability to engage in slavery-like abuses with virtual impunity.

In addition, despite the high level of government attention to the issue of trafficking, there has been little progress in responding to the human rights abuses endured by trafficked persons. Traffickers, when prosecuted, are typically charged with crimes related to immigration violations, not human rights abuses, and victims receive little in terms of assistance or justice. At the same time, most trafficked persons continue to be treated as "illegal aliens" when they come into contact with law enforcement officials, summarily deported without any investigation of the conditions of their migration or employment in the destination country. Dinan concludes that if governments are serious about combating trafficking in persons, a new approach is needed. Addressing the push factors of economic instability, poverty and inequality in countries of origin is important for reducing migration pressures over the long term. Increased efforts to investigate and punish traffickers are also needed, with penalties that reflect the gravity of the offence. And such efforts will not be successful until officials provide trafficking victims with the assistance and protection needed to gain their trust and cooperation as informants and witnesses. Most importantly, however, the incidence of trafficking in persons will not be reduced until governments shift their focus from reducing illegal migration to ending the slavery-like treatment and other abuse of migrants (and other workers). Therefore, she suggests, safe and legal migration opportunities must be expanded. Until countries address the mismatch between global migratory pressures and national immigration policies that makes trafficking and smuggling operations attractive to migrants and highly profitable for crime groups, little progress will be made.

A controversial topic in the debates which surround human trafficking is prostitution. Does prostitution inevitably generate human trafficking? Should it therefore be criminalized as a part of a policy for addressing trafficking? Or should prostitution be permitted but regulated, so that the welfare and rights of sex workers can be protected and demand for trafficked prostitutes can be reduced or eradicated? Should prostitution be recognized as legitimate work and thus respected in the context of anti-trafficking measures? Sally Cameron's chapter, "Trafficking of women for prostitution", grapples with these questions. As she observes, there is a fierce split among feminist academics based on whether prostitution can be considered work or whether it is innately exploitative and abusive. In addition to this pervasive ideological disagreement there is a lack of reliable data regarding the relationship between prostitution and trafficking. However, some observations are possible, including that trafficking in women for prostitution is driven by demand. The sex industry *per se* and workers within it have long been blamed for the exploitation of trafficked women. However, Cameron argues that this idea denies the complexity of intersecting factors which impact on individuals to make them vulnerable to trafficking. It also ignores the demands of the millions of purchasers of sex services, and the ruthless industry of those coordinating trafficking efforts who force people to live and work under highly exploitative, slavery-like conditions. In conclusion, she argues that prostitution must be disentangled from "migrant sex work" and human trafficking.

Human trafficking cannot be understood in isolation from the broader topic of migration, because trafficking exploits restrictive migratory policies and the desire of humans to travel to seek a better livelihood. Ratna Kapur's chapter, "Migrant women and the legal politics of anti-trafficking interventions", puts human trafficking into the context of the broader movement of people – both legitimate and illegitimate – across national and international borders. These movements, she argues, are exposing the porosity of borders, the transnational reality of women's migration and the questionable foundations of the laws regulating cross-border movements. Kapur claims that anti-trafficking initiatives have invariably failed to distinguish between consensual migration, albeit clandestine, and coerced movement. The result is that international trafficking initiatives have had a particularly adverse impact on women and their families. Treating all movement of women as coerced reinforces assumptions about ("third world") women as victims, infantile and incapable of decision-making. At the same time, their families are implicated in the trafficking chain and cast as criminals. As a result, these women and their families are excluded from access to legal recognition, rights and benefits, and rendered even more vulnerable and insecure.

If structural or underlying factors – such as poverty, social inequality and globalization – provide an explanation as to why communities are vulnerable to trafficking, proximate factors help to explain how trafficking actually occurs. Phil Williams's chapter, "Trafficking in women: The role of transnational organized crime", provides an important account of this. He argues that it is necessary to understand the structure of the human trafficking market in terms of supply and demand, the dimensions of the market, profitability issues and market trends based on opportunities, cost-benefit calculations and risk considerations. His analysis looks at the market actors, with particular emphasis on the supply networks that traffic in women and children. The market for commercial sex depends upon criminal networks that link the supply and demand sides and bring women and children to places where they are sold into and subsequently enslaved in prostitution. While the nature of the criminals who are involved varies, the trend has been towards greater organization and professionalism. His chapter demonstrates how traffickers recruit and transport women from source countries to destination countries. On this basis, Williams focuses on the balance between market facilitators and market inhibitors. For criminal markets to function effectively and criminal networks to operate efficiently, the facilitators must outweigh the inhibitors. Consequently, it is necessary to identify both kinds of factors before considering the ways in which facilitators can be reduced or removed and inhibitors can be expanded. In effect, by identifying and then manipulating facilitators and inhibitors it should be possible to reduce profitability and increase the costs and risks of trafficking. Through this, it is possible to adopt a holistic approach to the development of an effective policy response.

The second half of the book examines a number of case studies which illustrate the social background to trafficking in different regions – emphasizing structural factors – and the record of attempts to address trafficking. These cases show that different regions may display similar factors – and interrelationships of factors – but that patterns of trafficking can be different as a result of a number of local conditions. These cases are written by local scholars and practitioners directly involved in trafficking issues.

Helga Konrad's chapter focuses on "The fight against trafficking in human beings from the European perspective". She uses a framework of national security and human security as a dichotomy which exposes the shortcomings of attitudes and state policies towards trafficking. Despite consensus among policy circles that human trafficking is a serious crime and human rights violation, most countries organize their response to trafficking in persons in a narrow way, based almost exclusively upon prevailing notions of national security, national sovereignty and border control. Konrad argues that the protection of the fundamental rights of victims of trafficking takes second place to the promotion of state interests. The European Union and many destination countries in general put the emphasis on preventing irregular immigration and fighting asylum abuse. Governments very often see the battle against illegal immigration as their first priority, while pretending to fight human trafficking. Therefore victims of trafficking run the risk of being treated as illegal immigrants and immediately deported to their countries of origin. Even when victims are allowed to stay temporarily, support for them depends on whether they are useful to the prosecution of the traffickers and willing to cooperate with law enforcement authorities. As a result, victims are often instrumentalized in the interests of the prosecution. Again, state interests take precedence over the right of victims to protection of their physical and mental integrity. In conclusion, Konrad argues that there is equal need for short-term and long-term measures. Short-term measures, such as the immediate and urgent need to assist and protect the victims of trafficking, will only have the desired effect if they are based on serious research into the root causes of trafficking. On the one hand, the countermeasures have to be quick-acting. On the other hand, it is necessary to raise and address the issue of the structural roots of human trafficking – namely the global inequalities in the distribution of jobs, resources and wealth.

Maruja M. B. Asis's chapter is on "Human trafficking in East and South-East Asia: Searching for structural factors". Asis puts this into the context of increasing and diverse international migration in the region over the last three decades, and the push and pull factors generated by the forces of globalization. Of the world's 191 million international migrants, some 53.3 million are in Asia, making it the second-largest region hosting international migrants after Europe, which hosts 64.1 million. What is not reflected in these statistics is the huge numbers of unauthorized migrants as well as the suspected large numbers of men, women and children who are trafficked. Furthermore, under conditions of globalization, present migrations (including trafficking) are affected by factors that simultaneously push, facilitate and impede the movement of people across international borders. The displacing impact of globalization in developing countries results in increased economic dislocation. In the face of volatile or fragile national economies, families and households turn to overseas migration as a strategy to meet their needs. The facilitative processes come from improved communications and transportation that not only promote the movement of people (as well as ideas, goods, technology and capital) across borders, but also enable migrants to maintain linkages to their countries of destination and origin. Upon this basis, Asis's chapter proposes a framework examining the origins and development of human trafficking. She examines the patterns of human trafficking in East and South-East Asia in terms of what they imply about its structural factors, and examines the approaches of regional initiatives aimed at curbing trafficking.

Asis argues that both regular and unauthorized migration are part of the same system. Since migration is a transnational phenomenon, conditions and processes in the countries of *both* origin and destination must be considered. She concludes by observing that the global attention directed at trafficking has definitely created some awareness about it, but more awareness and educational campaigns are needed to go beyond a simplistic picture of such a complex phenomenon. A segmented and separate approach to trafficking, unauthorized migration and legal migration is likely to be counterproductive. Moreover, it is essential to devote more attention to the demand side of factors and processes of trafficking.

Gabriela Rodríguez Pizarro writes from the position of UN special rapporteur for the human rights of migrants. Her chapter focuses on "Human trafficking in Latin America in the context of international migration". The office of special rapporteur monitors the human rights situation of migrants and recommends activities and measures for the elimination of violations of their rights. From this perspective, the chapter has a unique insight into the dynamics of trafficking in the region. In terms of structural sources of trafficking, Rodríguez Pizarro emphasizes the social and economic exclusion of minorities, national and local economic underdevelopment, gender inequality, intra-family violence, xenophobia and a culture of impunity. She argues that the structural factors of trafficking in Latin America are related to the historical processes of poverty, economic crises, dependence on developed countries and scarce opportunities for human development in the local and national spheres. In addition, in South America the internal conflict in Colombia is the cause of a massive exit of migrants to bordering countries and Central America, the Caribbean and the United States. The proximate variables of the phenomenon of trafficking in Latin America are linked to the lack of adequate legislation in the countries of origin, transit and destination, lack of information, lack of documentation, criminalization of victims, impunity of agents of trafficking and unfamiliarity with principal international obligations which countries in Latin America have ratified. Corruption, too, is a major contributory factor. Noting that few specialized programmes for the rehabilitation of victims have been observed in the region, Rodríguez Pizarro concludes with an approach to addressing human trafficking from the perspective of empowering victims.

Renu Rajbhandari's chapter, "Human trafficking in South Asia: A focus on Nepal", finds similarities in the social and economic contexts of trafficking in Nepal. Her chapter presents practical examples, experiences and case studies with a view to deepening the understanding of the social, economic, gendered and political contexts of human trafficking in that country. It is based on the grassroots experiences of staff of the Women's Rehabilitation Centre (WOREC) and other NGOs working on the ground in Nepal. In terms of explanatory factors, the chapter highlights poverty, illiteracy and lack of awareness, issues of poor governance, discrimination based on class, caste and gender, widespread corruption, non-compliance with international commitments by national and international actors, international trade and labour and migration policies. Other structural factors, she argues, have been neglected in the discussion because many people are uncomfortable with them: for example, the strong patriarchal and semi-feudal social and political system, double standards about women's and men's sexuality, existing means of production and landowner relationships.

Some of these factors are also evident in Gulnara Shahinian's chapter, "Trafficking in persons in the South Caucasus – Armenia, Azerbaijan and Georgia: New challenges for transitional democracies". However, there are a number of historically unique features with the Caucuses. In particular, the collapse of the Soviet Union and the sudden transition to free market economics plunged the regions of the former Soviet Union into a painful social transition. At the same time, a liberalization of political systems allowed increased freedom of movement and a rising awareness of better economic opportunities overseas. A significant result of this has been vulnerability of people to deception and exploitation. Shahinian's chapter specifically illustrates the importance of factors such as unemployment, poverty and economic decline; the unequal status of women; traditional labour migration patterns exploited by criminal groups; the absence of comprehensive migration policies and monitoring; and the corruption of state officials and weak rule of law. She also identifies pull factors, in particular neighbours such as the United Arab Emirates and Turkey, which offer the prospect of lucrative migration. In line with this, Shahinian illustrates how the migration policies in the countries of destination are important factors in understanding trafficking.

Policy issues

The battle against human trafficking requires the development of coherent, multilayered strategies. The chapters in this volume raise a number of policy implications which have relevance for various actors, in particular governments and international organizations working on this issue.

Recognize the complexity of the practice

As Konrad points out, despite the problem being one of "breathtaking intricacy", governments have repeatedly attempted to reduce this highly complex and multidimensional problem to simplistic, often one-dimensional, terms. Trafficking involves diverse experiences. In addition to women, men and children are also trafficked; and all are trafficked into a large number of areas outside the sex industry. In some regions, trafficking occurs within borders. It is vital that morally driven agendas and the desire for a quick fix and to be "seen to be doing something" are replaced by laws, policies and programmes based on facts and (as far as possible) detached analysis. Responses must include human rights and development goals as well as legal enforcement. Little can be achieved without dialogue and cooperation between regional and international bodies, governments and NGOs.

Clarify definitions

Responses to trafficking are limited by the lack of clarity in terms and definitions used by governments, international agencies, NGOs, academics and the media. In particular, far greater efforts must be made to clarify and distinguish between trafficking and migrating, trafficking and prostitution and voluntary and forced prostitution. Far from being an "academic" issue, this confusion of terminology has two serious consequences for the development of trafficking responses. Firstly, it results in the collection of data which misrepresent (inadvertently or intentionally) reality because definitions are used loosely and without agreement. In the worst case, many individuals interested in this subject – and even some government agencies – routinely confuse human trafficking and smuggling, or use the terms interchangeably. Secondly, debates become infused with this lack of clarity, with unfortunate policy and public responses. For example, some debates concerning female migration have led to a presumption that women who migrate are victims of trafficking. This has had the effect of making the cross-border movement of women illegitimate in some contexts. Similarly, some anti-trafficking policies have focused upon "rescuing" migrant sex workers, some of whom have stated they were working consensually, have resisted the label "trafficked" and have perceived their treatment as something akin to a detention or arrest.

Rethink migration

As Dinan pragmatically states, "trafficking in persons must be understood within the context of the larger phenomenon of persons' movement across international borders". Trafficking debates must be embedded in notions of migration. In the words of Kapur, globalization is facilitating enormous movement, "exposing the porosity of borders, the transnational reality of ... migration and the contingent foundations of the laws regulating cross-border movements". The attitudes and assumptions of anti-trafficking policies need to be reconsidered in light of this. In particular, the relationship between the demands and advantages of globalization (including cheap imported labour and remittances) and state sovereignty with fixed borders needs to be reconsidered and reconciled. In fact, some "anti-trafficking" strategies appear to be thinly disguised battles against illegal immigration, with the possibility of addressing the human cost of trafficking as a secondary outcome.

Framing trafficking within the context of migration allows for the reality that, as Shahinian observes, "more and more people see migration as their only option". Victims often consider trafficking networks as people "helping" them to migrate, and this is at the heart of their vulnerability. Diasporas and migrant networks facilitate the process. Migration patterns develop networks and systems, spurring further migration. This calls for a review of migration policies, particularly a rethinking and possibly expansion of entry laws. Rather than stopping trafficking, limiting legal migration drives the activity further underground. Restrictive migration policies strengthen the use of irregular migration channels. As Dinan notes, "Europe saw flows of undocumented migrants increase tenfold to 500,000 per year in the 1990s, a period of dramatic increases in immigration controls."

In current trafficking debates, trafficked migrants are usually considered vulnerable, infantile, backward, outlaw, in need of protection and/ or a threat to national security. They are rarely considered whole, complex people. Asis argues that migrants can be "transnationals who can play a vital part in the creation of 'transnational communities' by maintaining links between their countries of origin and destination". Framing trafficking within migration debates allows a clearer understanding of the image many trafficked victims have of themselves when embarking on their legal or illegal migration, and holds greater possibilities for anti-trafficking initiatives.

As many of the authors in this volume argue, the protection of the human rights of victims is essential, but so too is protecting the rights of people to seek a living safely and make decisions for themselves. It is important to be aware of the danger of simplifying especially women as disempowered victims. The emphasis should be more on providing safe avenues for people to pursue their right to travel and work.

Make labour exploitation central

Trafficking debates would benefit from a clearer understanding of the fact that trafficking is essentially about labour exploitation. Trafficking is simply a means to provide that labour. People are moved to work, in exploitative or slavery-like conditions. Trafficking provides a supply, but it also increases people's vulnerability and makes them less likely to complain, escape or lobby for improved conditions by taking them out of the protected realm (where they have legal protection and a familiar cultural and linguistic environment) and either literally entrapping them or, more commonly, dangling the carrot of economic "freedom" in front of them. Asis suggests that "Demand is actually more critical in migration than supply-side factors." It is the unmet demand for migrant workers in the destination that drives the market for trafficking. Trafficked people are pushed into the dirty, dangerous and undesirable industries for which their destination country requires labour.

Include the economics of the industry

Many analysts and academics from a range of fields have engaged in the trafficking debate. Economists, however, have largely and noticeably been absent. Enormous figures have been floated relating to the number of people trafficked and the income their exploitation generates, but most of these are without accompanying data about how such figures have been reached. These figures appear to gain legitimacy as much through their use (being quoted again and again) as through any sincere belief in their sound methodological base. One wonders why exactly the trafficking market, which at a rough guess is worth at least billions of dollars each year, is not of greater interest to economists.

The swift spread of free markets, driven by liberal economic globalization, has resulted in enormous progress in living standards and lifted millions out of poverty. It has also produced increased levels of inequality within and between states, and, in many areas, economic instability. Liberal economic pressures have resulted in reforms which have exacerbated economic insecurity and left communities vulnerable to trafficking. Human trafficking reduces people to the status of commodities. Furthermore, economic theory can be more broadly applied to trafficking industries to enable consideration of market structure and dynamics: supply and demand, the dimensions of the market, profitability issues and even market trends based on opportunities, cost-benefit calculations and risk considerations. Such framing would then facilitate development of means to disrupt the market.

From an economic perspective, human trafficking raises some interesting facts. Undocumented migrants (some of whom have been trafficked) are fundamental to the economies of many states. In the United States, for example, some 10 million undocumented migrants account for nearly 10 per cent of the low-wage labour force. International remittances from migrants produce enormous domestic revenues while alleviating unemployment rates by reducing domestic labour supply. Moreover, the citizens of host countries enjoy the purchase of cheap goods and services (including sex from trafficked women) without accountability.

Recognize that trafficking is gendered

Gender analysis offers increased possibilities to understand the specifics of why certain women are trafficked into certain regions/industries and develop appropriate (often long-term) responses. As a starting point, women are being trafficked from states offering them limited opportunities outside the hard toil and drudgery of the home, the farm and unregulated markets. "Rescuing" women and sending them home does not affect that, and thus will not alter the principal push factors which make women vulnerable to trafficking. At the same time, there is a failure to understand and acknowledge fully the trafficking of men. While there is some writing about men working in exploitative, indentured or slave-like conditions, much of this has not been contextualized within a trafficking framework. Similarly, there must be greater recognition that children are trafficked. For too long the popular image of trafficking victims – young women coerced into prostitution – has influenced policy responses, but this is only a part of the reality.

Grapple with the issue of prostitution/sex work

It is somewhat ironic that trafficking into the sex industry dominates research and media alike, but that corresponding policies and programmes are notoriously lacking. The blurring of debates about trafficking and sex work has resulted in flawed legal strategies that are both anti-migrant and anti-sex work. Some respond by assuming that all migrant women working in the sex industry have been trafficked, while others imply that trafficking is only punishable (or should be more punishable) if the sex industry is involved. Notions of trafficking and prostitution must be disaggregated. Perhaps one means is to frame the industry in terms of coercion and consent. Put simply, sex without consent is sexual assault, and women who experience such assault have been victimized.

Policing and governance

Given that tens, if not hundreds, of thousands of individuals are trafficked each year, it is surprisingly difficult to find accounts of trafficked persons' experiences. Not surprisingly, research that has been carried out has been synthesized and analysed before making it into print, sometimes with a few case studies attached. Perhaps in the push to drive home to governments and policy-makers the urgency of addressing trafficking practices, many of the voices heard by researchers have been lost to a broader audience. In fact, when the UNU conducted interviews – as a part of an earlier trafficking project – with women who had previously been trafficked, researchers encountered varied tales of coercion and desperation, but to some extent it was the stories of resistance and coping that stood out. These are stories which are not often heard and which paint a clearer picture of the way different individuals respond to the similar circumstances in which they find themselves – thus putting the "human" back into human trafficking.

Notes

1. The Protocol to Prevent, Suppress and Punish Trafficking in Persons, especially Women and Children (supplementing the UN Convention against Transnational Organized Crime), adopted by resolution A/RES/55/25 of 15 November 2000 at the fifty-fifth session of the UN General Assembly, article 3, paragraph (a). The protocol entered into force on 25 December 2003.
2. US State Department, *Trafficking in Persons Report 2006*, Washington, D.C.: US State Department, 2006, p. 6.
3. The US State Department suggests that "the majority of transnational victims were trafficked into commercial sexual exploitation", ibid.

Part I
Themes

2

Trafficking in humans: Structural factors

Sally Cameron and Edward Newman

To develop an understanding of human trafficking it is necessary to consider the operation of, and interaction between, a range of factors that combine to enable individuals and organizations to traffic vulnerable people through the use of deception, coercion and exploitation. There is enormous intersection between these factors and, in fact, it may be the mode of this intersection that makes a particular region more or less likely to be targeted by traffickers. Broadly speaking, these factors can be divided into two categories: structural and proximate. Structural factors include issues of economic deprivation and market downturns, the effects of globalization, attitudes to gender, the demand for prostitutes and situations of conflict. Proximate factors include lax national and international legal regimes, poor law enforcement, corruption, organized criminal entrepreneurship and weak education campaigns. An understanding of this structural context is vital for addressing the problem at both the site of origin and the destination, as well as at the international level. Any assessment of the dynamics of the trafficking business, as well as existing and possible remedial efforts, must be made in this comprehensive context. If structural factors prove to be fundamental conditions of human trafficking, then policies must factor them in, for example by ensuring domestic migration policies take account of issues of labour demand and supply, by developing local industries that offer opportunities for citizens' advancement, thus reducing the attractiveness of migration, and by developing and implementing prostitution laws that offer protection to sex workers and decrease the industry's attractiveness to

Trafficking in humans: Social, cultural and political dimensions, Cameron and Newman (eds), United Nations University Press, 2007, ISBN 978-92-808-1146-9

organized crime. This chapter will focus primarily on illustrating structural factors.

Poverty

> A family in desperate need of money is inclined to say yes, even without knowing the full nature and circumstances of the work.[1]

It is broadly accepted that poverty is one of the key factors which places people at risk of human trafficking. Poverty acts as a catalyst for trafficking in a range of ways.

- Poverty places people in situations where they have few alternative opportunities. Their desperation may increase their vulnerability to deception and coercion. It may also increase their powerlessness to extricate themselves once they find themselves in a highly exploitative situation.
- Individual vulnerability may be exacerbated by lack of education, being one of many children within a family and limited understanding of life outside the local environment – all of which are often linked to situations of poverty.
- Visible differences in people's standards of living may lead people to question their own situation, which might be understood as an issue of "relative poverty".
- Poverty may motivate individuals to consider migration as one of the few viable means to increase their income.
- Floundering national economies may induce governments to promote labour migration, as expatriates' remittances have the potential to become a fundamental component of national income.
- Weak national economies and poor wages in the public sector may motivate corruption among public officials, increasing the ease with which criminal networks can operate.

The director of UNICEF for West and Central Africa states that poverty is a "major and ubiquitous" causal factor behind child trafficking. In those West African countries classified as "sending" states – Togo, Benin, Mali, Nigeria and Burkina Faso – anywhere from 33 to 73 per cent of the general population live on less than US$1 a day.[2] In basic terms, trafficking flows are generally from underdeveloped regions to more affluent regions.

Income levels, for example the simple $1 a day measure of poverty, create a snapshot of the world's disproportionate distribution of wealth, which is certainly relevant when considering the globalized nature of trafficking and the attractiveness of possible salaries in destination countries.

However, income levels provide only a limited explanation of people's circumstances. Measures of poverty include adequate nutrition, water, sanitation, education, employment and health care.

Also, poverty is not a static state. Poverty strikes those in seemingly stable, relatively affluent situations. For example, in parts of Asia and the countries of the former USSR, economic crises have had a dire effect on many people's living standards. Conversely, given fortuitous circumstances, people can make their way out of poverty, which is almost uniformly the goal of those who find themselves trafficked. Poverty encourages families to identify means to secure additional income. It also encourages them to find ways to reduce costs, for example reducing childcare costs by sending children away. Poor families may employ their children in the fields because they need additional labour, they do not see the benefits of education or the opportunity cost of sending a child to school is too high. Absence of education, a direct result of poverty (sometimes in combination with other factors, such as gender discrimination), can lead to greater vulnerability to recruitment by traffickers.

Lack of options

As outlined above, poverty challenges neo-liberal notions of individual choice. For example, a study of Central and West African countries found that in all countries studied, poverty was recognized as "the main factor that forces parents to send their child with an intermediary. The decision is taken without considering the consequences, or counting the price they will pay in the future, for they simply do not have a choice."[3] Similarly, in a Nepalese study, while more than 94 per cent of the parents acknowledged that their children's living standards were very poor at their workplace, "they pointed out that they have no other better option. They further stressed that this is being practised not because of their will but by compulsion created by the abject poverty that they are compelled to live in."[4]

The above Nepalese study raised a further point. The same group of parents acknowledged that the living standards at home were very poor. This raises the issue that even though people may be trafficked into highly exploitative and abusive conditions, these conditions may be no worse than, or may even be preferable to, the conditions they have left. In the Mekong subregion, "cases have been found of trafficked minors in highly abusive situations who considered themselves to be better off than had they remained in their home or village environments".[5] Similarly, a study of Nepalese girls trafficked into prostitution in India found that although a majority were exposed to "severe physical and mental torture ... a few of the respondents reported that they were much better off in the brothel than in their present lives, either at home or in rehabilitation centres".[6]

Sometimes the home environment is unacceptable for reasons which may or may not be linked to poverty, for example low education levels of parents, mistreatment, psychological and physical abuse, alcoholism, multiple marriages and remarriage. A Nepalese study of trafficked girls found that that one of the main causes of trafficking was location in a "dysfunctional family". A considerable number of respondents reported that they were maltreated in their maternal households, and a large proportion of them had migrated to urban areas due to step-parents' physical torture, domestic violence, sexual abuse, beating and/or alcoholism.[7]

The role of parents

Central to the vulnerability of people to trafficking is their position within their family, particularly if the family is living in poverty. While this is true of adults, who may for example feel an obligation to support their family, it is particularly true of children, who by definition live under the direction of their parents. There is no doubt that parents play a vital role in their children's vulnerability to trafficking. A Nepalese study of trafficked boys found that 33 per cent were "talked into migrating" by their own family members, 25 per cent by relatives and 21 per cent by friends.[8] A study of Nepalese girls trafficked into prostitution found that the majority of the parents "gave silent consent or were somehow involved in the trafficking of their daughters".[9] In the Central and Western Africa study, 67 per cent of all the children forced to work had been "handed over" to the employer by a family member or someone they knew.[10]

Throughout the world, and throughout existing literature, there are a range of opinions as to parents' culpability for the trafficking of their children. In Central and Western Africa a number of factors intersect to produce a high rate of child trafficking. Aside from grinding poverty, the region has the highest fertility rates in the world, and research has shown that children are more at risk when they are members of a family with five or more children.[11] Additionally, cultural traditions "make child work socially acceptable ... Social values are transmitted through work, and from the age of four onwards children are expected to help in the household and in the fields."[12]

Not all analysts are as sympathetic. A Moldovan study states that "sometimes parents will send their daughters abroad. They know that their daughters are working in prostitution in Moldova and they are not getting paid well. They want them to get paid more money."[13] Similarly, Nepalese girls "are frequently seen as family commodities who, like property, can be bought and sold".[14] A report from Ghana states that "mothers not only give away their children as a response to poverty but also out of greed, covetousness and self-fulfilment. They try to achieve through their children, what they have not been able to do themselves."[15]

Absolute versus relative poverty

While some measures of poverty may be absolute, others are relative. "Poverty is as much about perceived inequalities and relative deprivation as it is about low levels of material welfare."[16] In Asia, for example, many were bypassed by the growth in the region's economies.[17] CIS citizens are not only aware of the economic securities they have lost, but of their proximity to Europe's economic powerhouses. Similarly, the ILO suggests that the economic growth of African countries like Gabon, Côte d'Ivoire and Nigeria may have contributed to the aggravation of trafficking in children for labour exploitation.[18] In Thailand the surge of the urban economy swelled the size of the professional and skilled white-collar workforce and gave them a higher level of consumption denied to rural and low-waged urban workers, who have become increasingly dissatisfied with their low level of consumption.[19] The uneven pattern of development must be acknowledged as a strong motivator for migration, and associated vulnerabilities to trafficking. This reality is inextricably linked to globalization.

Globalization

> I think it's right and proper that people should try to develop, to try to attain a better life for themselves.[20]

The forces of globalization pervade contemporary social reality, including the function and operation of trafficking.

- While globalization has increased cross-border trade and the demand for cheap, low-skilled labour, migration policy has not allowed the free flow of people to fill that demand. This situation of high demand for labour and an absence of legal means for individuals to migrate to fill those positions creates ideal conditions for organized criminal networks to operate.
- Globalization has affected local industries. Economic liberalization has resulted in the influx of mass-produced foreign products into local markets in developing countries, while trade barriers have remained to protect producers and workers in industrialized countries. This has seriously affected local employment opportunities for many poorer regions.

- Globalization has changed the way many people see the world. As people become more aware of living standards and lifestyles in other parts of the world, for example through television or the stories (and sometimes wealth) of returning expatriates, their understanding of their "relative" poverty has increased and their expectations have changed. This motivates people to migrate to secure greater income. There is also evidence that young people in particular consider migration because they want to escape the drudgery of subsistence living and see "the bright lights of the big city".
- In conjunction with increases in the capacity of technology, globalization has facilitated the ease with which criminal networks can operate. Mobile phones and the internet have increased the speed and ease with which different parties can communicate, and have changed the nature of recruitment.

Local/global economies

Globalization has changed the nature of local economies, in part as a result of the enormous market demand for cheap, low-skilled labour. Companies have taken advantage of globalization by relocating operations to, or outsourcing to subcontractors in, low-wage economies. Firms have moved to "flexible" employment through increased use of casual and part-time work, and have adopted enterprise-based bargaining models that effectively reduce unions' capacity to protect wages and conditions.[21] While some firms may operate with integrity, fierce competition to cut costs has the potential to establish industries which are highly exploitative. Such industries need labour, some of which is attracted from communities with little capacity to generate cash income – a factor that was not highly problematic until recently. This too is a result of globalization and the monetarization of economies everywhere, including impoverished areas of poor countries. The need for cash cannot be satisfied in local labour markets, so families send family members out into the global workplace.[22]

Chasing remittances

The desire for hard currency has not only motivated individuals to consider the benefits of a globalized workforce. It has effectively motivated governments to chase foreign currency as a means to "develop" or prop up struggling economies. The Philippines is one example. Migrant workers remit billions of dollars to the Philippines each year – the equivalent of some 9 per cent of GDP – and the country is the world's third-largest recipient of remittances in absolute terms.[23]

The Migrant Workers and Filipinos Act of 1995 states that the Philippines "will no longer promote" overseas employment as a means to sustain economic growth and achieve national development; however, the Philippine government is proactive in its promotion of labour migration.[24] In 2003 Labor Secretary Patricia Santo Tomas said that her department was "targeting to deploy a million Filipinos abroad".[25] The government has substantial infrastructure to facilitate the process, and there are also hundreds of independent (government-licensed) recruitment agencies which arrange migrant workers' travel and employment, many of which operate outside the law.[26]

Of course, most Filipino migrant workers are not trafficked, although some of these legal migrants find themselves employed in exploitative conditions in states which offer them minimal protection. Others, however, are trafficked – a fact confirmed by the deputy executive director of the Commission on Filipinos Overseas in 2000: "Trafficked Filipinos include women who are 'legitimately' recruited, promised high-paying jobs, but end up as prostitutes; women who leave as tourists and end up as domestic helpers, exotic dancers, or bar girls; and women who are willing or coerced victims of the mail-order bride trade."[27] Of greatest concern is that traffickers are able to use the legitimate structures established by governments (source and destination countries) to their own ends.

Migration

Trafficking must be squarely positioned within the context of migration and labour demand. Trafficking can be considered a consequence of what has been called "the commodification of migration".[28] Although there are real cases of abduction, "in most cases, the potential trafficking victim is already seeking a chance to migrate when [she/he] is approached by an acquaintance or lured through an advertisement".[29] This fact prompted Dr Radhika Coomaraswamy, the UN special rapporteur on violence against women, to describe traffickers as "fishing in the stream of migration".[30]

Globalization has affected migration in a number of ways. Macroeconomic policies create the push and pull factors that generate labour migration, and where that movement is illegal, people are vulnerable to trafficking.

The current contradictions in trade policy are a good example of the problem. Economically marginalized people, particularly women, in developing countries are unable to realize their human right to a decent livelihood in their own country partly due to global inequities in trade. On the one hand, the economic liberalization being promoted by industrialized countries exposes them to competition from imports in local markets. On the other, their own products continue to face trade barriers in the markets of those same industrialized countries. The result is strong pressures in those poor countries to migrate to the industrialized economies in search of the means of livelihood, [with people] often becoming victims of trafficking in the process.[31]

While it is widely accepted that globalization has led to increased movement of labour across borders, it is not as widely acknowledged that in some instances this has resulted in exploitation and forced labour – a failure of both labour migration and labour markets. People are trafficked into certain regions because there is a demand for their services. Thousands of women worldwide are trafficked into the sex industry, but the demand for trafficked labour is far more diverse than that one industry. Children are also trafficked into domestic service, armed conflict, service industries like restaurants and bars and hazardous work in factories, agriculture, construction, fishing and begging.[32] In Brazil, sectors include mining, seasonal work in forest clearance, charcoal production and agricultural activities such as cane cutting, grass-seed growing and cotton and coffee harvesting.[33] Girls from Nepal are trafficked into circuses in India, which may involve sex work.[34] In China women are trafficked for marriage. Rural men are willing to pay substantial sums for a trafficked bride who can bear children and extend the family line. Similarly, families will pay traffickers for infants, almost always boys, who they will adopt as their own.[35]

The issue that links trafficking's regional specializations is that in all instances it is addressing particular labour demands; regionally driven demand satisfied by globally mobile labour. Effective targeting reaps big profits. In the United Arab Emirates, for example, girls of 13 or 14 have a high market value, as a female virgin can be sold for US$40,000 for a month's service, after which she may be sent to an ordinary brothel.[36] Outside the sex industry, the trafficking of children results from the unmet demand for cheap and malleable labour in general. For example, researchers interviewing traffickers of Nepalese boys (some as young as 6 years old) to Indian sari embroidery factories were told that the traffickers preferred young boys over adults because they were cheaper, their eyes were sharper and they could work for longer – more than 17 hours a day. Interviews with trafficked boys revealed that their working day had ranged from 10 to 14 hours, without rest.[37] Though children may be less productive than adults, they are less assertive and less able to argue for their legal rights: they can be made to work longer hours with little food, poor accommodation and no benefits.[38]

Not only is child labour intrinsically exploitative, but the levels of exploitation of trafficked children are severe. Children from Mali working on plantations in Côte d'Ivoire worked all day in intolerable heat in the full sun, were housed at night with 15–20 children in only 3 or 4 square metres, had very limited washing facilities and consequently were highly susceptible to skin diseases.[39] Nepalese girls trafficked into sex work in India worked from 3 to 24 hours a day (averaging 13 hours) servicing from 3 to 40 clients per day (averaging 14), the majority of whom did not regularly use condoms. Many of the girls were hungry and they were given almost none of their earnings.[40]

Globalization has not only meant mobility of labour to meet diverse demands, but also diversity of sources of that labour. When one source dries up, traffickers are able to find new victims. For example, the director of the Thai Office of Child Promotion and Protection noted a simultaneous reduction in the number of Thai women and children tricked into prostitution and an increase in the number of foreign victims, especially from Cambodia and Burma.[41] Organized crime has effectively harnessed people's mobility.

Globalized expectations – Relative poverty

Another way in which globalization has increased people's vulnerability to trafficking has been a change in people's expectations, particularly young people, as they become familiar with standards of living in other regions. In some cases, this has also been directly linked to development strategies. For example, the Sebangfai district in Laos has participated in development programmes for up to nine years, yet in a recent study it had the second-highest number of illegal migrant workers in Thailand in Khammuane province. "One of the push factors is that the villagers now have access to electricity, which brings consumerism through, and the influence of Thai television has a certain impact on the youths to seek for work in Thailand."[42]

Aghatise refers to this as "the issue of cultural colonialism; when television programmes create a certain image of the Western world. And then you compare it to the kind of life women live, in which there are only a few possibilities. Every day, they can choose only whether to eat once or twice a day."[43]

The effect is not only created by television. The *Nepal Trafficking in Girls with Special Reference to Prostitution* report refers to a similar effect created by Nepalese village families gaining tin and stone roofs as a result of their children's income. This "demonstration effect"[44] operates across the world.

- In Laos, villages reported that when school children "see others or their friends come back from Thailand with some good changes (e.g. looking better, dressing nicely, becoming popular among their friends), they become attracted to city life and wish to go to seek jobs in Thailand, too".[45]

- In Ukraine, NGO staff maintained that young women are enticed into going abroad by "women who earn money abroad and tell their friends about it when they return home".[46]

- In West Africa, "the attraction of urban areas or supposedly wealthy countries with their facilities and promise of comfort are definitely attracting children. These ideas are reinforced by visits of former inhabitants of a village who return, loaded with presents and who tell tempting stories about city life. This appeals to children who are searching for adventure."[47]

- In Thailand, a woman who had been trafficked expressed her frustration at her neighbours' flaunting of wealth: "'I just hate those parents who keep bragging about how much money they receive from their daughters. Didn't they know how much suffering their daughters must go through, how many men they had to sleep with so the parents can show off their latest models of mobile phones and their huge gold necklaces?'... She herself admitted, however, that back in her prime she never told anyone what she went through either. 'I just couldn't,' she sighed. 'I just told them I was doing fine.'"[48]

Growing consumerism is significantly impacting on people's willingness to put themselves at risk of trafficking, particularly children and young people. In Sebangfai district (Laos), the community stated that the problem of trafficking was not the result of lack of access to schools or job opportunities but was caused by young people's lax morals and ideology: "They take the issue as fashion. Many parents have tried to stop children leaving them but they still leave without the consent of their parents. Most of them will go in a group of friends."[49]

Technology

The technological change that is inextricably linked to increased globalization has facilitated the ease with which criminal networks operate. The development of communication technology, such as mobile phones, has greatly increased the speed and "safety" of criminal communications. The rapid decrease in price and increase in availability of these devices means access for even those at the local and poorer end of criminal networks.

The ILO cites the case of a village in Thailand where traffickers provide two mobile phones to the village and the phone number of the traffickers in Thailand to make appointments and arrangements. Anyone interested in going to work in Thailand can ring them directly to make arrangements. (Traffickers take their salary and they are not paid until the contract is completed. If they leave before the end of the contractual period, for whatever reason, they are not paid.[50])

The internet has not only increased the speed and ease with which different parties can communicate, it has also changed the nature of recruitment. Santos states that in the Philippines, technological advances have been an avenue for a serious rise in trafficking of women and children, one example of which is the internet's use for negotiations for "mail-order brides",[51] now also called "internet brides".

Gupta states that organized criminal networks are using the internet "to market girls all across the world, through all kinds of Internet sites which auction girls ... It is easy for buyers and clients to log on to Internet portals to find out where to go."[52]

Prostitution

> Whether opting to migrate voluntarily to sites of sex trade, or trafficking through means of deceit or coercion, prostitution has increasingly become a means of sustaining and maintaining vast numbers of third world women and their families.[53]

The debates surrounding prostitution among policy-makers, social scientists and feminist academics are fraught to say the least. What is generally agreed upon is that the sex industry has gone global and increasing numbers of women from developing countries are being recruited into it. Some of these women are victims of human trafficking. Compared to other industries, the sex industry has attracted a disproportionate share of traffickers' interest.

- The sex industry is frequently illegal or only partially decriminalized, and generates huge profits for those in control; a perfect *locus operandi* for criminal networks. Aside from other illegal purposes, these profits can be used to expand local sex industries or identify new locations for such industries, expanding the market for trafficking victims.
- There is enormous demand for prostitutes. The work is unattractive or unacceptable to many women and prostitutes frequently have a relatively short working life (youth is prized, some women become ill), so demand is seemingly endless. Criminal networks actively recruit and sometimes force vulnerable women into the industry.
- Like most industries, there is strong demand for cheaper services. Many prostitutes chose to work in the sex industry, but their choices involve consideration of whether income and working conditions are acceptable or not. Trafficked women are frequently moved into situations that other prostitutes would not be prepared to occupy.

• In some instances the sex industry operates like any other industry, with high demand for cheap services and a glut of available workers. Due to enormous disparities in income in different countries, some women are prepared to migrate and work as prostitutes because the possible profits seem enormous. These women's vulnerabilities are exploited because they are not aware of the harsh conditions and levels of control under which they will be forced to work.

For the purposes of this chapter, the key question that needs to be asked is whether the existence of the sex industry makes trafficking inevitable, or more particularly whether the existence of a sex industry in a particular location makes trafficking to that location inevitable. The chapter argues that while the sex industry is an enormous driver of trafficking, the two are not inextricably linked. There are certainly areas in the world where prostitution exists and trafficking does not. Sex work is diverse and context-specific.[54] The way in which the local sex industries intersect with other factors is crucial.

Many local sex industries now operate within a global context. Sangera refers to this as "one mammoth and contiguous structure with its tentacles spread in different regions, globally":

> As in the case of every major multinational enterprise under global capitalism, the principal players and beneficiaries of the sex industry are cohesive and organized ... And therefore, while women are still selling sex in the market, the magnitude, expanse, organization, rate of capital accumulation and range of market strategies employed to sell sexual services make the contemporary transnationalized sex industry qualitatively different from the old practice of prostitution and sex trade.[55]

Of course governments have responsibility for their prostitution-related legal structures and policies and their implementation, but governments and international agencies, particularly banks, are also responsible for allowing environments to develop in which trafficking for prostitution has flourished. The issue of remittances was addressed earlier, but another example is that of (sex) tourism. Tourism is a favoured development strategy, as a source of both employment and hard currency, and significant "development" loans have been made to enable countries to develop their tourism and entertainment industries. In many of these countries the development of the tourism industry has included development of the sex trade. Enloe suggests that "sex tourism is not an anomaly; it is one strand of the gendered tourism industry". Further, the service economy has not necessarily developed as a result of a decline in manufacturing but has been actively encouraged "before manufacturing industries mature. Bar hostesses before automobile workers, not after."[56] Sangera goes further: "Prostitution is no more simply the means of survival or material gains for sections of underprivileged women; it is the chosen strategy for survival, and indeed development, by nations."[57]

Trafficking for prostitution differs from trafficking for most other purposes, because in most other industries the trafficked person generates a saleable good. In reality prostitutes provide a service, but to a customer a prostitute may be objectified to the extent that she becomes the "good". Consumers generally seek cheaper goods but they derive no specific satisfaction from, and may in fact reject, goods produced by trafficked labour. This is not the case with child prostitution, where the age of the children is crucial to the transaction. While some customers may be deterred by knowing that a woman is not voluntarily a sex worker, for others this may be part of the attraction. After all, "prostitution is an industry in which fantasy is an important part of the product".[58]

Is prostitution work?

Just as there is no "standard" victim of trafficking, there is no standard method of recruitment. Some women and girls are literally or ostensibly abducted, some agree to be smuggled for a type of work other than prostitution, while others understand they will be engaged in sex work without understanding the conditions and the degree of exploitation and abuse they will experience. What women who are trafficked for prostitution have in common is that they are from developing countries or countries undergoing severe structural economic changes, and they are satisfying local demand in destination countries.

Many reports (particularly by media and anti-prostitution groups) detail numbers of migrant women working as prostitutes, and assume that these women have been trafficked. Such literature presumes that trafficking, prostitution and labour exploitation are synonymous. It fails to question whether the women concerned wanted to migrate to work as sex workers, whether they knew the conditions under which they would be working and whether they are able to extricate themselves.

It is broadly held that prostitution is different from other work and, for many, the fact that a woman agrees to migrate so that she might work as a sex worker negates any possibility of her being a trafficking victim. This is not the case. She is a victim of trafficking if she is deceived about the conditions of work and then coerced or forced to work in exploitative conditions.[59] This is, in fact, the same standard that is generally applied to definitions of "trafficking" for all other types of work.[60]

The Australian national peak body of community-based sex worker organizations, Scarlet Alliance, estimates fewer than 400 sex workers enter Australia in any 1 year on contract, and that the majority of these women consent to work. Despite its extensive networks, within 1 year the alliance had direct contact with fewer than 10 women who had been deceptively recruited.[61]

The designation of prostitution as different from other work emphasizes the distinction between sex work and other forms of dangerous, low-status labour undertaken by women, such as domestic or factory work. "It hides the commonality, the shared experience of exploitation, which links people in all such work."[62] The fact that some third world women choose to migrate and seek work as prostitutes is firmly rejected by some anti-trafficking campaigners. Nowhere is this more apparent than in the reports of recent "rescues" of trafficking victims by well-intentioned organizations which appear to have been carried out against the will of those being "rescued". One Indian NGO has been publicly criticized "for 'saving' women against their will".[63] The Thai NGO Empower, which has been working with sex workers for 18 years, has detailed another such "rescue" and insists the organization concerned was "unable or unwilling to differentiate between women who have been trafficked and migrant workers". Empower claims that police raided a brothel, accompanied by journalists and photographers who used the women's images in the local papers and on TV the next day. The "rescued" women believed they had been arrested. Empower states that a number of the women later interviewed were emphatic that they had not been trafficked, and that they were satisfied with the wages; an average of 600 baht/day compared to the minimum wage in Chiang Mai of 133 baht/day. To add weight to their claim, prior to the "rescue" the women had had daily contact with Empower, including Thai classes, workshops and outdoor activities, and none had talked about being trafficked or shown any desire to be rescued.[64] Finally, many of the women ran away from the building in which they were held post-"rescue", first a group of 4, then 11 (who strung sheets together to climb from a second-floor window) and then 9 more.[65]

Is prostitution abuse?

The nature of prostitution is unfortunately "undertheorized".[66] Arguments are often polarized, to the extent that it is difficult to source reliable data. Much of this relates to a failure to disaggregate effectively migration, trafficking, prostitution and labour exploitation. Anti-prostitution advocates in particular appear so desperate to make a resounding argument that there is enormous slippage between these categories. In part, prostitution debates among different feminist academic schools are heated because the issues surrounding prostitution involve:

> many of the issues that remain unresolved in feminisms: the relationship between feminists and female "victims of oppression"; the construction of the female subject in terms of "agency" (choice, autonomy, desire, "voice"); the public/private dimension of work/sexuality; the conceptualization of First World/Third World difference; and the sameness in women's status.[67]

As academic as the source of these disagreements may seem, these debates determine the arguments used about appropriate regulation of the sex industry, and consequently the capacity of traffickers to operate within the industry. They have been enormously influential at the international level, some argue, holding up the release of the UN Protocol to Prevent, Suppress and Punish Trafficking in Persons, Especially Women and Children by more than one year.[68]

Feminism (if for a moment we can presume such a singular theory exists) seeks to speak for the best interests of all women; however, many women in fact do not agree with feminist ideology. In the case of prostitution there has been an unfortunate divide between radical feminist theorists and (women) prostitutes, prostitution advocates and liberal feminist theorists.

Radical feminist theorists reject sex work as innately exploitative; effectively denying that prostitution can ever be considered a form of work (views represented, for example, by the Coalition against Trafficking in Women). What this approach misses, however, is the participation of women as actors in prostitution. By failing to distinguish clearly between objectification and abuse, sexual exploitation and sexual violence, this approach fails to reflect the reality that many prostitutes do not identify as victims but as sex workers, and that many women want to migrate to work as sex workers.

Liberal feminists argue that prostitution need not be exploitative (views represented by, for example, the Global Alliance against Traffic in Women). Prostitution involves women's management of their sexuality and their bodies, both of which they have the right to control. Prostitution is a service offered under specific terms, so it is these terms which must be the focus. Industry standards, laws and regulations put women at greater or lower risk of abuse. Criminalizing sex work has the most negative impact. For example, a ban on sex bars can force prostitutes to work in secluded areas – such as public parks – with a higher risk of brutality. Decriminalizing sex work and facilitating sex workers' involvement in the development of industry regulation offers the greatest opportunities for a safe, healthy working environment.

Government and international agency responses

Around the world, governments have markedly different systems of regulation in place to "control" prostitution. In many states prostitution is illegal yet the industry thrives, although some of this may be the result of a lack of enforcement. Women are trafficked into industries that are illegal, legal and decriminalized, but to date no systematic analysis has been undertaken to reveal which of these systems (and the myriad of options available under each system) provides the greatest disincentive to traffickers of women for prostitution.

Illegality may or may not result in fewer women being trafficked, but if women are trafficked they may face greater levels of isolation, stigmatization and marginalization and be at greater risk of violence[69] and control by their traffickers. Legalization may provide greater safety and less exploitative conditions for sex workers. Certainly a healthy, effectively governed legal sector should be of little interest to traffickers, although it is possible that trafficking may fill a niche dictated by the more exploitative end of the industry (which may then be operating illegally).

The Netherlands and Sweden are two first world countries that have taken radically different approaches, both based on extended, considered debate and a sincere desire to reduce violence against women and human trafficking across their borders. Of note, they are two of only a handful of countries which have appointed a rapporteur on trafficking in human beings, despite this being a recommendation of the Hague Ministerial Declaration in 1997.[70] There is no clear evidence to date to suggest which of their approaches has been more successful in reducing trafficking in human beings into the sex industry.

The Netherlands

In the Netherlands prostitution is legal, reflecting the government's position that prostitution "requires a realistic approach, without moralism".[71] Working hours, health and safety regulations, paid leave entitlement, tax law and social security regulations are all regulated by government. Workers are obliged to pay income tax.

While there are certainly many non-Dutch women working as prostitutes, it is difficult to identify accurate figures about how many of these women have been trafficked. Sites such as that of the CATW[72] primarily give statistics that pre-date the legal reforms of the late 1990s and confuse data on prostitution and trafficking. The Dutch national rapporteur on human trafficking quoted various sources identifying up to 371 registrations of trafficking victims in 2002, including some who had been domestically trafficked.[73] A recent report notes that "since the legalization of prostitution in the Netherlands, it has become increasingly difficult to find the victims of trafficking ... On the other hand, there is now a chance for trafficked women to work legally as sex workers",[74] which should minimize the degree of exploitation under which they work.

Sweden

The Swedish government has taken a radically different approach. It maintains that prostitution is an "undesirable social phenomenon", and created a new offence, "gross violation of a woman's integrity", which includes prostitution as a type of violence against women. As of 1 January 1999, the "purchase of sexual services" was prohibited and made punishable by fines and/or imprisonment for up to six months.[75]

Sweden's actions stemmed from a desire to get to the "root cause" of prostitution, which was identified as demand. Currently there is no agreement about whether the strategy has worked. When asked, Gunilla Ekberg, special adviser on issues of prostitution and trafficking in women at the Swedish Division of Gender Equality, replied: "Look around, did you see any women standing on the streets on your way here?"[76] Erndahl of the National Criminal Investigation Department says "the law has definitely had a disruptive effect on the customers",[77] but Martens of the National Council for Crime Prevention has suggested that the law has not reduced prostitution but merely hidden it.[78] There is some concern that if the industry goes underground it may result in greater exploitation of workers, and other issues of crime and safety have been raised. One escort told Reuters: "There are maybe two or three serious escorts in Sweden. The rest are run by organized crime and the clients are often robbed and then they can't go to the police and complain."[79]

The National Criminal Investigation Department estimates that between 200 and 500 women are trafficked to Sweden each year.[80] One of the challenges for Sweden is policing its extensive borders, including a 400-kilometre unguarded border with Finland which sees crossings of 18 million people a year, and the use of Finnish Schengen visas which allow the holders to travel into Sweden. Police have documented busloads of women arriving, the implication being that they work as prostitutes.[81]

Gender

Men, women, girls and boys are victims of human trafficking, but while this fact may imply some universality of risks and experiences, trafficking operates in a highly gender-targeted way. Unlike "sex", i.e. people's

biological difference, "gender" refers to the social and cultural constructions of human beings, their roles, behaviours and expectations associated with their gender status. While men and women differ biologically,
they are also evaluated differently, and these supposed differences in
characteristics and capabilities often become a source and means to sig-
nify and justify their rights, roles, responsibilities, etc. Logically, gender
is a social category that significantly contributes to a person's life chances
and participation in society.

An individual's gender impacts upon his/her vulnerability to trafficking
in different regions in different ways. There are, however, a number of
general observations which can be universally applied.

- Men and women frequently have different access to resources, different social responsibilities and different understandings of their own
  capacities – making them more or less likely to accept offers of work
  which may place them at risk of trafficking.
- Gender has a direct impact on the type of employment people are able
  to access. Most industries are gendered because employers seek male
  or female employees based on the presumption that the performances
  of men and women differ.
- Legal migration options are frequently gendered as a response to industry demands. Male-dominated sectors such as construction and agricultural work usually offer opportunities for men, while legal migration
  into domestic work and the adult entertainment sectors is far more limited. As a consequence, women are more likely to resort to illegal and
  more dangerous forms of migration that make them highly vulnerable
  to trafficking.[82]

Economic inequality is gendered

The majority of the world's poor are women. At a local level this has
meant that many women are without employment options. Such economic inequality "ensures a supply of desperately poor women and girls
willing to do anything to survive".[83] The Asian Development Bank states
that "the number of women living in poverty [in the Asia Pacific region]
has increased disproportionately over the past decade, compared to the
number of men".[84] Similarly, structural economic changes in the CIS
have had a disproportionate impact on women. Where old Soviet economic systems have been disrupted or discarded there has been
economic contraction and hyperinflation, which have wiped out people's
savings and security.[85]

For example, between 1994 and 1997 Moldovan men experienced a
slight decrease in their unemployment rate from 37 per cent to 32 per
cent, while the unemployment rate for women increased from 62 per

cent to 68 per cent. The effects of rapidly deteriorating economic conditions were compounded during that time by discrimination against women in the labour market. In Ukraine, by 1996 70–80 per cent of the unemployed were women, two-thirds of whom had post-high school degrees.[86] Both Moldova and Ukraine have become source countries for women trafficked into prostitution.

Industries are gendered

Most industries into which people are trafficked are highly gendered. Generally women are trafficked into sweatshops, domestic work and prostitution because of the gendered perception of skills that are desired in those industries, for example being gentle, caring, paying attention to detail, etc. Men are more likely to be trafficked into industries such as agricultural labour and mining, as a result of their expected capacity to tolerate hard physical work. The trafficking industry also targets by gender individuals who are trafficked outside the formal notion of "employment"; for example, in China women are trafficked as brides and infant boys are trafficked for adoption.[87]

The targeting of men, women, boys and girls into different industries also contributes to the different experiences of these groups, as the operation of each industry differs. An obvious example is trafficking of Nepalese girls to India for prostitution and Nepalese boys to India to work in sari embroidery factories. Both practices are exploitative, but the experiences of these two groups are clearly very different. One simple example is from Togo, where girls are trafficked as domestic servants and boys as farm labourers: a recent study found that "most of the girls … fled their traffickers following prolonged periods of physical and mental abuse, [while] most boys were released after a period of time and told to find their way home to Togo".[88]

While some people are aware of the industries into which they will eventually be trafficked (but not the degree of exploitation they will suffer), others are not. Gender roles and the gendered nature of industries are so readily accepted in many societies that traffickers are able to use this notion to their advantage in their deceptions. For example, traffickers might say they are recruiting for one highly gendered industry, such as domestic work, when they are actually recruiting for another highly gendered industry, prostitution. This example applies to many, including those women trafficked to South Africa who "generally believe that they are migrating legally for work in a variety of jobs, usually in the hospitality sector, but are exploited in the sex industry".[89]

The gendered nature of industries also has the capacity to change both the inbound and outbound nature of migration. In the Philippines, for example, the legal migration stream had become highly feminized by the mid-1980s as a result of the demand for nurses, domestic helpers and other types of "care-givers" in East Asian countries, the Middle East and Europe.[90] Additional to this was the demand for "entertainers" in Japan, the majority of whom were women and many of whom ended up coerced or forced into prostitution. While the Philippines is an interesting example, internationally most legal channels of migration provide opportunities in male-dominated sectors such as construction and agriculture. Women are relegated to the informal labour market (domestic labour, entertainment industry, prostitution). This means that internationally more men are able to migrate legally but women who wish to migrate are more likely to consider migration options which make them vulnerable to trafficking.[91]

Of course, gender targeting also intersects with other factors, for example age. This is true of domestic service, although this industry operates differently in different regions. In the Philippines adult women are trafficked as domestics to Singapore and the Middle East (although it is important to note that much of this migration is legal). In Central and Western Africa young girls are trafficked as domestics. In fact, the ILO estimates that more girl children under 16 are in domestic service than in any other category of work or child labour.[92] The intersection of age and gender is, however, nowhere more apparent than in the sex industry. Around the world, young women frequently have greater value than older women. In Africa this has taken on a further dimension influenced by the prevalence of HIV/AIDS and "the mistaken belief that having sex with a child is not only 'cleaner' and therefore 'safer', but even that it can cure the disease".[93]

Gender roles

Traditional gender roles frequently work to girls' disadvantage. Often poverty forces parents to choose which of their children to send to school and which to have at home to assist with labour. In many countries, including India, Nepal and those of Central and West Africa, strong societal gender bias means that parents choose to educate their sons. Sometimes parents send girls to work in part because the girl's income helps to support the schooling of her brothers.[94]

Gender roles include the belief that the most important thing a girl/woman can achieve is to be married before she is too old to attract a husband, and that to make a good match she must bring a dowry. In Togo more girls than boys are trafficked not only because parents consider domestic work as good preparation for married life but also because of parents' perceived need for girls to earn their dowry.[95] In many South

Asian communities there is strong preference for sons over daughters, in part because "marrying off a daughter – with a dowry and all requisite gifts – can put an unsustainable strain on family finances".[96] The need to earn a dowry pushes families to consider employment options that make their daughters vulnerable to trafficking. Additionally, the urgency of finding a good match can itself lead to such circumstances. In many regions there are cases of young women accepting offers of marriage to people they do not know well, which result in their being trafficked. In Nepal fake marriage was the second most prevalent means of trafficking girls.[97]

The trafficking industry has also been affected by the changing status of women and gendered expectations of women in destination countries. As women have moved into the paid labour force, and particularly into "professional" occupations, in certain regions of the world demand has increased for labour to take up their slack. This is also partly a consequence of men clinging to gendered notions of work/house responsibility and not increasing their share of domestic work. The wages offered for domestic service and other service sector occupations, including home-based care of the elderly and disabled, are often not attractive to women nationals.[98] In some countries this has created a strong legal structure to facilitate migrant women's entry for this type of work; in others it is not possible to gain legal entry for this purpose. In both circumstances it seems that some workers are employed in highly exploitative situations, and some women are trafficked for this explicit purpose. As well as the standard isolations of being in a foreign country (not speaking the language and being unaware of legal rights), domestic work presents particular difficulties in terms of monitoring labour standards – individuals can be completely isolated, being the only worker living and working at their house/workplace.

Changing gender roles and associated expectations have not only affected the first world. In China, gendered perceptions of men's and women's roles have had a significant impact on the marriage market for trafficked women. This has resulted in part from the highly distorted gendered perception of boys' and girls' "intrinsic" value, which might be more accurately understood as men's responsibility in later life to provide for their parents and continue the family line. The highly distorted sex ratio at birth and the millions of "missing women" that resulted from the "one-child" population policy and strong son preference leading to widespread abortion of female foetuses[99] have meant a lack of women available as marriage partners. Additionally, many of the women who have moved from rural to urban areas to work (often as waitresses or domestics – again highly gendered industries) want to stay in the cities. As a consequence, many rural men cannot find a local wife to carry on the family line.[100]

While in China gendered expectations of women's role in marriage have created a domestic market for trafficked women, in other parts of the world it is one of the push factors that encourage women to consider migration options that place them at risk of trafficking. As noted above, many women are "lured" by the promises of paid employment, disposable income and city life as an alternative to the drudgery of their current environment, which may include early marriage, multiple childbirth, infant mortality and hard physical labour. For others, the marriage contract includes the unstated obligation to tolerate domestic violence. In Ukraine, for example, it seems some women choose to seek work abroad to escape their situations of domestic violence. Hotline workers at the Women for Women Center in Donetsk, Ukraine, explained:

> If a woman wants to leave a violent relationship or household she has to start from scratch. She has to change everything including where she lives and where she works. This is why women are so attracted by ads for jobs in other countries. They are often desperate to get out and go somewhere new. If you tell them that they are likely to be forced into prostitution they say "well better to be a prostitute than to be raped and abused by my husband".[101]

Finally, rescuers and retrainers are often blind to their own gendered interpretation of "what women need", doing little to reduce women's vulnerability to further trafficking. Instead of treating women as adult actors in their situations, some "rescuers" appear to consider women only as "victims" who need "saving", at times infantilizing their vulnerability and treating them as children. This does little to address the complexity of their lives or empower them to make positive decisions for their future. Similarly, programmes for trafficking returnees tend to provide training in occupations that are traditional for women, and hence low skilled and poorly paid – in no way competitive to the wages offered by traffickers. Programmes that offer returnees, particularly returning commercial sex workers, training in crafts or sewing are unlikely to be effective unless they are able to offer relatively high earnings. The "solution" of a subsistence lifestyle leaves women vulnerable to retrafficking.

Race/ethnicity

> If she's light-colored, then she is sexually attractive to this population.[102]

Race, ethnicity, cultural identity, caste and the like contribute to people's vulnerability to trafficking in a range of ways.

- Discrimination can make it difficult if not impossible for a person to secure work, particularly well-paid work, in their country of origin, leading them to consider migration options.
- Traditional values based on cultural identity may influence a person's perceptions of what constitutes appropriate work, behaviours, rights and entitlements, and consequently influence the kind of employment they aim for and conditions they experience.
- Race/caste-based stereotypes may directly affect people's employability in destination countries.

It is also important to note that analysts' subtle racist lenses may contribute to their perception of people's vulnerability to trafficking, and consequently arguments that certain groups of people are "real" trafficking victims and thus deserving of rescue. Kempadoo and Doezema make this point in relation to various analyses that have been applied to the sex industry.[103] Frequently analysts have confused some women's lack of economic choice and non-Western cultural practices and morals with a denial of those women's capacity to utilize their own agency. This neo-colonial temptation to (inadvertently) frame arguments in terms of the perceived liberation of some peoples and the backwardness of others has the potential to skew both data and arguments. One possible means to bypass this problem is by remaining focused on the issue that people are trafficked into certain labour markets, and it is the conditions in those markets (i.e. their unacceptability) which define whether they have been trafficked.

Discrimination – At home

Race-based discrimination that exists within a state/society is likely to impact on a person's legal rights and entitlements, and ability to access and complete education and find employment. This same discrimination affects people's vulnerability to trafficking. Membership of an ethnic minority may mean lack of access to employment, which can in turn push people to look for opportunities to find work elsewhere, particularly the possibility of migration. Such race-based discrimination exists in varying degrees in most if not all countries, but it reveals itself differently in different parts of the world. For example, in Bolivia, Ecuador, Guatemala and Peru indigenous people are often among the most at risk of trafficking and labour exploitation.[104] In other regions race-based discrimination combines with state-prescribed laws of residence and citizenship to exacerbate people's disadvantage. In the Greater Mekong subregion, UNESCO has described lack of citizenship as "the single greatest risk factor for hill tribe women in Thailand being trafficked".[105] Bindman makes the point that slavery is closely associated with a lack of full citizenship rights.[106]

While discrimination is often overt, at times it is also an unintended consequence of a lack of acknowledgement of the diversity of a population group (their experiences, values, languages and needs) and/or lack of resources. In ethnically diverse regions, governments may struggle to guarantee an equitable spread of resources. Laos, for example, has a population of less than 5 million, but 47 official ethnic subgroups:[107] considerable diversity (not yet disaggregated by age, gender, income, etc.) to be resourced by an economically weak government, and a population from which traffickers recruit.

There has been considerable debate about whether caste-based discrimination should be included as a form of racism, as evidenced by the proceedings of the World Conference against Racism held in Durban in late 2002. *Human Rights Features* states that despite the fact that caste is an issue in a number of countries, including Nepal, Japan (Burakus), Senegal (Groits) and Nigeria (Osu and Oru), the Indian government maintained that the caste issue was being turned into a "country-specific" issue, and that reference or the absence of reference to caste became "an issue of victory or defeat".[108] The final Durban Declaration and Programme of Action does not mention caste-based discrimination.

This chapter considers that caste fits squarely within the broad definition of race-based discrimination, as does ethnicity and cultural identity, and there is certainly evidence that membership of a particular caste contributes to people's vulnerability to trafficking. For example, the *Nepal Trafficking in Girls with Special Reference to Prostitution* report estimated that 12,000 children are trafficked from Nepal every year, and while that trafficking crosses many caste/ethnic groups, members of the hill ethnic group and lower castes are most at risk.[109] In Nepal, as in other countries, the caste system operates to marginalize groups of people, making them more vulnerable to trafficking. Capital is generally controlled by a limited group, while those from "'lower" castes face economic discrimination and a sense of subordination.[110] "In remote rural areas, the hierarchical caste system is fundamentally exclusionary. Lower caste people face economic exploitation, social discrimination and high risk of sexual exploitation."[111] Location within the caste system has a direct relationship to earning potential and poverty, and consequently to vulnerability to trafficking.

As is the case with other forms of racism, at its worst caste-based prejudice not only locks people out of earning opportunities, it also ascribes particular (negative) attributes to them, as though such attributes were "natural" given their position in the caste hierarchy. For example, in a Nepalese study one girl from the "untouchable" caste reported that men of higher castes forced her into prostitution and claimed it was her "caste occupation".[112] Conversely, this system operates to the disadvantage of girls from "higher" castes if they are found to be engaged in prostitution. "Girls engaged in prostitution in Nepalgunj were reluctant to tell their names and their caste/ethnic identity due to fear of police brutality if it became known they were of higher castes."[113]

Cultural values

Cultural values, based on a person's race or ethnic identity, also impact on vulnerability to trafficking as these values may make a person more or less likely to consider certain actions or conditions as acceptable, more or less likely to migrate for work and more or less vulnerable to traffickers' deceptions. Another way of considering this is that there is frequently conflict between contemporary international human rights standards and those values which people describe as "traditional" to their race or ethnic group.[114] For example, in West and Central Africa putting children to work is socially acceptable, it being "customary to assign tasks to children as young as four years old".[115]

> The role of traditions such as placement of children in extended family, compulsory work in religious schools, compulsory labour exacted under traditional systems of governance and long-established notions of "slave" and "slaveholder" make the acceptance of the concept of forced labour and associated trafficking difficult to achieve.[116]

In many parts of rural China human rights awareness is low and "few people perceive purchasing a woman or child as criminal or immoral".[117] In these areas such behaviour is considered a "normal" part of cultural practice, which then directly affects (i.e. expands) the market for trafficked women and children. In Nepal many children "feel and think like adult breadwinners",[118] which puts immense pressure on them, increasing their vulnerability to trafficking. In fact, a WOREC study which interviewed boys who had been trafficked and subsequently returned to Nepal found that most of the boys did not feel that they had been victims of trafficking until after the initial sensitization sessions.[119]

Discrimination – At the destination

Race/ethnic identity frequently has a direct impact on a person's employability in a destination country, and consequently their usefulness to traffickers and their vulnerability to being recruited and trafficked. In many countries different industries reveal a clear hierarchy of employability, salaries and conditions based on race. The race-based labour hierarchy not only determines whether a person is employable in a given market, but also affects the conditions and degree of exploitation under which they are forced to work.

Firstly, a racist and xenophobic lens is frequently applied to compare foreign workers, including victims of trafficking, to nationals/local workers. This has the potential to reduce the foreign/racially/ethnically different worker to someone who is perceived to deserve fewer human rights, or at worst someone who:

> is not perceived as an equal human being and so can be used and abused in ways that would be impossible in respect to workers of the same race/ethnicity ... Racism, xenophobia and prejudice against ethnic minorities make it much easier for clients and employers to convince themselves that such practices are justified.[120]

Secondly, the race-based labour hierarchy frequently operates so that foreign workers are compared against each other. A recent IOM study revealed that certain groups or nationalities were found generally to be preferred by employers in all the European and Asian countries studied:

> In India, tribal Christians were typically considered desirable employees because they are stereotyped as professional, hardworking and disciplined. In Sweden, there was a preference for girls from the Baltic States because they need social and economic aid. Meanwhile in Thailand, the Burmese were stereotyped as particularly desirable as domestic workers.[121]

Such general preferences, while appearing sympathetic, are based on simple racist stereotypes.

Similarly, the globalized sex industry relies heavily on racist stereotypes of women and cultures, which translate into radicalized hierarchies. In the Caribbean, the Curacao sex industry is structured in a clear hierarchy of race/skin colour descending from white Europeans to light-skinned women from Colombia and the Dominican Republic and then to locals of Afro-Caribbean descent. Similar patterns appear in Haiti and Cuba.[122] In other sex industries, Asian women are frequently constructed and marketed as undemanding, demure, exotic, childlike women, particularly to non-Asian clients. Their construction is diametrically opposed to that of the demanding, emasculating woman of the first world. Such underhand racist generalizations about Asian women (effectively all reduced to "Asian woman") then work to reassure the customer that the power relation is "natural", assuaging any guilt he might otherwise feel.

In Asia the market differentiates more effectively but no less simplistically and hierarchically between workers from different Asian countries.

The Thai delegation to the World Conference against Racism raised the issue that in Thailand women of certain racial or ethnic groups were likely to be subjected to greater abuse than other women, and that "trafficking in women and girls, frequently involved racist attitudes and perceptions".[123] This assertion is supported by a quote from recent IOM research, where a Thai government employee stated:

> I prefer Thai sex workers because I feel more comfortable with them, and I don't feel proud of myself if I go with migrant sex workers. Socially it is looked down to be with Burmese sex workers because they work in particular types of establishments which are lower, and friends look down on it. Poorer men have to go to migrant workers because they are cheaper.[124]

War/state collapse

Surely this cannot be one of the peace dividends in the Balkans?[125]

The degree to which war and conflict greatly increase people's vulnerability to trafficking has only recently been recognized. In fact, Rehn and Sirleaf suggest that trafficking/sexual slavery and conflict are inextricably linked.[126] This interrelationship operates in a range of ways during times of conflict.

- Government strategies to reduce human trafficking are likely to be given a low priority (along with many other functions of governance in peacetime).
- Normal immigration procedures and border controls may be disrupted.
- Breakdowns in governance may facilitate corruption among officials and provide openings for organized crime to take control of various markets, including the trade in arms, drugs and people.
- Normal employment is frequently disrupted, leaving people in a precarious economic situation and more likely to look at options that would otherwise be considered unnecessary or risky. People may become more inclined to consider the option of migration as a means to find employment and earn an income.
- The desire for a safe and secure environment may also prompt people to consider means of migration.
- The influx of troops may lead to an increase in prostitution, which may include trafficked prostitutes. This may actually be more acute during reconstruction.
- Military groups may utilized child soldiers and may also use trafficked people to undertake other undesirable dangerous tasks.

Breakdown of governance

Given the newness of the recognition that conflict makes people vulnerable to trafficking, much of the available literature focuses on occurrences in Bosnia and Herzegovina, where in 2002 the UN mission estimated that between 750 and 1,000 trafficked women and girls remained trapped in brothels across the country. NGOs estimated the figure as 2,000 or more.[127] By April 2002 the IOM had assisted more than 300 women and girls who had been identified as victims of trafficking in Kosovo.[128]

Reports document the post-conflict increase in the activities of organized crime and the complicity and corruption of government officials. Corruption of individual officers allowed trafficking to flourish. "In Bosnia, involvement of local police ranged from visiting brothels as 'gratis' clients to facilitating the trafficking of women in the country."[129] However, the matter goes further than the actions of individual officers to suggest that by default (rather than intention) the state became complicit in the trade. How else is it possible that, with unemployment at over 40 per cent, local police stations throughout Bosnia and Herzegovina were allowed to issue work permits to nightclub owners for "dancers" and "waitresses"?[130] Strong governance was absent. Trafficking laws that existed went largely unenforced.[131]

Migrating populations

Not surprisingly, political turmoil and conflict act as a catalyst for people to leave their homes to ensure their own safety and identify ways of achieving a livelihood. Such increases in irregular migrants and asylum-seekers have been documented internationally from conflicts in numerous regions, including Colombia,[132] Africa,[133] the Middle East[134] and Kosovo.[135] People's desperation may not only make them likely to consider work outside their country, but also to accept offers of work with some risks attached. Asylum-seekers and refugees are not immune. In particular, young displaced women – especially those not under the protection of the UN High Commissioner for Refugees and those without the support of family members – are at risk of recruitment.

Criminal groups are quick to take advantage of new "opportunities":

> According to news reports, criminal gangs began infiltrating refugee camps as they were created for the fleeing Kosovars. Repeating a pattern seen during the Bosnian conflict, these criminals will persuade young refugee women – many of whom have been separated from their families – to leave the camps for promises of new homes and higher paying jobs. Some reports indicate that traffickers have abducted women who were unwilling to leave the camps.[136]

Almost 900,000 refugees fled Kosovo. Camps included a significant number of unaccompanied children, war widows and women and children whose male family members had returned first to their homes. These women and children constituted a particularly vulnerable population and were targeted by established trafficking networks already operating in the region. Some of them at least were included in groups of people smuggled into Italy.[137]

The practice of preying on young women who have experienced conflict-related trauma is not specific to Kosovo. In Guatemala traffickers exploited gendered stigmas attached to rape by targeting girls raped in the course of armed conflict and exploiting their concern about their damaged marriage prospects.[138]

Troops – Prostitution

In Bosnia and Herzegovina trafficking of women appears to have arisen not during the conflict but in the chaos that followed formal fighting. A similar pattern has recently been reported in FYR Macedonia, where the conflict which broke out in March 2001 appears to have triggered a reduction in the trafficking in women, as dealing in arms became more profitable.[139] This may have been exacerbated by the decrease in UN and KFOR personnel on leave from Kosovo, resulting in a drop in numbers of prostitution customers.[140]

It is accepted by many that "the main perpetrators of sexual violence and exploitation in conflict situations are typically the armed forces",[141] and even while the vast majority of peacekeepers carry out their duties with professionalism, the UNIFEM *Women, War and Peace* report quotes documented violations relating to sexual violence in Angola, Bosnia and Herzegovina, Cambodia, the Democratic Republic of Congo (DRC), East Timor, Liberia, Mozambique, Kosovo, Sierra Leone and Somalia.[142] To date, however, there has been little substantive research on the relationship between the stationing of troops (including peacekeeping troops) and the intersection of sexual violence, prostitution and trafficking.

Troops frequently feed a demand for prostitution, and in some instances prostitutes include victims of trafficking. Human Rights Watch states that since the end of the war and the stationing of international troops, Bosnia and Herzegovina has become a major trafficking destination. Trafficked women and girls reported that 30 per cent of their clients were "internationals". Local NGOs believe that the presence of thousands of expatriate civilians and soldiers has been a significant motivating factor for traffickers.[143] Prostitution increases, however, not simply because of the enormous number of "single" men and their attitudes, but also because of the absolute disparity in the economics of the two groups: well-paid personnel and women without other employment options, in local economies that have been devastated.[144]

The nature of recent conflict and UN peacebuilding initiatives has added another actor to the equation – civilian contractors. In Bosnia and Herzegovina a number of civilian contractors to the US military (employed by DynCorp) were found to have "purchased" women from brothels and kept them in their accommodation.[145] The incidents were serious enough to prompt eight members of the US Helsinki Commission to write to Deputy Secretary of State Richard L. Armitage "requesting information about State Department efforts to ensure that US contractors do not participate in prostitution or human trafficking related activities in Iraq [where Dyn Corp is active] or elsewhere".[146]

Trafficking for war

In other regions human trafficking operates right through conflict, and even forms a fundamental part of the strategy to build up armed forces. ILO Director-General Juan Somavia has stated that "perhaps there is no greater challenge or more pressing charge than freeing the 300,000 children who are caught in the crossfire of conflict" as child soldiers.[147] Children become soldiers for a range of reasons. A recent ILO report states that some 64 per cent of children in armed groups said they had made a personal decision to enrol. However, on closer examination half of these said they took the decision under extreme psychological pressure for their immediate survival, while the other half saw a long-term means of earning a living.[148] Twenty-one per cent of the remaining sample had been abducted, often by rebel groups.

The Coalition to Stop the Use of Child Soldiers believes that more than 120,000 children under 18 years of age are currently participating in armed conflicts across Africa, some no more than 7 or 8 years old. Affected countries include Angola, Burundi, Congo-Brazzaville, the DRC, Ethiopia, Liberia, Rwanda, Sierra Leone, Sudan and Uganda.[149] Human Rights Watch has reported that Myanmar's army includes some 70,000 children, many of whom appear to have been forcibly recruited. Likewise, armed ethnic groups use child soldiers, again many of whom are forcibly conscripted.[150]

In some of the worst cases of trafficking in conflict, people are abducted by armed groups and forced to accompany them on raids and to provide everything from food to sexual services. In Sierra Leone there is clear evidence of armed groups having abducted girls and young women to use as prostitutes. Many sexual slaves are also used for dangerous work like demining contested areas, "forced to risk their lives to make a field or hillside safe for soldiers".[151]

Conclusion

This chapter has illustrated the broader social and political forces which are fundamental to understanding human trafficking. It also displays the diversity of types of trafficking and the difficulty of generalizing about the phenomenon. Of course, the structural factors here do not form a direct causal relationship with trafficking. However, an examination of documented cases of trafficking suggests patterns which point to the significance of these structural factors. A more precise consideration of when and why these factors explain human trafficking can only be attempted in conjunction with proximate factors, such as inadequate national and international legal regimes; poor law enforcement, immigration/ migration laws and policies; inadequate as well as poorly enforced labour laws and standards; corruption and complicity of the state in criminal activities; support by state officials of underground criminal networks; and organized criminal/parallel entrepreneurship. This conjunction is illustrated in the case studies which feature in this volume.

Notes

1. B. Kumar KC, G. Subedi, Y. B. Gurung and K. P. Adhikani, *Nepal Trafficking in Girls with Special Reference to Prostitution: A Rapid Assessment*, Geneva: International Labour Organization, 2001, p. 20.
2. Human Rights Watch, *Borderline Slavery – Child Trafficking in Togo*, New York: Human Rights Watch, 2003, p. 10.
3. International Labour Organization/International Programme on the Elimination of Child Labour, *Combating Trafficking in Children for Labour Exploitation in West and Central Africa – Synthesis Report*, Geneva: International Labour Organization, 2001, p. 43.
4. Women's Rehabilitation Centre, *Cross Border Trafficking in Boys*, Kathmandu: International Labour Organization, 2002, p. 18.
5. International Labour Organization/International Programme on the Elimination of Child Labour, "Labour Migration and Trafficking within the Greater Mekong Subregion: Proceedings of Mekong Subregional Experts Meeting and Exploratory Policy Paper", Bangkok: International Labour Organization, 2001, p. 11.
6. Kumar et al., note 1 above, p. 26.
7. Ibid., p. 35.
8. Women's Rehabilitation Centre, note 4 above, p. 10.
9. Kumar et al., note 1 above, p. 2.

10. International Labour Organization/International Programme on the Elimination of Child Labour, note 3 above, p. 8.
11. Ibid., p. 14.
12. Ibid., p. 3.
13. Minnesota Advocates for Human Rights, *Trafficking in Women: Moldova and Ukraine*, Minneapolis, Minn.: Minnesota Advocates for Human Rights, 2000, p. 19.
14. Kumar et al., note 1 above, p. 2.
15. Quoted in International Labour Organization/International Programme on the Elimination of Child Labour, note 3 above, p. 28.
16. International Labour Organization/International Programme on the Elimination of Child Labour, note 5 above, p. 35.
17. Asian Development Bank, *Fighting Poverty in Asia and the Pacific: The Poverty Reduction Strategy*, 2004, available at www.adb.org/Documents/policies/poverty _reduction/default.asp.
18. International Labour Organization/International Programme on the Elimination of Child Labour, note 3 above, p. 5.
19. Satoko Watanabe, "From Thailand to Japan: Migrant Sex Workers as Autonomous Subjects", in Kamala Kempadoo and Jo Doezema, eds, *Global Sex Workers: Rights, Resistance, and Redefinition*, New York: Routledge, 1998, p. 122.
20. Esohe Aghatise, quoted in Pamela Shifman, "Trafficking and Women's Human Rights in a Globalised World", *Gender and Development* 11(1), 2003, p. 127.
21. Lorraine Corner, "A Gender Perspective to Combat Trafficking – An Integrated Approach to Livelihood Options for Women and Girls", unpublished paper, 2002, p. 13.
22. Ibid., p. 11.
23. Robert Burgess and Vikram Haksar, "Migration and Foreign Remittances in the Philippines", IMF Working Paper No. 111, Washington, D.C.: IMF, 2005.
24. Kristof Van Impe, "People for Sale: The Need for a Multidisciplinary Approach towards Human Trafficking", in *Perspectives on Trafficking of Migrants*, Geneva: International Organization for Migration, 2000, p. 116.
25. Burgess and Haksar, note 23 above.
26. "Coalition against Trafficking in Human Beings in the Philippines – Phase 1", UNICRI, project document, 21 March 2000, p. 5.
27. Catherine Paredes-Maceda, "Prevention of Trafficking, Protection, and Rehabilitation of Victims", in Ministry of Foreign Affairs, *Japan, Asia-Pacific Symposium on Trafficking in Persons* (proceedings), 20 January 2000, p. 29.
28. Majid Tehranian, "Cultural Security and Global Governance: International Migration and Negotiations of Identity", in Jonathan Friedman and Shalini Randeria, eds, *Worlds on the Move: Globalisation, Migration and Cultural Security*, London: I.B. Tauris, 2004, p. 15.
29. UN Department of Public Information, "Backgrounder to the World Conference against Racism, Racial Discrimination, Xenophobia and Related Intolerance", New York: UN Department of Public Information, March 2001.
30. Jubilee Campaign, "Peers Press for an End to Trafficking", Jubilee Campaign, 14 March 2002, available at www.jubileecampaign.co.uk/world/traf.htm.
31. Corner, note 21 above, p. 25.
32. ILO, *World of Work* 47, 2003, p. 5.
33. International Labour Organization, *Trafficking in Human Beings – New Approaches to Combating the Problem*, Geneva: International Labour Organization, 2002, p. 38.
34. Kumar et al., note 1 above, p. 20.

35. International Labour Organization/International Programme on the Elimination of Child Labour, *Yunnan Province, China, Situation of Trafficking in Children and Women: A Rapid Assessment*, Bangkok: International Labour Organization, 2002, p. vii.
36. An OSCE official, Cerasela Nicolas, quoted in Roland Eggleston, "Armenia: Government Pressured to Toughen Laws on Human Trafficking", Radio Free Europe/Radio Liberty, available at www.rferl.org/nca/features/2001/07/30072001112827.asp.
37. Women's Rehabilitation Centre, note 4 above, pp. 2, 14, 26.
38. ILO, note 32 above, p. 5.
39. International Labour Organization/International Programme on the Elimination of Child Labour, note 3 above, p. 31.
40. Kumar et al., note 1 above, p. 2.
41. Bhanravee Tansubhapol, *Bangkok Post*, 2 April 2003, p. 1.
42. International Labour Organization/International Programme on the Elimination of Child Labour, *Preliminary Assessment on Trafficking of Children and Women for Labour Exploitation in Lao PDR*, Laos: International Labour Organization, 2003, p. 36.
43. Aghatise in Shifman, note 20 above, p. 128.
44. Kumar et al., note 1 above, p. 36.
45. International Labour Organization/International Programme on the Elimination of Child Labour, note 42 above, p. 34.
46. Minnesota Advocates for Human Rights, note 13 above, p. 17.
47. International Labour Organization/International Programme on the Elimination of Child Labour, note 3 above, p. 29.
48. Mae Sai and Mari Nyota, "Coming Home to Disappointment", *Bangkok Post*, 21 August 2003, p. 1.
49. International Labour Organization/International Programme on the Elimination of Child Labour, note 42 above, p. 37.
50. Ibid., p. 32.
51. Aida Santos, quoted in Shifman, note 20 above, p. 126.
52. Ruchira Gupta, quoted in Shifman, note 20 above, p. 126.
53. Jyoti Sangera, "In the Belly of the Beast: Sex Trade, Prostitution and Globalization", Discussion Paper for South Asia Regional Consultation on Prostitution, 17–18 February 1997, unpublished.
54. Alison Murray, "Debt-Bondage and Trafficking: Don't Believe the Hype", in Kamala Kempadoo and Jo Doezema, eds, *Global Sex Workers: Rights, Resistance, and Redefinition*, New York: Routledge, 1998, p. 52.
55. Sangera, note 53 above.
56. Cynthia Enloe, *Bananas, Beaches and Bases: Making Feminist Sense of International Politics*, Berkeley and Los Angeles: University of California Press, 1990, p. 34.
57. Sangera, note 53 above.
58. Harriet D. Lyons, "The Representation of Trafficking in Persons in Asia – Orientalism and Other Perils", in *Trafficking, Sex-Work, Prostitution: Discourses and Representations of the Sub-Continent, Re/productions*, No. 2, April 1999, available at www.hsph.harvard.edu/grhf/, p. 1.
59. Examples might include being forced to work 7 days/week, 24-hour shifts, when ill or injured, or having threats made to kill family members if the woman does not comply.
60. Of course, arguments about choice do not apply to children, who are not "able" to consent to such practices. This standard must be applied despite the fact that they are ostensibly trafficked into (an extension of) the adult sex industry, although there may be specific demand for their services.

61. Scarlet Alliance, "Submission to Parliamentary Joint Committee on the Australian Crime Commission – Inquiry into Trafficking in Women and Sexual Servitude", Australia, September 2003.
62. Jo Bindman, "An International Perspective on Slavery in the Sex Industry", in Kamala Kempadoo and Jo Doezema, eds, *Global Sex Workers: Rights, Resistance, and Redefinition*, New York: Routledge, 1998, p. 65.
63. Maggie Jones, "Thailand's Brothel Busters", MotherJones.com, November/December 2003, available at www.motherjones.com/news/outfront/2003/11/ma_570_01.html.
64. Empower, *A Report by Empower Chiang Mai on the Human Rights Violations Women Are Subjected to When "Rescued" by Anti-trafficking Groups Who Employ Methods Using Deception, Force and Coercion*, Empower, 2003, available at www.nswp.org/mobility/mpower-0306.html.
65. Jones, note 63 above.
66. Rajeshwari Sunder Rajan, "The Prostitution Question(s) – (Female) Agency, Sexuality and Work", in *Trafficking, Sex-Work, Prostitution: Discourses and Representations of the Sub-Continent*, *Re/productions*, No. 2, April 1999, available at www.hsph.harvard.edu/grhf/.
67. Ibid., p. 1.
68. Ann D. Jordan refers to a "forced" year-long debate in *The Annotated Guide to the Complete UN Trafficking Protocol*, Washington, D.C.: International Human Rights Law Group, available at www.hrlawgroup.org/initiatives/trafficking_persons/, p. 9.
69. Marjan Wijers and Marieke van Doorninck, "Only Rights Can Stop Wrongs: A Critical Assessment of Anti-trafficking Strategies", paper presented at EU/IOM STOP European Conference on Preventing and Combating Trafficking in Human Beings, Brussels, September 2002, unpublished, p. 2.
70. Monika Smit, "Trafficking in Women, Dutch Country Report", paper presented at NEWR Workshop on Trafficking in Women, April 2003, available at www.newr.bham.ac.uk/pdfs/Trafficking/Netherlands1.pdf.
71. Ministry of Justice, quoted in Smit, ibid.
72. Available at www.catwinternational.org/factbook/Netherlands.php.
73. Anna G. Korvinus, *Trafficking in Human Beings – Third Report of the Dutch National Rapporteur*, The Hague: Bureau NRM, 2005, available at http://rechten.uvt.nl/victimology/national/NL-NRMEngels3.pdf.
74. European Migration Centre/Europäisches Migrationszentrum (EMZ), "Prevention and Fight against Trafficking: Institutional Developments in Europe – Netherlands Report 2003", Berlin: EMZ, 2003, available at: www.emz-berlin.de/projekte_e/pj37_1pdf/Netherlands.pdf.
75. Donna M. Hughes, "The 'Natasha' Trade: The Transnational Shadow Market of Trafficking in Women", *Journal of International Affairs* 53(2), 2000, p. 639.
76. Lisa A. Howard, "Prostitution: 'The Oldest Profession in the World' – Is it Possible to Reduce Demand?", Captive Daughters, available at www.captivedaughters.org.
77. Quoted in Ingmarie Froman, "Sweden's Fight Against Trafficking in Women", Stockholm: Swedish Institute, 27 February 2004.
78. Quoted in Patrick McLoughlin, "Sweden Seeks to Export Prostitution Legislation", Human Trafficking.com Forums, 13 April 2003, available at www.polarisproject.org/PolarisProject/forums/ShowPost.
79. Ibid.
80. Ministry of Industry, Employment and Communications (Regeringskansliet), "Prostitution and Trafficking in Women", factsheet, Stockholm: Regeringskansliet, January 2004, available at www.sweden.gov.se/content/1/c6/01/87/74/6bc6c972.pdf.
81. Froman, note 77 above.

82. Phil Marshal, "No Simple Solutions to Trafficking", *Choices: The Human Development Magazine*, UNDP, December 2003.
83. Shifman, note 20 above, p. 125.
84. Asian Development Bank, *The Challenge of Poverty Reduction*, available at www.adb.org/Documents/policies/poverty_reduction/challenge.asp.
85. Hughes, note 75 above, p. 635.
86. Minnesota Advocates for Human Rights, note 13 above, pp. 10–11.
87. International Labour Organization/International Programme on the Elimination of Child Labour, note 35 above, p. vii.
88. Human Rights Watch, note 2 above, p. 15.
89. International Labour Organization, note 33 above, p. 43.
90. Van Impe, note 24 above, p. 116.
91. International Labour Organization, note 34 above, p. 4; Wijers and van Doorninck, note 69 above, p. 2.
92. "Helping Hands or Shackled Lives", in International Labour Organization, note 33 above, p. 40.
93. Ibid, p. 41.
94. Human Rights Watch, note 2 above, p. 11.
95. International Labour Organization/International Programme on the Elimination of Child Labour, note 3 above, p. 27.
96. ILO, note 32 above, p. 6.
97. Kumar et al., note 1 above, p. 21.
98. Corner, note 21 above, p. 15.
99. Ibid.
100. International Labour Organization/International Programme on the Elimination of Child Labour, note 35 above, p. 19.
101. Minnesota Advocates for Human Rights, note 13 above, pp. 18–19.
102. *Campo* brothel client, quoted in Kamala Kempadoo, "The Migrant Tightrope: Experiences from the Caribbean", in Kamala Kempadoo and Jo Doezema, eds, *Global Sex Workers: Rights, Resistance, and Redefinition*, New York: Routledge, 1998, p. 131.
103. Kamala Kempadoo and Jo Doezema, eds, *Global Sex Workers: Rights, Resistance, and Redefinition*, New York: Routledge, 1998, pp. 11–12.
104. International Labour Organization, note 33 above, p. 37.
105. "UNESCO Responses to the Trafficking of Women and Children – UNESCO Projects Related to the Trafficking of Girls and Women", available at www.unescobkk.org/culture/trafficking/unesco.htm.
106. Bindman, note 62 above.
107. International Labour Organization/International Programme on the Elimination of Child Labour, note 42 above, p. 5.
108. *Human Rights Features*, "After the Deluge, the Damp Squib", *Human Rights Features* 5, October/December 2002, available at www.hrdc.net/sahrdc/hrfquarterly/Oct_Dec_2002/After_the_diluge.htm.
109. Kumar et al., note 1 above, p. 1.
110. Women's Rehabilitation Centre, note 4 above, p. 27.
111. Kumar et al., note 1 above, p. 37.
112. Ibid.
113. Ibid., p. 13.
114. This is not to suggest that cultural values are static and do not change.
115. International Labour Organization/International Programme on the Elimination of Child Labour, note 3 above, p. 27.
116. International Labour Organization, note 33 above, p. 40.

117. International Labour Organization/International Programme on the Elimination of Child Labour, note 35 above, p. 20.
118. Women's Rehabilitation Centre, note 4 above, p. 16.
119. Ibid., p. 11.
120. International Organization for Migration, "Study Finds Demand is a Factor Driving Human Trafficking", US Department of State, 6 January 2004, available at www.usembassy.it/file2004_01/alia/a4010606.htm.
121. Ibid.
122. Kempadoo, note 102 above, p. 131.
123. World Conference against Racism, "The Race Dimensions of Trafficking in Persons – Especially Women and Children", World Conference against Racism, available at www.un.org/WCAR/e-kit/issues.htm.
124. International Organization for Migration, note 120 above.
125. Orla Clinton, "Women's Bodies Have Become Part of the Battlefield", *Irish Times*, 13 January 2003, p. 7.
126. Elizabeth Rehn and Ellen Johnson Sirleaf, *Women, War and Peace: The Independent Experts' Assessment on the Impact of Armed Conflict on Women and Women's Role in Peace-Building*, New York: UNIFEM, 2002, p. 12, available at www.unifem.undp.org/resources/assessment/.
127. Testimony of Martina E. Vandenberg (Human Rights Watch) at House Committee on International Relations Subcommittee on International Operations, Human Rights Watch, 22 April 2002, available at http://hrw.org/backgrounder/wrd/trafficking-testim-april.pdf.
128. IOM Kovoso, *Return and Reintegration Project: Situation Report February 2000 – April 2002*, IOM Kosovo, 2002, p. 3.
129. Vandenberg, note 127 above, pp. 3–4.
130. Study between March 1999 and March 2000, quoted in Human Rights Watch, "Hopes Betrayed: Trafficking of Women and Girls to Post-Conflict Bosnia and Herzegovina for Forced Prostitution", Vol. 14, No. 9 (D), Washington, D.C.: Human Rights Watch, November 2002, p. 32, available at www.hrw.org/reports/2002/bosnia/.
131. Ibid., p. 4.
132. Rehn and Sirleaf, note 126 above, p. 13.
133. See, for example, a brief history of conflict in West Africa and its influence on migration in UNHCR, *The State of the World's Refugees: Fifty Years of Humanitarian Action*, UNHCR, 2000, pp. 260–261.
134. Ahmet Icduygu and Sule Toktas, "How Do Smuggling and Trafficking Operate via Irregular Border Crossings in the Middle East?", *International Migration* 40(6), 2002, p. 27.
135. Almost 900,000 refugees fled Kosovo into neighbouring countries to escape the ethnic cleansing campaign of the Serbian authorities.
136. Hearing before the Commission on Security and Cooperation in Europe, "The Sex Trade: Trafficking of Women and Children in Europe and the United States", 106th Congress, Fifth Session, 28 June 1999, Washington, D.C.: US Government Printing Office, 1999, p. 2.
137. Wendy Young (Women's Commission for Refugee Women and Children), in Hearing before the Commission on Security and Cooperation in Europe, "The Sex Trade: Trafficking of Women and Children in Europe and the United States", 106th Congress, First Session, 28 June 1999, Washington, D.C.: Commission on Security and Cooperation in Europe, 1999, p. 25, available at www.house.gov/csce.
138. Women, Health and Development Program, *Trafficking of Women and Children for Sexual Exploitation in the Americas*, Washington, D.C.: Women Health and Develop-

ment Program/Pan-American Health Organization, 2004, p. 2, available at www.paho. org/genderandhealth.

139. South East European Regional Initiative against Human Trafficking, *Former Yugoslav Republic of Macedonia*, South East European Regional Initiative against Human Trafficking, 2002, available at www.seerights.org/main.php?val=222.

140. Ibid.

141. Rehn and Sirleaf, note 126 above, p. 70.

142. Ibid.

143. Human Rights Watch, note 130 above, p. 11.

144. Rehn and Sirleaf, note 126 above, p. 11.

145. Vandenberg, note 127 above, pp. 5–6.

146. Commission on Security and Cooperation in Europe, "Commissioners Inquire of Administration Efforts to Combat Prostitution, Human Trafficking in Post-Conflict Iraq", *Scoop*, May 2003, available at www.scoop.co.nz/mason/stories/WO305/S00297.htm.

147. International Labour Organization, *World Day Against Child Labour 2003*, ILO, 2003, p. 4, available at www.ilo.ru/news/200306/docs/12JuneArticleENG.pdf.

148. Ibid.

149. CSUCS, "Global Report on Child Soldiers – 2001", 12 June 2001, quoted in *Out of the Shadows: Worst Forms of Child Labour Data*, available at www.globalmarch.org/worstformsreport/world/africa-region.html.

150. William Barnes, "Junta the Largest User of Boy Soldiers", *South China Morning Post*, 16 October 2002, p. 12.

151. Rehn and Sirleaf, note 126 above, p. 12.

3

Globalization and national sovereignty: From migration to trafficking

Kinsey Alden Dinan

This chapter explores the interaction between globalization and national sovereignty as a root cause of trafficking in persons: the transport of and trade in human beings for the purpose of forced labour, servitude and other forms of exploitation. The analysis focuses on transnational trafficking in adults, and does not attempt to explain the related phenomena of domestic trafficking or trafficking in children. Findings from case studies are used to illustrate the argument, with a particular focus on migration and trafficking in persons from Thailand to Japan, from Mongolia to other Asian and European countries and from Mexico to the United States.

Trafficking in persons must be understood within the context of the larger phenomenon of persons' movement across international borders. In most cases (including most cases of trafficking) this movement is motivated at least in part by the search for greater economic opportunity. Thus the vast majority of migrants move from developing nations to relatively wealthier countries in the developed or developing world. Over the past few decades the economic, political and social forces of globalization have played a major role in spurring this movement, thus contributing to the growing incidence of both migration and trafficking in persons.

Also essential to promoting human trafficking has been nation-states' selective resistance to globalization and assertion of national sovereignty. More specifically, governments' insistence on the right to determine who crosses national borders and the conditions under which they cross

Trafficking in humans: Social, cultural and political dimensions, Cameron and Newman (eds), United Nations University Press, 2007, ISBN 978-92-808-1146-9

provides a market for traffickers' "services" and facilitates their ability to engage in slavery-like abuses with virtual impunity. This chapter begins with a discussion of the role of globalization in explaining contemporary international migration patterns, followed by an analysis of the way restrictive national immigration policies (implemented in the context of strong migratory pressures) have fostered the human rights abuse of trafficking in persons.

Definitions

The definition of the term "trafficking in persons" has been the subject of significant debate. The most authoritative international definition comes from the UN protocol on trafficking, given in the introduction to this volume. The protocol, however, intentionally declines to address the most contentious definitional issue – the question of what constitutes "the exploitation of the prostitution of others or other forms of sexual exploitation" – leaving signatories to apply their own interpretation. On one side of the debate are those who argue that anyone who facilitates a woman's migration for the purpose of employment in the sex industry is guilty of trafficking, regardless of the existence or absence of coercive tactics, as commercial sex work is inherently abusive and a woman cannot legitimately "consent" to engage in it. The analysis in this chapter, on the other hand, holds that the concept of consent is central to the definition of trafficking, and reserves the term "trafficking" for situations in which coercive tactics are used to extract a person's labour, sexual or not. (Note that this applies only to adults; there is general agreement that a child cannot consent to sex work or other types of work that are injurious to its health and/or development.)

"Globalization" is also a term that evokes a variety of definitions. It is used to describe a wide range of international processes, from the transnational spread of free markets to the spread of (particularly Western) cultural values and norms. Globalization also refers to the growing sense that the world is interconnected: that events in one part of the world affect outcomes in another, and that economic activities and social networks operate without regard for national borders. Finally, globalization implies the retreat of nation-states from important areas of decision-making, so that economic and/or political decisions are made by actors or forces beyond national borders and national controls. In this analysis, the term "globalization" is understood broadly, but with a focus on the shift in decision-making power and control away from national authorities.

Globalization and international migration

Globalization and international migration are not new phenomena. At the end of the twentieth century the proportion of the world's population involved in transnational migration was higher than it is today.[1] However, after a decline in migration levels during the early to mid-1900s, the past few decades have seen rising migration in both proportional and absolute terms, along with new and increasingly complex migration patterns. Between 1960 and 2000 the number of migrants more than doubled from about 76 million to 175 million worldwide.[2] In developed countries, foreign-born persons comprise an increasing percentage of residents. At the same time, about half of all migrants move from one developing country to another.[3] There is increasing diversity in countries that have significant inflows and/or outflows of migrants, along with many more countries serving as major sites of both origin *and* destination for migration.[4] There is also more short-term migration,[5] and a growing proportion of the world's migrants are women.[6]

As most migrants travel abroad at least in part (if not almost exclusively) in search of greater economic opportunity, economic deprivation and a lack of economic opportunities at home are obvious underlying causes of migration. However, it must be noted that of the billions of people who suffer such hardships only a tiny fraction engage in international migration. Worldwide, less than 3 per cent of people live outside their country of birth.[7] Understanding the role that globalization plays in providing the motivation and means to migrate can help identify some of the factors that shape migration patterns and make certain people more likely to migrate than others. Since, as discussed below, trafficking in persons occurs primarily within the context of economically motivated migration, these same factors play a key role in shaping trafficking patterns.

Economic forces of globalization

Like contemporary migration, the modern era of globalization is marked by some distinctive characteristics. A key feature of globalization over the past three decades is the growing dominance of capitalist economic forces, including trade liberalization, currency deregulation, the privatization of national industry and the loosening of capital market controls. National economies have become increasingly dependent on foreign markets and foreign investment and, in the developing world, on foreign assistance. Currency exchange rates are set by global "market forces" rather than by government decree. Foreign investors shape the direction of industrial development, and real estate prices are subject to the judgements of foreign speculators.

While these changes have involved active decisions by national governments, they have also been powerfully promoted by international and regional institutions and the world's wealthiest nations. The two most important international institutions governing the spread of economic liberalization are the International Monetary Fund (IMF) and the World Bank. Created in 1944 to promote global economic stability, these institutions, along with the more recently established World Trade Organization, are powerful proponents of free market ideology. The impact of their decisions is most profound in developing nations, which depend on their loans as well as on the other resources that IMF approval can attract, such as regional and bilateral assistance and foreign direct investment. Notably, the decision-making structures of these institutions are dominated by highly developed countries – particularly the United States.

The results of economic liberalization have been mixed at best for developing nations. The swift spread of free markets has led to increased levels of inequality both within and between states and widespread economic instability. The rapid economic development that has occurred in countries such as the South-East and East Asian "tigers" could not have taken place without economic globalization. But even in these countries the disruption of traditional industries and the increased integration with (and dependence on) foreign markets has resulted in new economic winners and losers, along with rising economic instability and economic crises. Moreover, many other countries have seen not only rising inequality but also declining total levels of productivity and economic output.

It is increasingly understood that in many cases the economic "reforms" advocated by international institutions and powerful nation-states have created or exacerbated these problems by pushing for changes too quickly and in the wrong order. High levels of deregulation and privatization have been encouraged before the development of the necessary legal structures to prevent corruption or social safety nets to serve those who are inevitably displaced. Developing countries have been compelled to open themselves up to imports before sufficiently developing local industries even while wealthier countries' strict trade quotas and generous domestic subsidies in agriculture have been tolerated. Similarly, the rapid elimination of capital controls has left countries vulnerable to damaging speculation by international investors.[8]

Moreover, the IMF and the World Bank have conditioned the receipt of much-needed aid on austere economic reforms that have forced countries to *reduce* social spending while restructuring their economies. Such "conditionality" not only increases economic hardships but also effectively bypasses national legislative processes, thus undermining democratic development and ignoring the importance of establishing popular support for reforms. In addition, large economic development loans have left poor countries with a crippling debt burden, whether or not the programmes they financed succeeded.

The devastating currency crises in Mexico and East Asia in the 1990s illustrate the danger of rapid globalization even in countries otherwise viewed as economic success stories. The East Asian crisis was triggered by a sudden flight of foreign investment, causing first the crash of the Thai currency in 1997 and then expanding to plunge economies throughout the region into depression, with repercussions felt worldwide. The crisis may have had roots in national economic weaknesses, but the speed and overreaction of the market would not have been possible without the region's recent capital market liberalization. Moreover, the depth and length of the crisis were exacerbated by the IMF's "solution", which intensified economic downturns with spending cuts and interest rate hikes.[9]

The impact of Mexico's 1995 currency crisis was softened by a $50 billion bailout, financed largely by the United States and the IMF, which allowed Mexico to pay off American and other foreign creditors and restore confidence in the peso. By some measures the country's economic recovery was relatively swift, but nearly 10 years later wages had still not recovered to 1994 levels and income inequality continues to rise.[10]

In most former communist nations not only has inequality increased dramatically with the capitalist transition but overall economic output has declined significantly, leading to soaring rates of unemployment and poverty. In Russia rapid privatization led to the transfer of national industries to a corrupt élite, while capital market liberalization facilitated the transfer of these resources out of the country. The result has been billions of dollars worth of asset-stripping.[11] In Soviet satellite countries the difficulties of transition have been compounded by the loss of Soviet subsidies. Mongolia, for example, fell into a deep economic recession when the fall of the Soviet Union led to the sudden loss of subsidies that had once comprised 30 per cent of the country's gross domestic product.[12]

Contrary to the predictions of neo-classical economic theory, far from leading to economic "convergence", contemporary economic globalization (as implemented) has led to growing inequality. Between 1960 and 1990 the ratio of income between countries in the Organisation for Economic Co-operation and Development (OECD) and less developed nations *increased* by 45 per cent.[13] In the 1990s alone the number of people living in poverty increased by about 100 million.[14]

Political, social and cultural forces of globalization

Related to the global expansion of capitalism and the fall of communist economic systems has been the spread of democratic forms of government. More than 70 per cent of the world's population now live in countries with relatively democratic regimes.[15] One result has been a dramatic reduction in exit restrictions that hinder cross-border travel and migration. For example, until about 10 years ago Mongolia, like many other communist nations, permitted travel only with special government permission and generally only to other communist countries. Nowadays, 1994 legislation gives Mongolian citizens the right to travel abroad, to emigrate to a foreign country and to return to Mongolia at any time. With this new freedom and the other dramatic changes that occurred in the 1990s, the number of Mongolians travelling abroad has increased enormously, and a growing number of cases of trafficking in persons have been documented.[16]

Also integral to the modern era of globalization are dramatic technological advances that have made international travel and communications easier, faster and less expensive. It is now possible to travel quickly back and forth between "home" and "destination" countries – and to transfer money nearly instantaneously – allowing individuals and families to live "transnational" lives, simultaneously engaged in two or more nation-states. The same advances have facilitated the growth of transnational corporations and transnational organized crime groups whose activities include the traffic in persons across national borders.

Another result of communications and media advances is the pervasiveness of information (and misinformation) about lifestyles and cultural norms in developed, and particularly Western, societies. Some argue that this has led to increased perceptions of "relative" poverty, even when economic conditions remain stable in absolute terms, by expanding the comparison group against which individuals and families assess their economic position. The spread of Western media may also be a factor in the increased feminization of migration by contributing to changing societal norms regarding women's rights and roles that make it more acceptable for women to work outside the home and travel abroad on their own.

Root factors underlying migratory pressures

Contemporary international migration is both a manifestation and a consequence of globalization, and while many migrate safely, others find themselves subjected to trafficking abuses and other forms of exploitation. The forces of economic globalization described above foster strong "push" factors in migrants' countries of origin, such as economic dislocation and increased absolute and/or relative poverty rates. These hardships motivate millions of persons to seek economic opportunities abroad in order to maintain or regain their economic positions. In addition, high levels of economic and political instability and the experience of economic crises provide an incentive for families to reduce their overall economic risk by diversifying their sources of earnings across multiple countries.[17]

At the same time, destination countries exhibit important "pull" factors, such as significantly higher wages and a demand for migrant workers to perform low-wage (or otherwise undesirable) jobs. This is true in both developed countries and relatively wealthier developing nations, such as Thailand and Mexico, many of which serve as major countries of origin and destination for migration. In addition, the demand for migrant workers is often exacerbated by demographic changes, as declining birth rates in developed countries lead to shrinking populations with a growing ratio of elderly to working-age people.

In Japan a severe labour shortage in the 1970s and 1980s, coupled with the region's highest wage rates, led to an influx of foreign workers despite strong societal resistance to the idea of immigration. (This is the same period of time in which the trafficking of women into Japan became a large-scale phenomenon.) Migration rates fell with the beginning of the Japanese recession in the early 1990s, but nearly 10 years later, despite continued economic problems, there were an estimated 670,000 migrants in Japan (not including permanent residents).[18] Many Japanese commentators have noted that the country's ageing population is likely to renew immigration pressures in coming years.

International and regional economic crises commonly affect migrants' countries of origin as well as destination, with ambiguous implications for migration flows. The Asian economic crisis, for example, heightened migration pressures in Indonesia, but at the same time reduced the demand for migrant workers in Malaysia – the most common destination country for Indonesian migrants. The result was an initial decrease in the number of migrants in Malaysia, as the government initiated mass deportations. These policies were soon modified, however, as the government acknowledged that even with rising unemployment rates, migrant workers were needed to fill a variety of positions "shunned" by Malaysians. Indonesia, meanwhile, dubbed its migrants "foreign exchange heroes" and continued to promote emigration. Similarly, the Thai government responded to the 1997 crisis with efforts to deport migrant Burmese workers, but quickly faced pressures to relent from employers who relied on their labour.[19]

Along with the motivation to migrate, migration typically requires at least a minimal level of economic resources and connections to foreign countries or links to migration networks.[20] Even those who lack sufficient resources or networks to migrate independently – and who thus turn to transnational smuggling or trafficking operations – are generally not among the most disadvantaged in their countries. With globalization, the spread of market-based economic systems and the economic growth that has occurred in some countries (and in certain sectors of others) have increased access to the hard currency needed for international travel. At the same time technological advances in travel and communications have fostered a proliferation of transnational connections, and migration patterns tend to mirror other cross-border ties. The economic and social links forged by colonization, for example, are now reflected in strong patterns of migration from post-colonial countries to their former colonizers.[21] Similarly, connections built through international trade, foreign direct investment and transnational corporate activities often generate parallel migration flows.

Technological advances have changed the nature of migration as well, by allowing migrants to remain strongly connected to a community in one country even while seeking economic opportunity in another. For many, dramatic reductions in the financial and "emotional" costs of migration have resulted in a shift in the goals of migration from establishing a new life elsewhere to improving life at "home". This perspective is often encouraged by governments in countries of origin which recognize their migrants as important economic resources. In 2003 migrants' remittances to developing countries totalled close to $100 billion through official channels alone, with the actual size of transfers significantly larger. Remittances are now the second-largest source of external finance for developing countries after foreign direct investment, and greatly exceed the value of official development assistance.[22]

Emigration can also alleviate unemployment rates by reducing the domestic labour supply, and could theoretically lead to increased foreign investment in the long term as migrants establish themselves overseas but remain committed to their "home" country. Some countries have explicitly adopted "labour exportation" strategies to promote economic development. The Philippines provides the most striking example, with nearly 10 per cent of its population living abroad and sending home remittances equivalent to about 10 per cent of the country's gross domestic product.[23]

Many other countries have also taken significant steps to promote labour emigration and support their workers overseas. Mexico, for example, has greatly expanded consular services for its nationals in the United States and has lobbied public and private institutions in the United States to accept the Mexican identity cards issued by its consulates. These cards are issued without regard for immigration status, and, due in large part to the Mexican government's efforts, they can now be used in a number of US cities and states to open bank accounts (facilitating the transfer of remittances) and obtain driving licences.[24]

Reinforcing systems of migration

Complicating the task of identifying the "causes" of migration is the self-perpetuating nature of the phenomenon. As migration patterns become established, the transnational networks and systems that facilitate migration are strengthened, spurring further migration. Mexican migration to the United States, for example, dates back to the nineteenth century, when Mexicans were recruited by US employers to work on American railroads and farms. Migration levels subsequently increased in response to US labour shortages during the First and Second World Wars, and in the post-war period hundreds of thousands of Mexican workers were admitted into the United States each year through the Bracero Program. After this programme was terminated in 1964, levels of undocumented Mexican migration to the United States soared.[25]

By following the patterns established by previous migrants from their families or communities, new migrants have a better idea of what to expect in destination countries and how to locate employment and housing. (The desire for family reunification also provides another important motivation for migration.) In addition, as migration levels rise, various stakeholders become interested in ensuring that the flows continue.

In countries of origin, economic growth strategies that depend on labour exportation and the remittances of migrant workers serve as powerful incentives to encourage continued emigration. Similarly, in destination countries employers become dependent on migrant labour to fill positions that nationals are unwilling to take, often even during periods of relatively high unemployment. As dual-labour-market theorists have pointed out – and as the Malaysian and Thai examples above illustrate – immigration quickly becomes structurally embedded in national economies. Migrants perform low-wage and 3-D (dirty, difficult and dangerous) jobs in industries such as agriculture, construction, domestic service and the sex industry.[26] The benefits for destination countries include higher levels of productivity and lower prices for goods and services. (On the downside, the availability of a cheap and malleable labour force – which enjoys little protection from national authorities, as discussed below – reduces pressure on employers to make the kinds of improvements in wages and job conditions that would attract domestic workers.)

Also important are the highly profitable markets that develop around the facilitation of migration in countries of origin, transit and destination. As discussed below, national immigration regimes have created high barriers to migration, especially for low-skilled migrants from developing nations. As a result, an increasing range of services are available to assist potential migrants and their employers in navigating the complex process of migration, and the providers of these services have a strong financial interest in reinforcing migration trends. Some migration mediators assist people in accessing the limited legal migration opportunities that exist for low-skilled workers. Others facilitate illegal migration, and some of these "migrant smugglers" traffic persons into slavery-like employment situations.

The resistance of the nation-state

Despite important shifts in decision-making power from national governments to global forces over the last few decades, the authority of the nation-state remains paramount. National governments have the final word in determining which areas of decision-making can be ceded and which cannot. This is particularly true in wealthy countries that have the resources to resist international pressures and whose officials drive the decisions of powerful international institutions such as the IMF and the World Bank. The following pages describe how states' insistence on (selectively) asserting their national sovereignty in the face of globalizing forces provides the final essential condition for the growing incidence of trafficking in persons.

Restrictive immigration policies: Creating "illegal aliens" and other categories of immigrants

While national borders have become increasingly open to transnational flows of goods and money, governments have increasingly and forcefully asserted their sovereign right to control the movement of people across their borders. In recent years such stepped-up border control efforts have often been described as "anti-trafficking" measures. The current system of passports and visas is a twentieth-century phenomenon. During the peak migration period of the late nineteenth and early twentieth centuries there were few restrictions on cross-border movement. The past few decades, and the 1990s in particular, have seen dramatic efforts to tighten border controls, with the wealthiest countries setting the trend and developing nations increasingly following suit. In the United States and Western European countries, national spending on border control activities tripled or even quadrupled in the 1990s alone.[27] At the same time, new and tougher penalties have been imposed on migrants, employers and third parties who violate national immigration laws.

In some cases new restrictions have been placed on emigration as well, again often justified as efforts to prevent trafficking in persons. Thailand, for example, conducts extensive investigations of female passport applicants aged 14 to 36 (only), and denies passports, and thus the ability to travel abroad legally, to those whom public welfare officials believe are "being procured to sexual business in foreign countries".[28]

National immigration control efforts have been accompanied by a range of bilateral, regional and global instruments and agreements designed to enhance migration management and border control enforcement. These include bilateral agreements in which countries of origin agree to accept all deportees swiftly in exchange for financial aid or other assistance from wealthier destination countries. In "Fortress Europe" regional efforts to facilitate the movement of EU citizens between member countries have been accompanied by uniform and heightened restrictions on immigration from countries outside the European Union. And on a global level, the 2000 Convention on Transnational Organized Crime, supplemented by optional protocols on trafficking in persons and smuggling in migrants, compels state parties to take a range of steps to fight immigration violations and other transnational crimes.

Although there are a numerous international efforts to monitor and control migration, the right to determine who crosses national borders – and under what conditions – is still widely understood as the very essence of state sovereignty. And far from working towards a "global labour market", governments routinely impose limits on legal labour migration that are highly inconsistent with national labour market demands, particularly with regard to low-skilled work. Moreover, along with tightening immigration controls has come increasing differentiation in the rights accorded to a country's residents based on their "immigration status". Full rights are reserved for citizens, while more limited rights and protections are provided to various categories of non-citizens.

Thus migrants' status (and the meaning of that status) in destination countries is determined by national immigration policies, which differ substantially depending on migrants' country of origin, skills and wealth. Citizens of wealthy countries, along with wealthy and/or high-skilled citizens of developing nations, enjoy greater access to legal migration channels that offer many of the rights and protections of citizens and may also provide pathways to acquiring citizenship. Low-skilled migrants from developing nations, on the other hand, have limited access to legal migration opportunities. They are therefore more likely to become "undocumented" migrants – bypassing immigration controls and entering the destination country illegally, or entering through normal channels but either travelling on fraudulent documents or violating their terms of entry by, for example, working on a "tourist" visa or staying past their visa's expiration date.[29]

Government immigration policies and practices do not prevent – or even purport to prevent – all undocumented migration. In fact, increased flows of undocumented migrants are an inevitable result of restrictive immigration policies in the context of strong migratory pressures. Europe saw flows of undocumented migrants increase tenfold to 500,000 per year in the 1990s, a period of dramatic increases in immigration control efforts, and the United States has a net inflow of at least 300,000 "illegal aliens" each year.[30] The 10 million undocumented migrants in the United States account for nearly 40 per cent of the non-citizen population and close to 10 per cent of the country's low-wage workforce.[31] Employers in a variety of industries rely on the labour of undocumented migrants, who live and work in the United States with the implicit tolerance of the government, private corporations and the community. Similarly, in Japan, where overall levels of migration are much lower, more than one-third of the foreign-born population are undocumented.[32]

Despite their ineffectiveness – and in stark contrast to the pressures for free trade and capital market deregulation – nations' restrictive migration policies go largely unquestioned. And this is true even when such policies result in egregious (and predictable) consequences. Along the 2,000-mile US-Mexico border, for example, the United States has exponentially increased its border control enforcement efforts over the past two decades. Migration flows have not declined as a result – the number of undocumented migrants crossing the border has remained essentially unchanged over this period.[33]

Enforcement activities have, however, contributed to an increasing death toll in the border area, which reached a rate of 500 persons per year in 2000.[34] Border control efforts have also resulted in a growth of organized criminal activity as migrants increasingly turn to third parties to assist them in the difficult migration process. As discussed below, undocumented immigrants are particularly vulnerable to rights violations, including forced labour and other trafficking abuses, during the migration process and in destination countries. Moreover, for many who succeed in migrating, the militarization of the border increases the length of their stay in the United States by making it more difficult to travel back and forth between the two countries in response to seasonal labour market demands and other factors. Still, while there are calls for changes in US policies on humanitarian and other grounds, there are no major international institutions questioning the inherent right of the United States to guard its border heavily and keep visa quotas for Mexicans far below the demand for their labour among American employers.

Exploitative practices

As suggested above, one inevitable result of the mismatch between migratory pressures and legal migration opportunities has been an enormous growth in the migration mediation industry. Illegal migrant smuggling and trafficking operations yield an estimated $10 billion per year and serve approximately half of all undocumented migrants worldwide.[35] The result of such activities is not only increased rights abuses and increased resources for organized crime (only drugs and weapons smuggling bring in more money), but also an increased incidence of official corruption as bribing government officials is common practice in such operations.

The services of migrant smugglers and traffickers (the latter are discussed in more detail below) include obtaining fraudulent passports, visas and other documentation and providing escorts and transportation for illegal border crossings. Specific services also arise in response to particular border control strategies. For example, Argentinean immigration policies require Bolivians to show $1,500 in spending money in order to enter the country as tourists – as a result, short-term loan operations have emerged that charge 10 per cent interest for the hour it takes to cross the border.[36] And once migrants reach destination countries, their remittances provide another opportunity for profit, as migrants pay fees as high as 20 per cent to send money to family members at home, particularly when their undocumented status prevents them from using official channels.[37]

Restrictive immigration policies, coupled with lax enforcement of labour standards, also generate highly profitable opportunities for those who employ migrant workers. These policies and practices create a class of workers who will provide cheap and malleable labour to meet national labour market demands, but can be detained and deported at the government's discretion. Undocumented migrants have little or no recourse in the face of labour standards' violations and other abuses. Their fear of deportation makes them reluctant to turn to authorities for assistance, and when they do, governments routinely focus on their violations of immigration law over the violations they have suffered at the hands of the country's citizens. Furthermore, even the legal migration channels that exist for low-skilled migrants often provide only the most minimal protection against abuse. In particular, visas for low-skilled migrants are typically short term and contingent on work for a particular employer, making the migrants' legal status dependent on their employers' discretion.

Industries that employ large numbers of migrants, and particularly undocumented migrants, are more likely to violate safety and wage regulations and less likely to be unionized. The vulnerable position of migrants *vis-à-vis* their employers impacts on low-wage citizen workers as well, undermining their ability to fight for higher wages and better job conditions. Recognizing this, the American Federation of Labor-Congress of Industrial Organizations (AFL-CIO), which represents more than 13 million workers in the United States, recently reversed its long-standing position in favour of tough immigration policies. Rather than calling for sanctions against undocumented workers and their employers, the AFL-CIO now calls for the legalization of undocumented migrants and the strict enforcement of labour standards for all workers, regardless of immigration status.

Trafficking in migrants

Traffickers take advantage of national immigration policies and practices that render migrants vulnerable to exploitation both during the process of migration and after they arrive in the destination country. By operating across national borders, through networks that include recruiters and agents in countries of origin, escorts who accompany migrants as they travel and labour brokers and employers in countries of destination,[38] traffickers follow migrants from the beginning to the end of the migration process. The difficulty of migrating independently ensures a ready pool of recruits in countries of origin, and the lack of protections for undocumented migrants facilitates traffickers' exploitation of victims in destination countries. In some cases trafficking operations involve large-scale organized crime groups, such as the Russian mafia or the Japanese *yakuza*; in other cases smaller-scale networks are involved.

There are few reliable statistics regarding the incidence of trafficking. The criminal nature of the phenomenon and insufficient efforts by governments to identify and investigate trafficking cases make estimating the scale of the problem difficult. Compounding these factors, most "anti-trafficking" efforts concentrate on enforcement at national borders, where it is often difficult or impossible to distinguish traffickers from smugglers (who facilitate illegal migration but do not engage in slavery-like treatment of migrants). In addition, estimates of trafficking are undermined by overestimates that include voluntary female migrants consensually working in the sex industry (or those intercepted at the border and believed to be in danger of entering sex work), as well as by underestimates that focus nearly exclusively on trafficking of women and children for sexual purposes. Still, most agree that hundreds of thousands, and perhaps millions, of persons are trafficked into slavery-like conditions each year.

Research consistently indicates that in the vast majority of trafficking cases the "victims" initially cooperate with their traffickers and even actively seek out their services.[39] In the first step of the process, recruiters identify potential migrants and tell them about lucrative job opportunities (or sometimes marriage offers) abroad. In many cases recruiters are acquaintances or even relatives of the people they recruit, and they may approach people who have already expressed an interest in migrating but, like many other low-skilled potential migrants, are unable to navigate the migration process by themselves. The recruits are motivated by the same factors as other migrants: economic instability, a lack of economic opportunities and other push factors at home, coupled with the lure of higher wages abroad. Most seek short-term work in hope of achieving a better life for themselves and their family at home.

The recruiter introduces interested persons to a trafficking agent, who makes the official offer. After someone agrees to migrate, the agent is responsible for making travel arrangements, often including obtaining fraudulent travel documents, and for ensuring that the migrant is escorted to brokers in the destination country. Once the agent begins making arrangements, the agreement is generally binding. Nonetheless, the coercive nature of the situation is rarely fully apparent until after the migrants arrive in the destination country. In fact, in some cases trafficking agents are virtually indistinguishable from legitimate migration mediators, at least from the potential migrant's perspective.[40]

When trafficking victims arrive in the destination country, their escort delivers them to labour brokers who place them with "employers". Trafficked persons have no input into the choice of employer or the terms of employment, and they are generally forced to work for months, or even years, for little or no pay. In some cases the nature of the work differs drastically from what was initially promised; for example, women promised work as nannies or waitresses might find themselves compelled to work in the sex industry. And in all cases trafficked persons find that they have been deceived about the conditions of their labour, including the unpaid wages, coercion and other abusive treatment.

A slavery-like practice commonly employed by trafficking networks is debt bondage. Trafficked persons are told that they owe exorbitant debts, often tens of thousands of dollars, which must be repaid with their labour. Victims of trafficking often describe being "sold" by their brokers for a "price" that becomes the basis of their alleged debt. Until they repay this amount they are kept under constant surveillance, and repayment calculations are in the hands of their employers, who typically add living expenses, fines and other charges to the initial debt. Moreover, in a clear indication of the slavery-like nature of the arrangement, employers frequently claim the right to resell indebted workers, often further increasing their debt level.

Trafficked persons' ability to escape is hindered by their linguistic and cultural isolation, separation from family and friends, lack of financial resources and fear of local authorities in destination countries. Debt bondage and other types of servitude are also enforced by the threat and use of violence against both trafficked persons and their family members at home. In addition, traffickers capitalize on their victims' fear of law enforcement officials, holding their passports and other documentation and warning them of the dangers of falling into the hands of police or immigration officials. Research shows that this fear of authorities is not unfounded, as trafficked persons are commonly subjected to punitive treatment as "illegal aliens", detained and deported with little concern for the abuses they have endured (or the trafficking agents they may face at home). In other cases corrupt officials return escapees to their traffickers. In some instances authorities in countries of origin compound this problem by punishing their nationals when they return. Research regarding the recent increase in trafficking in Mongolian women, for example, found that after the women return to Mongolia they are commonly penalized for prostitution and immigration-related offences "committed" during the trafficking process.[41]

Trafficking networks flourish where migratory pressures are strong, legal migration opportunities are limited and existing migration networks are insufficient to overcome immigration barriers without assistance and provide protection for new migrants in destination countries. Traffickers also take advantage of gaps in labour law enforcement in destination countries, so trafficked persons generally work in sectors with weak labour protections, such as domestic service, agriculture and illegal sex work. As noted above, those who engage in international migration are rarely among the most disadvantaged in their country of origin, given the need for a certain level of resources and connections. However, trafficking victims are likely to be more disadvantaged than other migrants, and evidence indicates that they are disproportionately female and members of racial or ethnic minorities or other groups that suffer discrimination in the home country.

In Thailand women trafficked into Japan's sex industry typically come from the northern provinces where there are few economic opportunities, especially for women, and domestic migration for work in Thailand's sex industry is common. Many victims are members of hill-tribe groups who are typically denied Thai citizenship and many of the rights it affords. The large-scale traffic of Thai women to Japan began in the 1970s following the deepening of economic ties between the two countries and an increase in Japanese tourism, including sex tourism, to Thailand. The public outcry against sex tourism contributed to the demand for Thai women to work in Japan's sex industry, and huge wage disparities between the countries ensured a supply of willing migrants. Without legal migration opportunities or the networks necessary to navigate the process independently, trafficking operations became a major avenue for migration.

Decades later, trafficking networks between Thailand and Japan remain strong. There are tens of thousands of Thai women working in Japan, but the Thai community is relatively weak as nearly all are undocumented and most eventually return to Thailand rather than settling in Japan. In addition, Japanese authorities are reluctant to respond to abuses suffered by undocumented migrants (especially those working in the sex industry), who are viewed as criminals. In contrast, the

Philippines government has pushed for legal labour migration opportunities for Filipinas in Japan, and while abuses against Filipinas continue, evidence indicates that rates of trafficking and slavery-like abuses have declined.[42] (Recent moves by the Japanese government to reduce visas for Filipinas may reverse these gains – see more below.)

More recently, similar patterns have emerged in Mongolia. Exit liberalization after the fall of the Soviet Union means that Mongolians are now free to travel abroad, but there are few legal migration opportunities available, except for the wealthy and/or highly skilled. At the same time, dramatic transitions at home have led to extensive social upheaval and economic displacement. With these developments, there has been an increasing incidence of trafficking in Mongolian women to other Asian countries and Europe. Initial research by the Center for Human Rights and Development indicates that the victims tend to be young, single women who are unemployed, students and/or engaged in prostitution. The women's educational backgrounds vary, but many have some foreign language ability – though not in the language of the country where they are trafficked. In all documented cases the women have been promised highly paid work abroad, only to find themselves in coercive situations with their pay – as well as their passports – withheld until large "debts" are paid off.[43]

In the case of Mexican-US migration, migrant smuggling operations and labour standards' violations by employers in the United States are widespread. However, a long history of migration and large communities of Mexican nationals in the United States mean that most of the hundreds of thousands of undocumented Mexican migrants who enter the country each year are not subjected to slavery-like abuses. Nonetheless, with an undocumented population in the millions, and with a large percentage working in industries where US labour laws do not apply or are not enforced, forced-labour violations are common and numerous clear cases of trafficking have been documented. These include the trafficking of men into debt-bondage agricultural work, the trafficking of women and girls for forced prostitution and the trafficking of deaf adults and children for forced begging in New York.[44]

A new approach

The growth of large-scale migrant smuggling and trafficking operations, often involving organized crime, has generated intense international concern. And while the abuse of (often undocumented) migrants attracts less interest overall, the plight of girls and young women treated as "sex slaves" is an exception. In recent years governments around the world have implemented new policies and programmes in the name of combating trafficking. Wealthy nations have also provided foreign aid specifically targeted to support "anti-trafficking" activities in poorer countries, and a variety of bilateral and multilateral initiatives have been undertaken to combat transnational trafficking through cross-border information-sharing and law enforcement cooperation. At the international level, 107 countries have ratified the UN Convention against Transnational Organized Crime since it was adopted in December 2000, and the supplementary optional protocols on trafficking and smuggling have been ratified by 87 and 78 countries, respectively.[45]

Ironically, as suggested above, government "anti-trafficking" efforts (particularly in destination countries) have largely consisted of further tightening the immigration controls that drive migrants underground and into traffickers' hands in the first place. The Japanese government, for example, recently announced "anti-trafficking" measures that include making it much more difficult for Filipinas to obtain entertainer visas to work in Japan.[46] It has long been known that many Filipinas on entertainer visas work in Japan's sex industry (in violation of their visa terms). The evidence also indicates, however, that these women are less likely to be trafficked into slavery-like conditions than migrant women without such visas.[47] Nonetheless, Japan's recent actions are widely viewed as a response to criticism from the United States for Japan's failure to address adequately the problem of human trafficking. The new visa rules went into effect in March 2005, as efforts by the Philippines government to delay the rules failed. Together with heightened efforts to crack down on illegal immigration, the result was an immediate surge in arrests and deportation of Filipino migrants.[48]

Worldwide, law enforcement activities at international borders have been stepped up to prevent "potential trafficking victims" and other undocumented migrants from entering destination countries. Such measures are often combined with educational campaigns in countries of origin warning of the dangers of migration. However, these campaigns do not offer alternative economic opportunities, and they are largely ineffective in the face of the strong migratory pressures discussed above.

Despite the high level of government attention to the issue of trafficking, there has been little progress in responding to the human rights abuses endured by trafficked persons. Traffickers, when prosecuted, are typically charged with crimes related to immigration violations, not human rights abuses, and victims receive little in terms of assistance or justice. At the same time, most trafficked persons continue to be (mis)-treated as "illegal aliens" when they come into contact with law enforcement officials, summarily deported without any investigation of the conditions of their migration or employment in the destination country.

And even when trafficking victims are identified, "rescue and repatria-tion" efforts often differ little from arrest and deportation procedures. Only in rare exceptions – and typically with tremendous efforts on the part of non-governmental organizations and advocates – have victims had the opportunity to pursue justice and compensation from their abusers.

Unfortunately, the UN protocol on trafficking largely supports this approach. While it makes reference to providing assistance and access to justice for victims, the language in these provisions is weak and vague. State parties are asked merely to consider actions that are in fact central to meeting their obligations to trafficked persons under general inter-national human rights law. This language stands in stark contrast to the detailed and mandatory provisions in the protocol and main convention regarding cross-state information-sharing, the criminalization of organized crime groups, the seizure of proceeds from crime and various measures to combat money-laundering and corruption. Moreover, the protocol on trafficking fails to address the larger context of strong migratory pres-sures and restrictive state immigration policies within which trafficking abuses take place.

If governments are serious about combating trafficking in persons, a new approach is needed. Addressing the push factors of economic insta-bility, poverty and inequality in countries of origin is important for reduc-ing migration pressures over the long term and is a worthy goal in its own right. Increased efforts to investigate and punish traffickers are also needed, with penalties that reflect the gravity of the offence. And such efforts will not be successful until officials provide trafficking victims with the assistance and protection needed to gain their trust and cooper-ation as informants and witnesses.

Most importantly, however, the incidence of trafficking in persons will not be reduced until governments shift their focus from reducing illegal migration to ending the slavery-like treatment and other abuse of mi-grants (and other workers). Governments must recognize that migration is a historically normal process that can be highly beneficial for countries of origin and destination, as well as for the migrants themselves and their families. In destination countries the public should be educated regarding the benefits of migration. And in countries of origin awareness-raising ef-forts regarding safe migration are needed and should be integrated into development efforts that are likely to generate economic instability or disrupt traditional economic systems. Heightened efforts also are needed to enforce labour standards for both citizens and migrant workers, re-gardless of immigration status. A good first step would be ratifying the International Convention on the Protection of the Rights of All Migrant Workers and Members of Their Families; as of September 2005 only 33 countries were party to this convention – including very few major migration destinations.[49]

Finally, safe and legal migration opportunities must be expanded. Destination countries should reassess visa quotas based on labour market assessments and historical migration trends. Countries should also revise visa conditions that render migrants vulnerable to abuse by employers (such as the non-portability of visas to different employers). At the same time, countries of origin should actively push for legal rights and protections for their nationals overseas. Until countries address the mismatch between global migratory pressures and national immigration policies that makes trafficking and smuggling operations attractive to migrants and highly profitable for crime groups, little progress will be made.

Notes

1. UN Department of Economic and Social Affairs, *World Economic and Social Survey 2004*, New York: United Nations, 2004, p. ix.
2. Ibid., p. vii.
3. Philip Martin and Jonas Widgren, "International Migration: Facing the Challenge", *Population Bulletin* 57(1), 2002.
4. Peter Stalker, *Workers Without Frontiers: The Impact of Globalization on International Migration*, Boulder, Col.: Lynne Rienner, 2000, p. 7.
5. Graeme Hugo, "Circular Migration: Keeping Development Rolling?", *Migration Information Source: Fresh Thought, Authoritative Data, Global Reach*, Washington, DC: Migration Policy Institute, 1 June 2003.
6. Ninna Nyberg-Sorensen, Nicholas Van Hear and Poul Engberg-Pedersen, *The Migration-Development Nexus: Evidence and Policy Options*, Geneva: International Organization for Migration, 2003, p. 10.
7. Martin and Widgren, note 3 above, p. 4.
8. For a detailed discussion of these issues see Joseph E. Stiglitz, *Globalization and Its Discontents*, New York: W. W. Norton, 2003.
9. See Martin Khor, *The Economic Crisis in East Asia: Causes, Effects, Lessons*, San Francisco, Cal: International Forum on Globalization, available at www.ifg.org/khor.html; Milton Friedman, "How Asia Fell", *Hoover Digest* 2, 1999; Stiglitz, ibid., pp. 89–130.
10. See John Audley, Sandra Polaski, Demetrios G. Papademetriou and Scott Vaughan, *NAFTA's Promise and Reality: Lessons from Mexico for the Hemisphere*, Washington, D.C.: Carnegie Endowment for International Peace, 2003, pp. 12–13; Friedman, ibid.; Brett M. Humphrey, "The Post-NAFTA Mexican Peso Crisis: Bailout or Aid? Isolationism of Globalization?", *Hinckley Journal of Politics* 2(1), 2000, pp. 33–40; Stiglitz, note 8 above, pp. 86, 121.
11. Stiglitz, ibid., pp. 133–165.
12. US Central Intelligence Agency, *The World Factbook: Mongolia*, available at www.odci.gov/cia/publications/factbook/print/mg.html.
13. Stalker, note 4 above, p. 17.
14. Stiglitz, note 8 above, p. 5.
15. UN Development Programme, *Human Development Report 1999*, New York: Oxford University Press, 1999, p. 25.

16. Center for Human Rights and Development, *Combating Human Trafficking in Mongolia: Issues and Opportunities*, Ulaanbaatar: Center for Human Rights and Development, 2005, p. 9.

17. Note that while this chapter focuses on the economic motivations that drive the vast majority of transnational migrants, violence and civil conflict (in some cases caused in part by economic crises) also play a significant role in motivating migration. In these situations migrants typically remain within their countries of origin, contributing to the growing ranks of internally displaced persons, or move to neighbouring countries within the developing world. The connections between conflict and trafficking in persons are discussed in another chapter of this volume.

18. Martin and Widgren, note 3 above, p. 27.

19. See "Malaysia: Foreign Workers Stay", *Migration News* 5(8), 1998; "Thailand: Migrants Can Stay", *Migration News* 5(8), 1998; Sidney Jones, *Making Money Off Migrants: The Indonesian Exodus to Malaysia*, Hong Kong: Asia 2000, 2000; Martin and Widgren, note 3 above, p. 26.

20. The need for resources means that while economic growth should reduce migratory pressures over the long term, it can also lead to a "migration hump", initially spurring increased migration before reaching a level at which push factors are substantially dampened. See Nyberg-Sorensen, Van Hear and Engberg-Pedersen, note 6 above.

21. Martin and Widgren, note 3 above, p. 8.

22. Dilip Ratha, "Understanding the Importance of Remittances", *Migration Information Source: Fresh Thought, Authoritative Data, Global Reach*, 1 October 2004.

23. Martin and Widgren, note 3 above, p. 28.

24. Marti Dinerstein, *IDs for Illegals: The "Matricula Consular" Advances Mexico's Immigration Agenda*, Washington, D.C.: Center for Immigration Studies, 2003; National Immigration Law Center, "Driver's Licenses for Immigrants: Broad Diversity Characterizes States' Requirements", *Immigrants' Rights Update* 16(7), 22 November 2002; National Immigration Law Center, "House Appropriations' Committee Votes Against *Matricula Consular*", *Immigrants' Rights Update* 18(5), 9 August 2004. Note that as a result of the REAL ID Act, which became federal law in the United States in May 2005, many states may soon stop accepting Mexican identity cards as proof of identity: National Immigration Law Center, *Questions & Answers about Driver's Licenses Now That the REAL ID Act Has Become Law*, Washington, D.C.: National Immigration Law Center, 2005.

25. US-Mexico Migration Panel, *Mexico-U.S. Migration: A Shared Responsibility*. Washington, D.C.: Carnegie Endowment for International Peace, 2001, p. 6; Martin and Widgren, note 3 above, p. 14.

26. The discussion in this chapter focuses on low-skilled labour migrants, both because they comprise the vast majority of migrant workers and because they are the ones who are potentially vulnerable to the abuses of human traffickers. However, there are also substantial flows of highly skilled migrant workers who often are actively recruited by destination countries, even when barriers to unskilled labour migration are high. Among skilled migrant workers in the United States, Western Europe and Australia, an estimated 1.5 million are from developing countries. The loss of these workers in developing nations – often referred to as the brain-drain – can have significant negative consequences, feeding back into the problems of economic deprivation and disparities that promote migration flows: Stalker, note 4 above, pp. 107–114.

27. Martin and Widgren, note 3 above, p. 5.

28. Department of Public Welfare, Ministry of Labor and Social Welfare, "Welcome to the Department of Public Welfare, Ministry of Labor and Social Welfare", Thailand, 1998, p. 9, cited in Human Rights Watch, *Owed Justice: Thai Women Trafficked into Debt Bondage in Japan*, New York: Human Rights Watch, 2000, p. 189.

29. While most undocumented migrants come from developing countries, the number from developed nations is not insignificant. In the United States, for example, there are an estimated 47,000 undocumented migrants from Canada and thousands more from Western Europe: US Immigration and Naturalization Service, Office of Policy and Planning, *Estimates of the Unauthorized Immigrant Population Residing in the United States: 1990 to 2000*, Washington, D.C.: US Immigration and Naturalization Service, 2003, pp. 16–17.

30. World Bank, *Global Economic Prospects 2004: Realizing the Development Promise of the Doha Agenda*, Washington, D.C.: World Bank, 2004, p. 148.

31. Jeffery S. Passel, Randy Capp and Michael Fix, *Undocumented Immigrants: Facts and Figures*, Washington, D.C.: Urban Institute, 2004.

32. Martin and Widgren, note 3 above, p. 25.

33. US-Mexico Migration Panel, note 25 above, p. 5.

34. Ibid.

35. International Organization for Migration, *World Migration 2003: Managing Migration – Challenges and Responses for People on the Move*, Geneva: IOM, 2003, p. 60. In addition, legal international labour recruiters and brokers – such as government agencies and government-licensed organizations – often extract large commissions for assisting migrants in obtaining coveted work opportunities abroad.

36. Stalker, note 4 above, p. 126.

37. Ratha, note 22 above.

38. This model of a trafficking network is for explanatory purposes, and there may be variations in practice. In particular, in small trafficking networks the same people may perform more than one of the roles identified here.

39. This description refers to trafficking in adults. The dynamics involved in trafficking in children are somewhat different, though in those cases too the child's guardians typically cooperate in the initial phases of the trafficking process.

40. It is also possible for legal migration mediators to engage in trafficking, either by facilitating both legal and illegal migration or by placing legal migrants – with legal work visas – into coercive employment situations. More often, however, "illegal" immigration status is a key aspect of trafficked persons' vulnerability to abuse.

41. Center for Human Rights and Development, note 16 above, p. 23.

42. For more information about the trafficking of Thai women into the Japanese sex industry see Kinsey Alden Dinan. "Migrant Thai Women Subjected to Slavery-Like Abuses in Japan", *Violence Against Women* 8(9), 2002, 1113–1139; Human Rights Watch, note 28 above.

43. Center for Human Rights and Development, note 16 above, pp. 16, 23.

44. Amy O'Neill Richard, *International Trafficking in Women to the United States: A Contemporary Manifestation of Slavery and Organized Crime*, Washington, D.C.: US Central Intelligence Agency, Center for the Study of Intelligence, 2000, pp. 47–50.

45. These figures are as of August 2005. An up-to-date list of signatories and parties to the convention and protocols is available at www.undcp.org/odccp/crime_cicp_signatures.html.

46. Nojima Tsuyoshi, "Tokyo Rejects Delay in Visa Measures", *Asahi Shimbun*, 15 February 2005; "Tougher Restrictions on Foreign Entertainers to Be Enforced in March", *Japan Times*, 24 January 2005.

47. Human Rights Watch, note 28 above, pp. 46–49; Tony McNicol, "The Show's Over: Filipinos Under Pressure Amid Visa Crackdown", *Japan Times*, 26 April 2005.

48. Tsuyoshi, note 46 above; McNicol, ibid.

49. For an up-to-date list of signatories and parties to the convention see www.ohchr.org/english/countries/ratification/13.htm.

4

Trafficking of women for prostitution

Sally Cameron

Any consideration of the trafficking of women for prostitution is severely limited by a lack of reliable data. Those which do exist are scattered amidst the propaganda wars of players with polarized opinions and vested interests within trafficking debates. There is a fierce split among feminist academics based on whether prostitution (generally) can be considered work or whether it is innately exploitative and abusive. Governments routinely deny the reality of the sex industry's operation within their borders and paint their actions, ranging from non-existent to harshly prohibitive, as highly successful and generally the best possible available option. It is little surprise that traffickers are not revealing anything. Research-based studies drawing on interviews with trafficked women are few and far between. This is sometimes attributed to the difficulty of identifying victims given the clandestine nature of their situation and at times their shame, although it must be noted that when efforts are made, many trafficked women are prepared to give generous accounts of their experiences. In reality, the general lack of interest on the part of research bodies and research funders has played a larger part in limiting research. While it is now possible to source some reliable information on Europe and Asia, there are very few data from Africa, Latin America and elsewhere. Our "world view" is generally limited to a few regional locations.

When considering the operation of the sex industry and its effect on human trafficking, it is important that a broad perspective is not lost. The unfortunate equation of human trafficking with prostitution has

Trafficking in humans: Social, cultural and political dimensions, Cameron and Newman (eds), United Nations University Press, 2007, ISBN 978-92-808-1146-9

tended to mask the significant trafficking of men and boys, and the trafficking of women into industries other than the sex industry. The International Labour Organization (ILO) estimates that there are 12.3 million people enslaved in forced labour, bonded labour, forced child labour, sexual servitude and involuntary servitude at any given time. The nationalities of these people are as diverse as the world's cultures.[1] Men, women and children are trafficked into a broad range of industries and situations. For example (and unfortunately there are so many from which to choose), boys from Bangladesh, Pakistan and Afghanistan are trafficked to the Gulf states to work as camel jockeys, beggars and labourers,[2] boys in Togo are trafficked to work on farms,[3] girls from Nepal are trafficked into circuses in India,[4] Cambodian children are trafficked to Viet Nam and Thailand to work as street beggars,[5] Chinese boys are internally trafficked for adoption,[6] Laotian men are trafficked on to Thai fishing boats,[7] men from Central Asia and Russia are trafficked into the Russian construction and agricultural industries,[8] Burmese women are trafficked to a range of countries to work as factory labourers and household servants[9] and Chinese women are trafficked for marriage.[10]

Definition of trafficking

This chapter employs the definition of trafficking outlined in the Protocol to Prevent, Suppress and Punish Trafficking in Persons, elaborated in the introduction to this volume. Most importantly, this definition goes further than simply distinguishing between trafficking and smuggling by making it clear that an operation that begins as smuggling (with the willing participation of the person being moved) can become trafficking if coercion or deception is later used. Coercion or deception is enough to nullify a victim's consent to be smuggled or to migrate, because logically it is only possible to consent to something if you know all the facts and are free to consent or not.[11]

This point is often rejected by those arguing that an individual's desire to migrate is enough to exclude consideration of their later abuse; in reality, trafficking operates within the context of many people's desire to migrate for work and some people's willingness to employ illegal means to do so, including using the resources of people smugglers. Cases of abduction are rare.

At its most basic level trafficking involves the physical movement of people, usually across borders, but unlike people smuggling it involves significant deceptions and controls for the specific purpose of producing forced labour at the destination. While the exploitation of migrants is nothing new, trafficking is distinctive because traffickers control both the movement and the labour exploitation. The centrality of labour exploitation is key to this formula.

The equation of women's trafficking and prostitution, and the preoccupation with issues frequently associated with prostitution (morality, virtue, blame, etc.), dominated early trafficking debates to the exclusion of other vital considerations, for example the complex intersection of social and cultural forces that place people at risk of being trafficked, the experience and evidence of many of those who have been trafficked and the practices employed by traffickers. These flawed, simplistic concerns have slowed the development of constructive ideas, political action and programme responses.

Definition of sex work

Government, community and academic-led debates about the rights and wrongs of sex work, include sex work removed from trafficking, have had an enormous impact on strategies to reduce trafficking in women. The arguments of the polarized feminist "split" between radical feminist theorists on the one hand and (women) prostitutes, prostitution advocates and liberal feminist theorists on the other have been influential at the international level.[12]

Generally, radical feminists have condemned the sex industry *per se* as innately exploitative – "the marketing of the sexual exploitation of women"[13] – effectively denying that prostitution can be a form of work. This perspective is summed up by the comments of Kathleen Barry, a radical feminist academic who was instrumental in setting up an early feminist anti-trafficking conference[14] which did not include prostitutes among its participants. When challenged on that decision and her unwillingness to enter further debate, Barry stated that "the conference was feminist and did not support the institution of prostitution" and it would be "inappropriate to discuss sexual slavery with prostitute women".[15] In international debates this perspective continues to be represented by the Coalition against Trafficking in Women (CATW) and the European Women's Lobby, the latter of which organized an October 2005 conference with the stated aim of developing policy and best practices against prostitution and trafficking in Europe. The highly charged, emotive arguments continue, with the European Women's Lobby publicly stating its opposition to "any move that would create the idea that sex work is normal work that your or my daughter would be ambitious enough to do when she's 17 or 18".[16] Conference organizer Mary McPhail argues that 98 per cent of prostitutes have no choice but to turn to the sex trade, and insists that prostitution is fundamentally exploitative.[17] The source of the

98 per cent statistic is not clear and surely questionable unless McPhail has had the means to conduct such intensive research across the globe. What this approach misses is the participation of women as actors in prostitution: many prostitutes do not identify as victims but as sex workers, and many women want to migrate to work as sex workers.

Liberal feminists, whose perspective is represented by the Global Alliance against Traffic in Women (GAATW), argue that prostitution need not be exploitative, focusing on the capacity of women to control their sexuality and reproductive labour. They argue the possibility that sex workers can have greater control of their sexuality than women in other (non-commercial) heterosexual relationships. This argument claims that women have the right to control their body and sex work is a service offered under specific terms. Abuse is not intrinsic to the industry but is a result of the failure of industry standards, regulation, etc. If governments regulated effectively, exploitation (the abuse of labour standards) could be removed from the industry. This would make it less attractive to criminal networks and reduce trafficking. This position allows a focus on labour conditions, and a reminder that slavery-like conditions are unacceptable for all working in the sex industry, including those who have and those who have not been trafficked.

In the same month as the European Women's Lobby held its 2005 conference, some 120 male and female sex workers from across the European Union convened the Sex Work, Human Rights, Labour and Migration Conference to call for an end to "repressive policies" against prostitution and demand the same social rights as other employees: "What we do is work and we want it recognized as that."[18]

This chapter takes the position that prostitution is sex work, i.e. it is work, women have the right to choose sex work as a type of work and some women choose to work in the sex industry; taking into account that "choice" is not an absolute, and poverty, in particular, has a significant impact on the choices available to people. (Arguments about choice do not apply to children, who are not "able" to consent to such practices.) Perhaps this argument is most convincing when taken to its extreme, the case of first world women working in the upper echelons of the sex industry – for example a highly educated, articulate woman who has a range of employment options available, has no debilitating dependency (be it drugs, alcohol, gambling, etc.) and is generally removed from the various stereotypes of women presumed to fill the industry. While this chapter is not about such women, the fact that they exist makes the point that some women who have a wide range of choices available to them, even by first world standards, decide to work in the sex industry.[19] Internationally, studies have shown that women choose to work in the sex industry for a range of reasons, including access to relatively high income and a sense of "empowerment". There may also be other reasons, such as the relative freedom to work one's own hours to accommodate childcare or study responsibilities, and the high level of camaraderie sometimes experienced with other workers.[20]

This broad philosophy about sex work, however, cannot be applied to women trafficked into prostitution, as trafficked women lack the basic right of consent. They are not "choosing" their "employment" under specific conditions. Even so, broad sex work debates are crucial to understanding trafficking for prostitution. Firstly, trafficked women are moved into the sex industry, and an understanding of the industry's operation is vital to the development of policies, laws and standards to stamp out abuse. Secondly, sex work is recognized as work and the empowerment of workers and strong industry standards are demanded. Trafficking for prostitution is anathema. Trafficked labour is exploited labour. Rape and sexual abuse are violent crimes. Thirdly, much of the debate about trafficking, sex work and prostitution is muddled. It is vital that these definitions and the thinking that informs them be understood, so that further analysis and discussion might proceed with increased clarity and focus.

It is impossible to consider trafficking for prostitution separately from migration and labour demand. People are trafficked into certain regions because there is a demand for their services. It is perhaps stating the obvious that traffickers will not invest time, energy and resources in moving people into regions where there is no demand for their services and consequently no labour to exploit. Trafficking is targeted; in some cases highly targeted, for example by race,[21] by age[22] and/or by perceived virginity.[23] The degree of exploitation ranges greatly, but at the worst end of the market it is severe. A study of Nepalese girls trafficked to India found that the brothel-owners kept 90–95 per cent of their earnings, while the girls were given a small amount of "pocket money" and many did not get enough food to eat. The girls engaged in prostitution for approximately 13 hours/day (ranging from 3 to 24) and were forced to serve 14 men per day (ranging from 3 to 40). Three-fifths of the girls said their clients used condoms sometimes, rarely or not at all.[24]

Globalization has also enabled the increased mobility of traffickers in identifying new sources of labour. Traffickers are flexible enough to source their victims as required, moving from one location to the next if areas become better regulated, communities become wary or costs or transport conditions change.[25]

Of course, only a portion of those migrating for work become trafficked. Some women wish to migrate and are prepared to engage in sex work. Some of these women use people smugglers to arrange their transport. Rejection of the reality of migrant sex work (often linked to the rationale that all prostitution is intrinsically exploitative or that "foreign women" must be protected) has led to simplistic anti-trafficking policies as well as the unfortunate "rescues" of those with no desire to be removed from their place of residence and work.

Agency/choice

The degree of victimization and exploitation of trafficking victims varies but, fundamentally, *all* are victimized and exploited. This reality coexists with the fact that trafficking victims have "agency". The idea that a person may be responsible for some of the decisions that resulted in their finally being trafficked seems unattractive to media and governments alike. The simplistic view is that to be victimized one must be "blameless" in all regards. Trafficking victims who have displayed some agency (i.e. most) are treated as "co-conspirators". This distinction is universally unproductive as it denies the multiplicity of factors that facilitate the operation of trafficking networks worldwide. In particular, "much of the work on the sex trade has had a strong ideological bent towards women simply as victims rather than as actors in complex situations".[26]

There is no "typical" victim of trafficking.[27] An example from a study in Moldova and Ukraine makes this point:

> Some women go abroad knowing that they will work in the sex industry without knowing the terrible work conditions and violence that accompany the trafficking business. Other women answer job advertisements for positions abroad such as dancers, waitresses, and nannies, only to find themselves held against their will and forced into prostitution and sexual slavery. Still others are kidnapped and taken to other countries without ever consenting to travel.[28]

Similarly, in a study of 59 trafficked Armenian women recently returned from the United Arab Emirates and Turkey, most of the women told interviewers "they had been tempted into trafficking rings by offers of well-paid jobs as translators, waitresses, or nannies ... but not all women were fooled. Of the 59 ... some 17 per cent said they had suspected they would end up working in the sex industry."[29] Some were prepared to place themselves at risk. Of course, this neither makes them responsible for the system into which they were pulled nor mitigates the seriousness of the offences later committed against them.

Notions that an individual must be entirely "blameless" to be considered a victim of trafficking may arise in part as a result of confusion between notions of "agency" and "choice". Many people who are trafficked are active in seeking an escape from their current situation, particularly conditions of economic deprivation. An ILO/IPEC report states that in the Mekong subregion "the vast majority of people trafficked use trafficking networks of their own volition. They turn to traffickers because they are aware of the costs, including financial, legal and time, involved in legal migration."[30] Their desire to migrate places them at risk of exploitation.

The choices that people make are not only affected by factors of which people are conscious, i.e. "I am poor and need greater income." Lived experience creates the set of expectations and understandings on which choices are based, so that people have different expectations and understandings of issues such as their human rights and legal entitlements. For example, an ILO/IPEC study on trafficking in Yunnan province in China notes that the upbringing of poor girls in rural Mengha tended "to leave them unsophisticated, inexperienced, and naïve. Their parents, too are largely undereducated, and have little consciousness of the need to protect their daughters."[31] So while people clearly display agency, is it reasonable to accuse them of having chosen the circumstances in which they find themselves? De Troy argues that the word:

> "choice" is coming from the new liberalism. In the neo-liberal economic model, everybody has a choice and is responsible for their success. That's totally false, and ignores the difficulties, and the imbalance, both among and within countries, where not everybody has the same choices and the same chances ... The word "choice" has to be analyzed in the context of the economic model we are living in.[32]

For many, the risk of entering a potentially exploitative situation is balanced against the lack of possibilities, drudgery and exploitation inherent in their current lives.

Supply

A range of variables intersect with the operation of legal and illegal sex industries to make individuals vulnerable to targeting for trafficking.

Poverty

Poverty, or economic deprivation, is a key factor in individuals' and communities' vulnerability to targeting for trafficking. On a national scale, governments have recognized the enormous contribution expatriate remittances can make to GDP. Not surprisingly, countries including India, Mexico and the Philippines have developed legislation, institutions and programmes to promote migration for work. Low public sector wages in some source countries as well as countries of destination may also partially explain corruption and the capacity of criminal networks to circumvent official government policies.

For the individual, poverty usually means few alternatives to achieve survival or a modest improvement in living standards, which can make people more vulnerable to deception and coercion and may similarly leave them few options for extricating themselves from dreadful situations. Of course, poverty need not be absolute (if such a notion exists) to have a significant impact on vulnerability. In the Mekong subregion many are aware of greater affluence and higher levels of consumption "just across the border" or a short distance away, i.e. their relative poverty.[33] The impact of television, stories of returning expatriates and the "demonstration effect" (where people see the increased affluence of those returning and their families[34]) have contributed to people's awareness of living standards and lifestyles in other parts of the world, and sparked the desire to migrate for work.

Many countries of the former USSR suffered severe economic crisis which severely impacted on their citizens, many of whom had previously enjoyed relatively affluent middle-class lifestyles. The Ukraine *Prevention of Domestic Violence and Trafficking in Humans Training Manual* cites the causes of women's migration as including "the wish to professionally assert oneself, aspirations to obtain a prestigious education, 'to see the world', to fulfill one's dreams of a 'beautiful life', to marry successfully, etc.".[35] Women who are educated, ambitious and aware of their relative position and poverty may be proactive in looking for ways out of their situation and aware of the risks associated with taking up offers of overseas work, but may still find themselves deceived and becoming the victims of trafficking networks because, ultimately, the power of the individual is extremely limited in the context of the range of choices available to them and the strength and control of trafficking networks.

Gender

Although men, women and children are victims of human trafficking, trafficking for prostitution appears to involve almost exclusively the trafficking of women and underage girls. At face value this seems to be simple sex-based (as in man/woman) selection of victims, but it is better understood as reflecting men's and women's gendered roles, behaviours and expectations.

The Asian and Pacific Islander Institute on Domestic Violence makes the direct link between gender- and poverty-based vulnerabilities by stating that trafficking is about "the exploitation of female poverty (including mothers who 'sell' their children)".[36] Women frequently have less access to resources and limited understanding of their own capacities. Most industries are gendered, based on assumptions about the performances of men and women, and women are frequently locked out of higher-paid jobs. In practice, this leaves enormous numbers of dreadfully poor women and girls who are desperate for a way to survive.

Women's economic disadvantage is not necessarily the result of long-term, entrenched social practices. The economic collapse in the CIS has clearly had a devastating effect on women's economic (and thus "life") choices, revealing the intersection between poverty and gender discrimination. Women's empowerment has been "hampered by domestic violence and the treatment of women as a commodity".[37] In Ukraine, "young women who are would-be mothers are considered as having no prospects for professional improvement. Women are the first to be laid off and the last to be hired."[38] According to a 2000 UNESCO report,[39] more than half the jobs that vanished between 1989 and 1999 were women's jobs. The Central and Eastern European Harm Reduction Network asserts one of the main consequences has been that in many countries of the region sex work represents the only way for significant numbers of young women to earn a living.[40]

The intersection of poverty and gender is felt in homes, as parents are forced to choose which of their children to educate and which to have at home to assist with labour. In many countries, including India, Nepal and those of Central and West Africa, strong societal gender bias means that parents choose to educate their sons, and girls may actually be sent to work to earn income to support the schooling of their brothers.[41] The seeking of such work leaves them vulnerable to targeting by traffickers.

For some women, their vulnerability stems from their and their families' desire to achieve the goal of marriage. In many regions there are cases of young women accepting offers of marriage to people they do not know well, which result in their being trafficked.[42] In Colombia traffickers convince women to send their photographs and details for inclusion in catalogues for Japanese men seeking Colombian wives.[43] In Albania the sham-marriage-proposal recruitment tool is so common that the Association of Albanian Girls and Women produces an anti-trafficking education handout which reads:

> Considering a Marriage Proposal? Be careful. Be skeptical. In many cases, young Albanian girls who fall in love with an older boy are proposed to and are then sold to foreign brothels. The boy was not a dream husband but instead a pimp seeking to use the girl to make a profit for himself.[44]

In Nepal the ILO identified fake marriage as the second most prevalent means of trafficking girls.[45] Perhaps ironically, the social significance of marriage is clearly indicated by a posting on the website of the anti-trafficking NGO Maiti Nepal which celebrates the marriage ceremony of three previously trafficked "girls" who had successfully attended the Maiti rehabilitation centre and then gained employment. The Maiti site states: "in Maiti Nepal we believe that marriage is also a part of our rehabilitation program since our girls/women are getting socially accepted".[46]

In some cultures, for example Togo[47] and many South Asian communities, marriage requires a dowry, which pushes families to consider any means to raise the required funds. Alternately, women may be desperate to escape a life of subsistence living, early marriage, multiple childbirth and infant mortality, leading them to consider risky migration options. Others may be escaping violent marriages:

> If a woman wants to leave a violent relationship or household she has to start from scratch. She has to change everything including where she lives and where she works. This is why women are so attracted by ads for jobs in other countries. They are often desperate to get out and go somewhere new. If you tell them that they are likely to be forced into prostitution they say "well better to be a prostitute than to be raped and abused by my husband".[48]

The intersection of gender-based violence in a woman's home situation and women's vulnerability to trafficking has been under-researched, although its existence is acknowledged by agencies such as the Women's Consortium of Ukraine, which states "when examining the causes of women's migration abroad, one has to take into account one more gender aspect of the problem – the traditional approach to women as sex objects. This stereotype leads to violence against girls and women in Ukrainian families."[49] Similarly, the Asian and Pacific Islander Institute on Domestic Violence acknowledges that trafficked women "may have fled equally traumatic bonds with their families".[50]

Weak state apparatus

Not surprisingly, governance practices significantly impact on individuals and their vulnerability to trafficking, both directly, through laws, policies and programmes that increase or decrease vulnerability to trafficking, and indirectly, by governing (or not) the broad social and economic conditions under which individuals live.

The US Department of State, the self-appointed monitor of international anti-trafficking governance practices, publishes an annual assessment of governments' actions to prevent trafficking; the *Trafficking in Persons Report*.[51] The report provides useful comment, and may in fact have impacted on some governments' anti-trafficking measures.[52]

Although many countries have signed or ratified the international anti-trafficking protocol,[53] many lack the political will or capacity to create domestic laws, policies and programmes to see that its basic aims are implemented, let alone expand on its largely law and order focus. Frequently, anti-trafficking strategies continue to be undermined by crude analysis of what makes people vulnerable to trafficking and the development of simplistic laws or programmes (for example, denying women the right to independent movement or providing training in "skills" that offer limited options for employment or economic reward), the lack of resources to implement programmes and corruption of government officials. Two other issues of governance warrant particular mention.

Migration-for-work programmes

A number of governments now have programmes in place to promote the migration of their workers overseas. Ostensibly, such programmes simultaneously reduce the demand to create domestic employment while providing enormous revenue through the remittances overseas workers send home. Officially recorded remittances worldwide (including those from people recruited through government-endorsed migration programmes) exceeded $232 billion in 2005, with developing countries receiving $167 billion of that; more than double the amount of development aid they receive from all sources. Remittances sent through informal channels could add another 50 per cent to that figure, making remittances the largest source of external capital in many developing countries.[54] Unfortunately, these well-intentioned, highly lucrative programmes have in some instances proven fertile ground for trafficking networks.

The Philippines, for example, has a highly developed programme promoting migration for work which includes a number of substantial government agencies. Preliminary labour department data for 2006 suggested that 1.1 million newly hired Filipinos left to work overseas in that year, to become part of the more than 8 million Filipinos working overseas, or nearly a tenth of the population. In 2006 official remittances (not including funds sent informally) reached $12.8 billion.[55]

The government is aware that Filipino women are being trafficked through these systems[56] and has set in place numerous safeguards to minimize risk. One curious example has been the saga of entertainer visas used to gain entry to Japan. Filipino women have been one of the main groups of foreign women entering Japan to work in the entertainment industry, many of them travelling on entertainer visas; the conditions of these are very specific and based on the premise that labour must be "skilled". Entertainer visa holders must have passed Philippine government-controlled auditions and demonstrated that they have the professional-standard performance skills of a singer or dancer, and have a minimum of two years' experience outside Japan. It is questionable whether the majority of entertainer visa holders could satisfy these qualifications, particularly given the sheer number of such visa holders traveling to Japan each year.[57] The entertainer visa workplace regulations operating in Japan[58] are also stringent, but are not routinely met.

Since the introduction of the entertainer visa the governments of both Japan and the Philippines have taken actions to tighten its "skills" requirements, including a 1996 amendment to consolidate a clear distinction between "entertainer" and "hostess". Following the amendment, the number of Filipino entertainers entering Japan dropped sharply;[59] the number of applicants "passing" dropping from 95 to 45 per cent, or "20,000 applicants not making it to Japan and a loss of over P4 billion Philippine pesos in commissions to the OPA sector of the overseas placement industry".[60] Far more recently, in 2005 the Japanese government moved to restrict the issuing of entertainer visas to Philippine nationals, which, the US Department of State asserts, has resulted in a sizeable reduction in the trafficking of Philippine women to Japan.[61]

As in other source countries, many Filipino women are faced with a profound lack of job opportunities and little or no prospect of improving their circumstances. Poverty is widespread and sections of the population are undernourished.[62] In the case of the Philippines, the enormous size of the migrant worker "industry", its highly structured operation and the fact that it is government instigated may provide additional impetus for women to accept job offers for overseas work, which in some instances results in their being trafficked into prostitution (and other forms of servitude, including domestic work).

Conflict

Political turmoil and conflict have also played a role in exposing women to the risks of trafficking for prostitution. As many flee their homes to ensure their own safety and look for a means to earn a living, desperation sets in, making people more likely to accept offers of work with risks attached. Asylum-seekers and refugees are exploited by criminal groups seeking new "opportunities". Minnesota Advocates for Human Rights reported criminal gangs infiltrating refugee camps as they were being created for fleeing Kosovars, offering housing and employment, and when that failed resorting to abduction of unwilling women.[63] In Guatemala traffickers targeted girls raped during the period of armed conflict, exploiting their concern about the stigma attached to rape and damaged marriage prospects.[64] In South Africa refugees are both victims and perpetrators of trafficking. As male refugees encounter unemployment and xenophobia, they recruit female relatives from their countries of origin and move them to South Africa where they are sexually assaulted and forced into prostitution.[65]

Demand

> Trafficking in women and their compulsory involvement in prostitution will exist as long as developed countries have a sustained commercial demand for cheaper and more easily accessible sex services of women from poor countries.[66]

Trafficking in women for prostitution is driven by demand. Traffickers simply do not bother moving women to destinations where their labour cannot be exploited with relative ease. It is perhaps surprising, then, that only limited attention has been given to the factors which make particular destinations attractive to traffickers. Why are there many trafficked women in some destinations and few or none in others? Why do many governments do little to address the weaknesses within their states that facilitate the operation of exploitative work sites? And why do governments persist in focusing on "illegal" workers while ignoring their citizens' demand for sex workers' services?

In considering demand, it is important to note that in any destination the demand for sex worker services is not limitless. Like any industry, increased competition and market saturation can lead to cheaper prices and reduced benefits. European-citizen sex workers have blamed migrants for ruining commercial sex markets by accepting bad working conditions and undercutting the prices of established (European) workers.[67] The *Purchasing of Sexual Services in Sweden and the Netherlands* report notes instances in both Sweden and the Netherlands where competition for services between local and foreign sex workers led to conflict. The report states that from the mid-1990s there was an influx of foreign prostitutes to Sweden, which in Stockholm developed into a problem of law and order as tension rose between Swedish and foreign sex workers.[68] In the Netherlands recent legislative changes meant that foreign sex workers without work or residence permits were pushed out of brothels, many ending up in "tolerance zones", triggering animosity and conflict between the sex workers originally in the tolerance zones and the new foreign prostitutes.[69] Similarly, Rijal reports that Nepali women sex workers in India have faced "serious threats to their survival" as the result of a big decline in the number of clients in Mumbai and Calcutta due to an increase in the number of street call-girls, flying sex workers and bar girls.[70]

The issue of restricted demand has not gone unnoticed by sex worker advocates, with the International Committee on the Rights of Sex Workers in Europe recommending that:

> the issue of competition in sex markets ... is one that needs to be addressed among all workers, since it is obvious that migrants coming from poorer countries, under pressure to pay back debts and in fear of being thrown out at any moment may well request lower fees for sex than established Europeans. As long as migrants feel they are under constant fire and socially excluded, they may not feel they can benefit from asking for higher prices charged by those who enjoy security (and possibly losing clients).[71]

Market competition is likely to affect trafficking debates among sex worker advocacy groups. Australia, for example, has seen little trafficking of women into the sex industry. Scarlet Alliance, the Australian national peak body of community-based sex worker organizations, estimates that there are fewer than 400 sex workers entering Australia in any one year on contract, and that the majority of these women consent to work. Despite its extensive networks, within 1 year the alliance had direct contact with fewer than 10 women who had been deceptively recruited.[72] While the *Trafficking in Persons Report* states that Australia is a destination country for women from South-East Asia, South Korea and China, it also recognizes that some of these women travel to Australia voluntarily to work in both legal and illegal brothels, and are then deceived or coerced into debt bondage or sexual servitude.[73] Scarlet Alliance has strongly argued that sex slavery in Australia is largely a myth and most Asian sex workers working illegally in Australia are in fact migrant sex workers who should be granted working visas. This argument is interesting in the context of Australia's borders being basically closed (unlike the European Union), except for those migrating for specific purposes, i.e. not sex work, and the number of migrant sex workers being low, thus providing little competition for local sex workers. Perhaps informed by an understanding of the difficulties caused by unregulated market competition, Scarlet Alliance has suggested a cap of 300 visas per year. At this point, the immigration minister's office has said that sex workers, "like fruit pickers", would not be eligible for working visas because they offered low-level skills and Australian industries had no demand for them.[74]

Sex industry regulation

The structure of domestic sex industries impacts on women's vulnerability to trafficking as they are the industries into which women are generally trafficked. Internationally, governments have debated the merits of criminalization, legalization and decriminalization of their domestic sex industries, although many have tended towards simplistic law and order responses despite their obvious lack of success and proven poor health outcomes.

Model 1 – Criminalization and prohibition

Criminalization or prohibitionist arguments remain the most common legislative responses to prostitution. They usually have a strong moral premise (e.g. selling sex is wrong, women must be protected) and include an assumption that prohibition is the mechanism most likely to lead to eventual abolition of the domestic sex industry despite the fact that, as Harcourt, Egger and Donovan note:

> with the possible short-term exceptions in totalitarian settings such as the Taliban regime in Afghanistan and during the Cultural Revolution in China, prohibition has neither eradicated prostitution nor markedly reduced the other social ills traditionally associated with the industry.[75]

Criminalization attempts to address complex criminological, social and economic factors with a basic "law and order" solution. It places all power in the hands of the police and government officials, and consequently increases the likelihood of corruption and abuse of sex workers. It completely disempowers sex workers and, in practice, removes many of their human rights. If enforced it is administratively expensive, and if not enforced it leaves workers vulnerable to uncertainty, threats, extortion and abuse. It impedes the provision of health care, including HIV/AIDS prevention and care, by driving people engaged in prostitution underground.[76] Clearly, an underground industry or a splitting of the industry into two – legal and illegal – parts is particularly detrimental to trafficked women, as it makes available an illegal sector into which they can easily be moved and ensures their employment in that sector only.

In Japan prostitution is "illegal" but operates widely through various loopholes (prostituting vaginal sex is illegal but anal sex, masturbation, etc. are not) and a lack of policing. Prostitution is largely provided in "restricted sex-related businesses", which are businesses defined under the Law on the Control and Improvement of Amusement Businesses as providing services aimed at fulfilling "the sexual curiosity of clients of the opposite sex".[77] Bars and nightclubs where hostessing is provided are "entertainment businesses". According to police statistics, in 2003 there were around 32,340 shops registered as "entertainment businesses".[78]

The broad Japanese entertainment industry, including the sex industry, reflects a globalized world, as young women contribute to a substantial migrant labour force. Women from all over the world, including developed countries such as Australia, Canada, the United Kingdom and the United States, are employed in the entertainment industry. There is no evidence to date to suggest that trafficked women make up more than a small proportion of those working in the entertainment industry, and prostitution is only a part of that industry.[79]

Anti-trafficking laws aside, in most countries sex workers are those most heavily targeted by criminal laws against prostitution. Although it is now also illegal to *purchase* sex services in some countries, even in those jurisdictions the weight of the law usually falls on sex workers. In Canada the exchange of sex for money is technically legal, but ss. 210–213 of the Criminal Code make almost every prostitution-related activity illegal. It is illegal to keep a brothel or transport someone to a brothel, to encourage or force a person to participate in prostitution, to live on the money earned by prostitution by someone else and to "communicate" in public (sex workers and customers) for the purpose of prostitution. Enforcement of the communication charge reveals a strong gender bias. Roughly an equal number of men and women have been charged, but the sentences given to women have been much harsher than those given to men. Women receive custodial sentences at a much higher rate – approximately 90 per cent of women are incarcerated compared to only 10 per cent of men, with men being more likely to be ordered to pay fines (compared to incarceration) and to receive probation.[80]

Canada has also made the interesting decision to follow the lead of the United States and introduce "john schools" where men charged with attempting to purchase sexual services may be referred and have charges against them stayed or dropped. In practice, this means that men are diverted from the criminal prosecution process in exchange for "spending a few hours in a classroom setting, being informed about the legal, medical and social ramifications of their activities".[81] The rationale and effectiveness of these schools is open to debate.[82] Indeed, the operation of john schools can be construed as reflecting the confusion of the government's legal versus moral responsibilities, and indeed confusion about issues of morality. Is it the government's responsibility to lecture men on the damage caused by sex work, or should it be instructing johns on how to purchase sex legally?

While some governments are now prepared to punish traffickers, many have proven reticent to punish men who buy sex, including those who pay for the services of trafficked women, i.e. those who create the demand. Sweden is an interesting exception. Since 1999 it has taken a radical approach to the criminalization of sex work by addressing demand and making it illegal to buy sex, while decriminalizing the selling of sex.[83] The Swedish government maintains that prostitution is a social ill and a form of men's violence against women. Women who sell sex are victims requiring protection by the state.[84]

Debate continues about whether the strategy has worked. Erndahl of the National Criminal Investigation Department says "the law has definitely had a disruptive effect on the customers",[85] but whether it has actually reduced prostitution is open to question. Sex work appears to have moved off the streets but into other venues. A 2003 Goeteborg-based study found that the internet was becoming the favourite way to advertise and buy sexual services in Sweden.[86] Martens of the National Council for Crime Prevention maintains "the law has hidden prostitution. We don't see it much on the streets, but it is increasing in the cities after initially going down."[87] Martens states that the number of sex workers operating in 1998 (2,500 workers) "is unlikely to have changed".[88]

In interviews with female Swedish sex workers, Östergren found that most were unhappy with the current legal and social situation, saying they felt "discriminated against, endangered by the very laws that seek to protect them, and ... under severe emotional stress".[89] The difficulties for street workers are multiple:

- difficulty accessing clients
- clients being more stressed so negotiations are more rapid, reducing sex workers' capacity to gauge and avoid dangerous clients
- apprehension about seeking help from the police
- fewer workers on the street having resulted in a breakdown in informal networks and reduced ability to give support and warn of dangerous clients
- lower prices because of fewer customers, resulting in more desperate women agreeing to engage in unsafe sex and sexual activity they usually would not perform.

Lowman refers to Östergren's work and concludes that "by ruling out harm reduction strategies, the Swedish approach exposes prostitutes to harm".[90]

There is little information available about the effect of Sweden's prostitution laws on trafficking, although it is broadly acknowledged that Sweden is very active in anti-trafficking movements and has specific anti-trafficking laws and training for police. According to the National Criminal Investigation Department, between 200 and 500 women are trafficked to Sweden each year.[91] Further details are not easily available. The national rapporteur Kajsa Wahlberg states that "few foreign women are found in open prostitution in the street [and] are instead being escorted to clients' homes or other places indoors".[92] The US *Trafficking in Per-*

sons Report states that women and children are trafficked into Sweden for prostitution from Eastern and South-Eastern European countries, the Baltics, Russia and (to a lesser extent) Thailand. Sweden also is used as a transit point for a limited number of victims.[93]

Sweden's strong anti-trafficking legislation has proven disappointing in at least two aspects. Firstly, despite expanding the legislation in July 2004 to include labour exploitation (and internal trafficking), trafficking for prostitution has continued to be defined by sex/prostitution rather than labour exploitation, with "procurement" being the focus of prosecutions. Secondly, and of greater concern, the judicial interpretation of Swedish law reveals a reluctance to apply the rationale of the international anti-trafficking protocol which outlines that an individual can be considered a victim of trafficking despite having initially agreed to a process of illegal migration. Sweden's anti-trafficking legislation requires prosecutors to prove that traffickers used improper means. "Judges commonly rule that improper means were absent in cases involving victims who consented at some point during their trafficking ordeal."[94]

Model 2 – Legalization and licensing

Legalization or licensing of aspects of the sex industry is generally perceived as a means of bringing the industry into the mainstream, excluding criminal involvement and increasing government control. It allows workers (in legalized sections of the industry) access to legal protections, and governments to set conditions relating to public and sexual health and workplace conditions, including occupational health and safety.

Unfortunately, licensing regimes have not always delivered the full range of anticipated positive outcomes[95] and they come with costs attached, which may include significant administrative, police and health resources, particularly if they involve health screens and criminal history checks. Under some regimes individual sex workers are stigmatized through "licensing" of individuals, which may include restriction of movement, identification on travel documents and medical care limited to approved clinics. Individual licensing also increases the chances of corrupt officials exploiting individual workers.

Licensing requires the government to take the difficult position of ensuring the number of workers effectively meets demand. Too many or too few workers may result in the development of illegal operators, as too many workers will see pressure on some to agree to lower payment and worse conditions, and too few licensed premises will see workers working outside the legal sector. Previous studies of Australian states found that in two states workers were pushed into illegal work when the number of brothel licences fell short of demand. From a public health perspective, licensing systems may be preferable to criminalization but they raise a number of concerns, not the least of which is that money spent on administration and unnecessary health screens is lost to more productive health programmes. At the same time a false sense of security may be engendered by an apparently comprehensive system of regulation.[96]

Deciding exactly which aspects of the industry should be legalized or criminalized has proven fraught. A snapshot of Australian states and territories reveals the struggle that state governments have had in regulating the Australian sex industry. Despite the states' similar historical and cultural backgrounds, and at the time of writing all governments being ruled by the same political party, table 4.1 represents a hotchpotch of attempts to regulate/criminalize different aspects of the industry, presumably based on politicians' personal beliefs and anecdotal evidence. What is absent from legislative and policy development is detailed comparative research into the effect different legislative models have had and are likely to have on workers. In fact, such research is largely absent *per se*, with international debates on sex industry regulation suffering greatly from the same polarized opinions and vested interests that infuse trafficking debates, and a blatant lack of interest from funders to support research into this complex issue.

Model 3 – Decriminalization

Decriminalization, or the removal of most criminal penalties applying to adult prostitution, has been adopted in Denmark, Germany, New Zealand, parts of Australia and, most famously, the Netherlands. Decriminalization means that regulation of the sex industry occurs outside the criminal justice system.

Models of decriminalization are based on the rationale that some adults chose to work as sex workers and that it is not possible to eradicate prostitution, so sex work should be normalized as work and the industry regulated to ensure the highest degree of occupational health and safety possible. Proponents argue that decriminalization facilitates a separation of the sex industry from organized crime and police corruption while improving public health outcomes and workers' rights. There is some evidence that this has largely worked, in some locations at least. Fears that decriminalization would lead to a sex industry explosion and recruitment of workers has not occurred.[97] While it seems likely that systems of decriminalization have improved occupational health and safety outcomes, it is less clear that other standard industrial benefits, such as annual leave, sick pay and superannuation, have followed, partly as the result of brothel-owners treating sex workers as subcontractors.[98]

The government of the Australian state of New South Wales has attempted to instigate a model of decriminalization. It can be summarized as follows.

- *Brothel-based sex work.* Legal from a legal brothel. Local government controls permissions through planning policies and development approval.
- *Sole operator.* Legal but covered by the same zoning requirements as brothels. Consequently, permission to operate is at the individual discretion of councils.
- *Street work.* Legal, but it remains a criminal offence for a sex worker or a client to solicit or take part in sex (including in a vehicle) in or within view of a dwelling, school, church or hospital. Street sex workers can be fined for loitering under local by-laws by council staff. Police can fine street sex workers for not following a reasonable direction.
- *Escort.* Legal.

Evidence from Australia suggests that the decriminalization model has not been problem-free. Put plainly, many people do not want any obvious (or even inconspicuous) prostitution in their neighbourhood. Street-based "zone" laws and local government planning laws are interpreted rigidly to minimize the opportunities for sex workers and premises to operate. Some state regulations around sole workers or home-based businesses force workers to work alone (rather than with one or two other workers or support staff for safety) and/or to apply to local government for planning permits to operate a home-based business. It is not surprising that many sex workers operating sole businesses from home are not prepared to go on the public record, a process which includes having a planning permission notice placed outside their home for a period of time.

The Netherlands offers another, fuller model of decriminalization. Prostitution has been legal since 1988, sex workers have paid income tax since 1996 and prostitution has shared the same status as other forms of labour since 1999.[99] In basic terms, the Dutch government has stated: "that prostitution exists is a given fact, even for the government. That requires a realistic approach, without moralism."[100] Conditions such as working hours, health and safety regulations, paid leave entitlement, tax law and social security regulations all apply. In October 2000 the government lifted its ban on brothels, its rationale being that this would improve legalization and intensify the fight against unwanted phenomena in the sector. Responsibility moved to local authorities to formulate and implement policies tailored to the circumstances prevailing in their area and issue licences to brothels. Regulations specify safety and hygiene standards, fire precautions, minimum working area size and measures to prevent "excessive nuisance in neighbourhoods". The Association of

Table 4.1 Legalizing the sex industry in Australia

	ACT	New South Wales[a]	Northern Territory	Queensland	South Australia[b]	Tasmania	Victoria	Western Australia[c]
Working in a brothel	Legal from a legal brothel	Legal from a legal brothel	Illegal	Legal from a legal brothel	Illegal	Illegal	Legal	Illegal
Sole operator	Legal from own premises Must register	Legal but regulated by local councils Same zoning requirements as brothels	Legal Must register Must work alone	Legal but must work alone except for licensed bodyguard	Illegal	Legal and may work with one other worker	Legal but must register Regulated by local councils	Legal from own premises Must work alone
Working from the street	Illegal	Legal, but zoning restrictions apply	Illegal	Illegal	Illegal	Illegal	Illegal	Illegal
Working as an escort	Legal Must register Register open for public inspection	Legal	Legal from licensed agency if worker issued with police certificate stating no violence or drug-related criminal history	Illegal	Ambiguous Agencies operate on the condition that they provide staff for the company of clients	Ambiguous Agencies operate on the condition that they provide staff for the company of clients	Legal for workers employed by an agency or working as a small owner-operator	Ambiguous Agencies operate on the condition that they provide staff for the company of clients

Brothel regulation	Must publicly register Must operate within a prescribed location	Controlled by local council through planning policies	Illegal	State zoning laws apply Brothels cannot have more than 5 rooms	Illegal	Illegal	Controlled by local council through planning policies Generally limited to 6 rooms	Illegal

Notes

[a]Sex work is decriminalized in New South Wales.

[b]The act of commercial sex itself is not illegal in South Australia but a number of laws relate to commercial sex in a brothel (e.g. living on the earnings, soliciting, keeping a brothel), effectively rendering brothel-based sex work activities illicit.

[c]The Western Australian government is at April 2007 considering significant changes to sex work laws. The government's Prostitution Law Reform Working Group's thorough *Prostitution Law Reform for Western Australia* report recommends that sex work be largely decriminalized.

Netherlands Municipalities has published guidelines for the regulation of prostitution. The national government publishes booklets for sex workers and their employers on social insurance and related matters.[101] It was envisaged that the lifting of the ban on brothels would have the spin-off advantage of also combating trafficking in women.[102]

> Labour laws offer the most effective protection against exploitation, violence and coercion ... Abuses are easier to detect when prostitutes operate publicly and legally rather than in clandestine subculture ... Through regular inspections to ensure that brothels conform to the licensing conditions, the police are in a position to pick up signs of human trafficking. They obtain invaluable information that can be used immediately to trace and prosecute offenders in both the regulated and unregulated sectors.[103]

There are estimated to be some 25,000 sex workers in the Netherlands, with 12,500 working at some 6,000 locations at any one time. Migrant sex workers are not new although patterns of migration have changed over time, with sex workers arriving from Thailand and the Philippines in the 1970s, from Latin America and the Caribbean in the 1980s and from Central and Eastern Europe in the late 1980s/1990s. Their representation in the sex industry is significant, with the government giving a 1999 estimate that no more than one-third of sex workers were Dutch nationals, the remainder representing some 44 nationalities.[104] Thérèse van der Helm concludes that over the last few decades prostitution in the Netherlands has become a profession mostly practised by migrants from countries with unstable economic or political situations.[105]

While the new Dutch laws may have resulted in reduced trafficking, they may also have unintentionally triggered an increase in the vulnerability of illegal foreign sex workers. The law introduced in October 2000 had a direct effect on these women. Thérèse van der Helm states that migrant sex workers without residence permits were forced to leave brothels, which were illegal but relatively stable and well tolerated. As a result many now work in illegal brothels or travel around various cities in the Netherlands and abroad.[106]

There are certainly cases of human trafficking into the Dutch sex industry, but it is difficult to identify accurate figures. A 2002 study examined the impact of the lifting of the brothels' ban, but the government maintained it was too soon to draw conclusions about its impact, and notes "rehabilitating a sector that has been operating illegally for almost a century requires more than new laws or new policy".[107] Police have reported a decrease in trafficking in the legalized sector, but the government did not carry out a 2004 recommended systematic screening of foreign prostitutes in the red-light districts, so comprehensive data on the number of trafficking victims are unavailable.[108]

Foreign sex workers working without a valid residence permit (who are not victims of trafficking) are asked to leave or deported. There are no available figures differentiating the percentage of foreign-born sex workers who are working legally/working illegally/victims of trafficking. Of some concern, the 2005 US Department of State *Trafficking in Persons Report* states that "a significant percentage of the 25,000 individuals engaged in prostitution reportedly are trafficking victims. Most victims are trafficked from Central and Eastern Europe, with some victims from Nigeria and Brazil."[109]

The detailed third report of the Dutch national rapporteur on human trafficking includes a number of sources for 2002 statistics, identifying 343 (possible) victims of trafficking registered with the Dutch Foundation against Trafficking in Women, 163 victims who came into contact with support services, 371 (possible) victims registered with police and 258 victims who reported to the police or made witness statements.[110] The report also details cases of internal trafficking, as also reported by the US Department of State.[111]

Weak state apparatus

Laws are what they are: they mean nothing without strong, consistent enforcement. Weak governance, be it the result of an ill-equipped public sector, corruption or conflict, is a major facilitator of human trafficking. Many governments struggle to find the financial resources to equip a strong public sector. Income fed to corrupt government officials effectively "oils" the global human trafficking industry, while human trafficking helps perpetuate systemic government corruption.[112]

Research and anecdote-based examples of corrupt governance are plentiful (see for example Kazakhstan,[113] Bosnia,[114] the Philippines[115] and Cambodia[116]). Interesting index-based research by Vital Voices clearly reflects a commonly held belief that countries with limited government corruption perform better in terms of anti-trafficking measures, while those with more corrupt governments are less successful.[117]

War and conflict impact enormously on states' capacities to govern. Conflict drains state resources and can lead to a total breakdown of governance structure. Strong governance is absent. Trafficking laws go unenforced.[118] Organized crime is able to flourish. Armed forces and related civilian contractors have also been implicated.[119]

Conclusion

The sex industry – as an "institution" and the individuals who control it – has long been blamed for the exploitation of trafficked women. Such crude assertions deny the complexity of intersecting variables that impact on individuals to make them vulnerable to trafficking, the demands of the millions of purchasers of sex services and the ruthless, focused industry of those coordinating trafficking efforts who force people to live and work under highly exploitative, slavery-like conditions. Detailed research is required into the experiences of women trafficked into prostitution, and consideration of those strategies which have provided the most effective management of sex industries in different locations around the world. "Prostitution" must be disentangled from "migrant sex work" and "human trafficking". Only then can considered debate ensue and real progress be made on the reduction of trafficking in women for prostitution.

Notes

1. US Department of State website, available at www.state.gov/g/tip/rls/tiprpt/2005/46606.htm.
2. US Department of State, *Trafficking in Persons Report 2006*, available at www.state.gov/g/tip/rls/tiprpt/2006/65989.htm.
3. Human Rights Watch, *Borderline Slavery – Child Trafficking in Togo*, New York: Human Rights Watch, 2003.
4. International Labour Organization/International Programme on the Elimination of Child Labour, *Nepal Trafficking in Girls with Special Reference to Prostitution: A Rapid Assessment*, Geneva: International Labour Organization, 2001, p. 20.
5. Human Rights Watch, "Cambodia", available at www.humantrafficking.org/countries/cambodia.
6. International Labour Organization/International Programme on the Elimination of Child Labour, *Yunnan Province, China, Situation of Trafficking in Children and Women: A Rapid Assessment*, Bangkok: International Labour Organization, 2002, p. vii.
7. UNICEF, *Broken Promises, Shattered Dreams, A Profile of Child Trafficking in the Lao PDR*, UNICEF, 2004, available at www.unicef.org/media/files/BrokenPromisesFULLREPORT.pdf, p. 33.
8. US Department of State, "Report Details Mixed Human Trafficking Picture in Europe, Eurasia", US Department of State, 2006, available at http://usinfo.state.gov/gi/Archive/2006/Jun/07-205905.html.
9. Human Rights Watch, "Burma", available at www.humantrafficking.org/countries/burma.
10. International Labour Organization/International Programme on the Elimination of Child Labour, note 6 above, p. vii.
11. Ann D. Jordan, *The Annotated Guide to the Complete UN Trafficking Protocol*, Washington, D.C.: International Human Rights Law Group, available at www.hrlawgroup.org/initiatives/trafficking_persons/, p. 11.

12. For example, Marshall argues that it delayed the release of the international anti-trafficking protocol by more than a year. Phil Marshall, "Globalization, Migration and Trafficking: Some Thoughts from the South-East Asian Region", paper presented to Globalizaton Workshop, Kuala Lumpur, 8–10 May 2001, available at www.un.or.th/TraffickingProject/Publications/globalisation_paper.pdf, p. 10.

13. Kathleen Barry, quoted in Rajeshwari Sunder Rajan, "The Prostitution Question(s) – (Female) Agency, Sexuality and Work", in *Trafficking, Sex-Work, Prostitution: Discourses and Representations of the Sub-Continent, Re/productions*, No. 2, April 1999, available at www.hsph.harvard.edu/grhf/, p. 3.

14. A workshop entitled International Feminist Networking against the Traffic in Women: Organising against Female Sexual Slavery, held in Rotterdam in 1983.

15. Sunder Rajan, note 13 above, p. 3.

16. Mary McPhail, quoted in Stefania Bianchi, "Sex Workers Say They Have Labor Rights Too", Global Information Network, 2005, available at sex-work@eforums.healthdev.org.

17. Ibid.

18. Conference organizer Ruth Morgan Thomas, quoted in Bianchi, note 16 above. Further information on the Sex Work, Human Rights, Labour and Migration Conference is available at www.sexworkeurope.org.

19. Professional communication with Scarlet Alliance.

20. J. Jordan, *Working Girls: Women in the New Zealand Sex Industry*, Auckland: Penguin Books, 1991; P. M. Pyett, B. R. Haste, et al., "Who Works in the Sex Industry? A Profile of Female Prostitutes in Victoria", *Australian and New Zealand Journal of Public Health* 20(4): 1996, 431–433. Quoted in Jan Jordon, *The Sex Industry in New Zealand – A Literature Review*, Ministry of Justice, March 2005, available at www.justice.govt.nz/pubs/reports/2005/sex-industry-in-nz-literature-review/sex-industry-in-nz.pdf, p. 12.

21. "If she's light-colored, then she is sexually attractive to this population." *Campo* brothel client, quoted in Kamala Kempadoo, "The Migrant Tightrope: Experiences from the Caribbean", in Kamala Kempadoo and Jo Doezema, eds, *Global Sex Workers: Rights, Resistance, and Redefinition*, New York: Routledge, 1998, p. 131.

22. The ILO cites the HIV/AIDS-influenced African example of girls being forced into prostitution because of "the mistaken belief that having sex with a child is not only 'cleaner' and therefore 'safer', but even that it can cure the disease". International Labour Organization, *Trafficking in Human Beings – New Approaches to Combating the Problem*, Geneva: ILO, 2003, p. 41.

23. For example, an OSCE official states that in the United Arab Emirates girls of 13 or 14 have high market value as a female virgin can be sold for $40,000 for a month's service, after which she may be sent to an ordinary brothel: Cerasela Nicolas, quoted in Roland Eggleston, "Armenia: Government Pressured to Toughen Laws on Human Trafficking", Radio Free Europe/Radio Liberty, Munich, 30 July 2001, available at http://hyeforum.com/lofiversion/index.php?t845.html.

24. International Labour Organization/International Programme on the Elimination of Child Labour, note 4 above, p. 2.

25. In 2003 the director of the Thai Office of Child Promotion and Protection noted a simultaneous reduction in the number of Thai women and children tricked into prostitution and an increase in the number of foreign victims, especially from Cambodia and Burma. Bhanravee Tansubhapol, *Bangkok Post*, 2 April 2003, p. 1.

26. International Labour Organization/International Programme on the Elimination of Child Labour, "Labour Migration and Trafficking within the Greater Mekong Subregion: Proceedings of Mekong Subregional Experts Meeting and Exploratory Policy Paper", Bangkok: International Labour Organization, 2001, p. 33.

27. Minnesota Advocates for Human Rights, *Trafficking in Women: Moldova and Ukraine*, Minneapolis, Minn.: Minnesota Advocates for Human Rights, December 2000, p. 17.
28. Ibid., p. 3.
29. Eggleston, note 23 above.
30. International Labour Organization/International Programme on the Elimination of Child Labour, note 26 above, p. 15.
31. International Labour Organization/International Programme on the Elimination of Child Labour, note 6 above, p. 15.
32. Collette de Troy, quoted in Pamela Shifman, "Trafficking and Women's Human Rights in a Globalised World", *Gender and Development* 11(1), 2003, p. 125.
33. International Labour Organization/International Programme on the Elimination of Child Labour, note 26 above, p. 35.
34. International Labour Organization/International Programme on the Elimination of Child Labour, note 4 above, p. 36.
35. Natalka Samolevska, quoted in Ruslana Bezpal'cha, *Prevention of Domestic Violence and Trafficking in Humans Training Manual*, Winrock International, 2001, available at www.winrock.org/leadership/files/Dos_manual.pdf, p. 152.
36. Firoza Chic Dabby, *Trafficking Considerations and Recommendations for Domestic Violence Advocates*, Asian and Pacific Islander Institute on Domestic Violence, August 2004, available at www.apiahf.org/apidvinstitute/CriticalIssues/trafficking.htm.
37. Bezpal'cha, note 35 above, p. 1.
38. Ibid., p. 152.
39. *UNESCO Courier* 14, February 2000, available at www.unesco.org.
40. Central and Eastern European Harm Reduction Network, *Sex Work, HIV/AIDS and Human Rights in Central and Eastern Europe and Central Asia*, Central and Eastern European Harm Reduction Network, 2005, available at www.ceehrn.org/index.php?ItemId=15504.
41. Human Rights Watch, note 3 above, p. 11.
42. US Department of State website, available at www.state.gov/g/tip.
43. Polania A. Molina, "Japan, the Mecca for Trafficking in Colombian Women", Colombia: Global Alliance against Traffic in Women/International Human Rights Law Group/Foundation against Trafficking in Women, 2000, p. 10, available at www.december18.net/web/general/paper30ColombiaJapan.pdf.
44. Association of Albanian Girls and Women website, available at www.aagw.org/Education/Handouts/ConsideringMarriage.
45. International Labour Organization/International Programme on the Elimination of Child Labour, note 4 above, p. 21.
46. Maiti Nepal, "Maiti Nepal Organized Survivors' Marriage Ceremony", available at www.maitinepal.org/events/index.htm#e5.
47. The ILO found that in Togo parents needed to earn a dowry but also considered domestic work for girls to be good preparation for married life. International Labour Organization/International Programme on the Elimination of Child Labour, *Combating Trafficking in Children for Labour Exploitation in West and Central Africa – Synthesis Report*, Geneva: ILO, 2001, p. 27.
48. Minnesota Advocates for Human Rights, note 27 above, pp. 18–19.
49. Bezpal'cha, note 35 above, p. 152.
50. Chic Dabby, note 36 above.
51. 2005 edition available at www.state.gov/g/tip/rls/tiprpt/2005/.
52. Although whether "countries ... have been inspired to greater action against human trafficking as a result of this unique compendium", as Secretary of State Condoleezza Rice claims, is a matter for debate.

53. List available at www.unodc.org/unodc/en/crime_cicp_signatures_trafficking.html.
54. World Bank, "Migration Can Deliver Welfare Gains, Reduce Poverty, Says Global Economic Prospects 2006", 16 November 2005, available at http://web.worldbank.org/WBSITE/EXTERNAL/NEWS/0,,contentMDK:20724214~pagePK:64257043~piPK:437376~theSitePK:4607,00.html.
55. AFP, "Philippine 2006 Overseas Remittances Hit Record 12.8 Billion Dollars", *Yahoo Asia News*, 15 February 2007, available at http://asia.news.yahoo.com/070215/afp/070215073037eco.html.
56. For example, in early 2000 the deputy executive director of the Commission on Filipinos Overseas acknowledged that trafficked Filipinos include women who are "legitimately" recruited and promised high-paying jobs but end up as prostitutes; women who leave as tourists and end up as domestic helpers, exotic dancers or bar girls; and women who are willing or coerced victims of the mail-order bride trade. Catherine Paredes-Maceda, "Prevention of Trafficking, Protection, and Rehabilitation of Victims", in *Proceedings of Asia-Pacific Symposium on Trafficking in Persons*, 20 January 2000, Tokyo: Ministry of Foreign Affairs, Japan, p. 29.
57. In 2002 73,246 Filipinos left for Japan using an entertainer visa, 99 per cent of whom were women. Carmelita G. Nuqui, "The Vulnerabilities of Filipino Women as Potential Trafficking Victims", paper presented at Conference on Human Trafficking in Asia, Tokyo, 23–24 June 2004, unpublished.
58. For example, they state that entertainers must not act as hostesses or serve food or drinks, and venues must provide a sizeable stage and waiting room.
59. International Organization for Migration, *Trafficking in Women to Japan for Sexual Exploitation – A Survey on the Case of Filipino Women*, Geneva: IOM, May 1997, p. 9.
60. *Daily Tribune*, "DoLE Official Admits Gov't Part in Trafficking of Women", *Daily Tribune*, 3 February 2003, available at www.trafficking.org.ph/resources/feb03/dole.htm.
61. US Department of State, note 2 above.
62. "The *2000 Family Income and Expenditures Survey* in the Philippines found that between 1997 and 2000 the poverty level actually rose to 33.7 per cent. More than 20 per cent of the population (or over 15 million people) are considered undernourished." Quoted in "About the Philippines", available at www.freefromhunger.org/philabout.html.
63. Hearing before the Commission on Security and Cooperation in Europe, "The Sex Trade: Trafficking of Women and Children in Europe and the United States", 106th Congress, 5th Session, 28 June 1999, Washington, D.C.: US Government Printing Office, 1999, p. 2.
64. Women, Health and Development Program, *Trafficking of Women and Children for Sexual Exploitation in the Americas*, Washington, D.C.: Pan-American Health Organization, 2004, available at www.paho.org/genderandhealth, p. 2.
65. IOM Regional Office for South Africa, *Seduction, Sale and Slavery: Trafficking in Women and Children for Sexual Exploitation in Southern Africa*, IOM South Africa, May 2004, available at www.queensu.ca/samp/migrationresources/gender/documents/martens.pdf.
66. Bezpal'cha, note 35 above.
67. International Committee on the Rights of Sex Workers in Europe, *Migration and Sex Work*, April 2006, available at www.sexworkeurope.org/website/BackgroundPapers/Migration.htm.
68. Working Group on the Legal Regulation of the Purchase of Sexual Services, *Purchasing Sexual Services in Sweden and the Netherlands: Legal Regulation and Experiences*, Oslo: Ministry of Justice and the Police, 2004, p. 20.

69. Ibid., p. 25.
70. Sangeeta Rijal, "Quitting Impossible for Nepali Sex Workers", *Kantipur Online*, 9 November 2005, available at www.kantipuronline.com/kolnews.php?&nid=56649.
71. International Committee on the Rights of Sex Workers in Europe, note 67 above.
72. Scarlet Alliance, "Submission to Parliamentary Joint Committee on the Australian Crime Commission – Inquiry into Trafficking in Women and Sexual Servitude", Australia, September 2003.
73. US Department of State, *Trafficking in Persons Report 2005*, Washington, D.C.: US Department of State, 2005, available at www.state.gov/g/tip/rls/tiprpt/2005/46614.htm.
74. AAP, "Union Pushes for Sex Worker Visas", AAP, 14 October 2005, available at www.scarletalliance.org.au/media/News_Item.2005-10-17.1833.
75. Christine Harcourt, Sandra Egger and Basil Donovan, "Sex Work and the Law", *Sexual Health* 2(3), 2005, pp. 121–128, available at www.publish.csiro.au/nid/164/paper/SH04042.htm.
76. UNAIDS/Inter-Parliamentary Union, *Handbook for Legislators on HIV/AIDS, Law and Human Rights*, Geneva: UNAIDS/Inter-Parliamentary Union, 1999, pp. 56–59.
77. Article 2 defining the categories of "restricted sex-related businesses" (*sei-kanren tokushu eigyou*). International Labour Organization, *Human Trafficking for Sexual Exploitation in Japan*, Geneva: ILO, 2004, p. 38.
78. Ibid., White Paper on Police 2004, p. 119.
79. Sally Cameron, "Trafficking of Filipino Women to Japan: A Case of Human Security Violation in Japan", paper presented at International Conference on Globalization, Migration and Human Security: Challenges in Northeast Asia, Tokyo, 6 October 2003, available at http://gsti.miis.edu/CEAS-PUB/2003_Cameron.pdf.
80. UNAIDS/Inter-Parliamentary Union, note 76 above.
81. Ibid.
82. For example, see the arguments of Ian Mitchell in "Dealing with Prostitution in Canada", *Canadian Medical Association Journal* 172(1), 4 January 2005, available at www.cmaj.ca/cgi/content/full/172/1/13; J. Marlowe, *What's Wrong with John School?*, Sex Workers Alliance of Vancouver, August 1996, available at www.walnet.org/csis/groups/swav/johnschool/johnschool.html.
83. As of December 2005, it seems India may also be considering travelling down this path.
84. Ministry of Industry, Employment and Communications (Regeringskansliet), *Prostitution and Trafficking in Women*, factsheet, Stockholm: Regeringskansliet, January 2004, available at www.sweden.gov.se/content/1/c6/01/87/74/6bc6c972.pdf.
85. Quoted in Ingmarie Froman, *Sweden's Fight Against Trafficking in Women*, Swedish Institute, 27 February 2004, available at www.sweden.se/templates/Article_6076.asp.
86. *The Age*, "Sweden's Prostitutes Ply Their Trade on the Net", *The Age*, 16 January 2003, available at www.theage.com.au/articles/2003/01/16/1042520720227.html.
87. Quoted in Patrick McLoughlin, *Sweden Seeks to Export Prostitution Legislation*, Human Trafficking.com Forums, 13 April 2003, available at www.polarisproject.org/PolarisProject/forums/ShowPost.
88. Ibid.
89. Petra Östergren, *Sexworkers Critique of Swedish Prostitution Policy*, available at www.petraostergren.com/english/studier.magister.asp.
90. John Lowman, "Dealing with Prostitution in Canada", *Canadian Medical Association Journal* 172(1), 4 January 2005, available at www.cmaj.ca.
91. Ministry of Industry, Employment and Communications (Regeringskansliet), note 84 above.

92. Kajsa Wahlberg, "Trafficking in Human Beings", *Rikskirimianpolisen*, available at www.nmr.ee/women/presentations/KajsaWahlberg.pdf, p. 2.
93. US Department of State, note 73 above.
94. Ibid.
95. Harcourt, Egger and Donovan, note 75 above.
96. Ibid.
97. Donovan, quoted in Jordon, note 20 above; Harcourt, Egger and Donovan, note 75 above.
98. B. Sullivan, "Prostitution Law Reform in Australia. A Preliminary Evaluation", *Social Alternatives* 18(3), 1999, pp. 9–14; Harcourt, Egger and Donovan, note 75 above.
99. Sex Work and Sexual Exploitation in the European Union, "The Situation in the Netherlands", available at www.ex.ac.uk/politics/pol_data/undergrad/aac/nl.htm.
100. Ministry of Justice, quoted in Monika Smit, "Trafficking in Women, Dutch Country Report", paper presented at NEWR Workshop on Trafficking in Women, April 2003, available at www.newr.bham.ac.uk/pdfs/Trafficking/Netherlands1.pdf.
101. Netherlands Ministry of Foreign Affairs, *Dutch Policy on Prostitution – Questions and Answers 2005*, available at www.minbuza.nl/default.asp?CMS_TCP=tcpAsset&id =DD4FBBCB6EE14102A58AAA13FEA22B43, p. 5.
102. Council of Europe, *Trafficking in Human Beings – Compilation of the Main Legal Instruments and Analytical Reports Dealing with Trafficking in Human Beings at International, Regional and National Levels*, National Texts, Vol. II, Strasbourg, July 2001, p. 108.
103. Netherlands Ministry of Foreign Affairs, note 101 above.
104. Ibid.
105. Thérèse van der Helm, "Migration and Mobility of Sex Workers in the Netherlands", *Health, HIV and Sex Work: The Influence of Migration and Mobility: Research for Sex Work* 5, June 2002, available at www.nswp.org/pdf/R4SW-05.PDF.
106. Ibid.
107. Netherlands Ministry of Foreign Affairs, note 101 above, p. 3.
108. US Department of State, note 73 above.
109. Ibid.
110. Anna G. Korvinus, *Trafficking in Human Beings – Third Report of the Dutch National Rapporteur*, The Hague: Bureau NRM, 2005, available at http://rechten.uvt.nl/ victimology/national/NL-NRMEngels3.pdf.
111. US Department of State, note 73 above.
112. Dr Louise I. Shelley, Testimony before the Commission on Security and Cooperation in Europe (Helsinki Commission), 28 June 1999, available at www.american.edu/ traccc/transcrime/humantraffic.html.
113. Available at www.stopvaw.org/3Jun2004.html.
114. Available at http://hrw.org/reports/2002/bosnia/.
115. Jorge Tigno, *Trafficking in Human Beings from the Philippines: Examining the Experiences and Perspectives of Victims and Non-Governmental Organisations*, UN Global Programme against Trafficking in Human Beings. available at www.unodc.org/pdf/ crime/human_trafficking/Exec_summary_ISDS.pdf.
116. Available at www.vitalvoices.org/DesktopDefault.aspx?page_id=214#II.
117. Available at www.vitalvoices.org/files/docs/Trafficking%20Alert%20May%202005 %20International%20Edition.pdf.
118. Human Rights Watch, "Hopes Betrayed: Trafficking of Women and Girls to Post-Conflict Bosnia and Herzegovina for Forced Prostitution", Vol. 14, No. 9 (D), Washington, D.C.: Human Rights Watch, November 2002, p. 4.

119. Elizabeth Rehn and Ellen Johnson Sirleaf, *Women, War and Peace: The Independent Experts' Assessment on the Impact of Armed Conflict on Women and Women's Role in Peace-Building*, New York: UNIFEM, 2002, available at www.unifem.undp.org/resources/assessment/, p. 11; Testimony of Martina E. Vandenberg (Human Rights Watch) at House Committee on International Relations Subcommittee on International Operations, Human Rights Watch, 22 April 2002, available at http://hrw.org/backgrounder/wrd/trafficking-testim-april.pdf, pp. 5–6.

5

Migrant women and the legal politics of anti-trafficking interventions

Ratna Kapur

Introduction

Globalization is resulting in extraordinary movements of people, legitimate and illegitimate, across national and international borders. These movements are exposing the porosity of borders, the transnational reality of women's migration and the contingent foundations of the laws regulating cross-border movements. This chapter examines the legal regulation of the border crossings of transnational migrants, with a specific focus on migrant women, and its implications for women's human rights. It analyses how the very foundations of liberal understandings of the state and the subject are confronted with the challenges posed by migrant women, whose movements reflect the contemporary manifestations of globalization, the ubiquitous quality of capitalism and labour and the ascendance of new international non-state actors.

The chapter explores how the legitimacy of migrant women is reshaped and reconfigured in the process of crossing borders – they are rendered vulnerable, stigmatized and even outlawed by efforts to stop them from crossing borders through the operation of anti-trafficking and anti-migration initiatives. These responses impact on the construction of migrant women. They are at times regarded as victims of their cultures and familial contexts, in need of protection. This approach is based on assumptions about women as weak and vulnerable and the "Other" – societies in the developing world – as backward and uncivilized in its treatment of its women. They are also regarded at times as genderless,

Trafficking in humans: Social, cultural and political dimensions, Cameron and Newman (eds), United Nations University Press, 2007, ISBN 978-92-808-1146-9

and constituted primarily by the overarching identity of the cultural "Other" as dangerous and a threat to the security of the nation. Migrant women are affected by an array of legal rules, such as anti-trafficking, anti-immigration and border security proposals emanating primarily, though not exclusively, from powerful countries in the global North that obstruct or arrest such movements and afford little recognition to women as complex subjects and transnational actors.

The intention in this chapter is not to provide a comprehensive global analysis of laws that regulate borders and border crossings. It is to highlight how transnational migrants, in particular migrant women, are addressed through a spectrum of legal rules and criteria designed to question their legitimacy at the point of crossing borders. International and domestic laws are serving as sites where the emergence of the transnational migrant on the global stage is being resisted and her legitimacy indicted. The discussion focuses on the international legal regulation of women who migrate for work, including sex work. It also explores the impact of legal interventions on the rights of the migrant woman, and the underlying assumptions about women, the "Other" and family on which such interventions are based.

The female "Other" and cross-border movements

The cross-border movements of migrant women have been primarily treated as an issue of trafficking. Anti-trafficking initiatives, including the Protocol to Prevent, Suppress and Punish Trafficking in Persons, have invariably failed to distinguish between consensual migration, albeit clandestine, and coerced movement. The result is that international trafficking initiatives have had a particularly adverse impact on women and their families. Treating all movement of women as coerced reinforces assumptions about ("third world") women as victims, infantile and incapable of decision-making. At the same time their families are implicated in the trafficking chain and cast as criminals. As a result, these women and their families are excluded from access to legal recognition, rights and benefits, and rendered even more vulnerable and insecure.

Keeping the "native" at home

On 3 March 2003 sex workers, transgendered, male and female, their families and support communities crossed international borders to converge on the city of Trivandrum to celebrate the International Sex Workers Rights Day. At the epicentre of their debates and protests was a challenge to the anti-trafficking initiatives being promoted by Western and South Asian countries, feminists and human rights groups. They argued that such measures targeted migration from the South, promoted a highly conservative moral agenda and denied sexual and other subalterns the right to work, to family and to mobility. This raises many fundamentally important issues, including the legal and non-legal barriers in the arena of trafficking that impact on the right to migrate, and the rights of migrants and their families. There is a danger that anti-trafficking initiatives are based on assumptions about trafficked persons, especially women, as "victims" incapable of choosing to cross borders; there is also a failure to address the push factors that compel such "unsafe" movements. These responses focus on border controls and the prosecution of "traffickers", who range from transport agents to the victims' families who consent to the movement. Discouraging women's mobility and stigmatizing her (third world) family therefore conveys a simple message: to keep the "native" at home.

Conflations and confusions

The distinctions between the issues of trafficking and migration and trafficking and sex work have been constantly blurred, resulting in the formulation of confused legal strategies that are both anti-migrant and anti-sex worker, and anti the families of both. They fail to recognize why people move, and what are the consequences of trying to stop movement using border controls and displacing the problem on to individuals and their families. The legal responses construct women's movement as primarily forced and for the purpose of sex work or prostitution. These responses are infused with assumptions about women's appropriate roles and conservative sexual morality. This narrow focus on women's migration excludes the complex social, economic, cultural and political factors that affect women's movement, and further stigmatizes the women and their families.

Transborder and in-country movements and migrations are occurring for a plethora of reasons: the reconfiguration of the global economy, displacement and dispossession of marginalized populations, the awareness through consciousness-raising that there are better options elsewhere, armed conflict and of course the basic human aspiration to explore the world.[1] The global patterns of economics and trade have increased the demand for low-wage labour, as well as the demand of poor countries for remittances from immigrants in the global North that will assist in social welfare which the state is neither able nor willing to provide.[2] Poorer countries thus have little interest in controlling outward movement, legal or illegal.[3]

Women move and are moved, with or without their consent, for a variety of reasons.[4] They frequently find their way into the job market doing domestic help or similar work. The impetus for this is not because they love cleaning other people's homes or taking care of others' children at the cost of being separated from their own, but because they need jobs and those are the only ones available in the market. Many women from the South also find their way into the sex industry, partly because the sex entertainment industry is one of the largest enclaves of the job market in receiving countries.

These movements across borders have triggered a flurry of activity on behalf of Western and South Asian governments and many human rights groups, and have been conflated with the spectre of trafficking, which is considered to be a growing phenomenon worldwide.[5] In contemporary discourse, human trafficking has come to be variously and yet integrally interwoven with migration, mainly illegal, clandestine border crossing and smuggling of humans. On a parallel plane, trafficking in women and girls is resoundingly conflated with their sale and forced consignment to brothels in the sex industry. The conflation of trafficking in persons with various manifestations of migration and mobility on the one hand and with prostitution and sex work on the other lies at the very core of the confusion that underpins the contemporary discourse on trafficking of women and girls, globally, regionally and nationally.

Equating migration with trafficking

In November 2000 the United Nations adopted an international definition of trafficking, set out in the UN Protocol to Prevent, Suppress and Punish Trafficking in Persons, Especially Women and Children, which supplements the UN Convention on Transnational Organized Crime. The definition reflects an important development and shift towards newer, relatively more widely acceptable and inclusive definitions of trafficking.[6] But the problems of lack of coherency and the conflation of trafficking with migration have not been eradicated. The protocol fails to address the fact that women move in part in search of more lucrative economic opportunities to support their families back home, and more specifically, if they are mothers, to provide educational support and opportunities for their children. Women's movement is intimately connected with their families.

The definition of trafficking fails to distinguish between trafficking and voluntary consensual migration, implying that trafficked persons will receive the same treatment as illegal migrants, who are subject to deportation and denied any legal rights. The protocol also foregrounds prostitution as the main site of trafficking and considers the consent of the "victim" irrelevant. And finally, it does not require state parties to provide any redress measures or services to trafficked persons or their families. In all these ways the trafficking definition delegitimizes women's cross-border movement.

The protocol reflects the tensions that characterize anti-trafficking initiatives. Equating trafficking with migration has led to simplistic and unrealistic solutions – in order to prevent trafficking there is a conscious or inadvertent move to stop those who are deemed vulnerable from migrating. Even when curbing migration is not a stated programmatic focus, an inadvertent impetus is to dissuade women and girls, in particular, from moving in order to protect them from harm. Anti-trafficking measures are frequently applicable to "women and girls", thereby failing to accord women an identity as adults and confer rights that flow from that status, including the rights to choose to move and to have control over one's life and body.[7] It also emphasizes women's role primarily as carers for children and fails to consider that this role has altered. Women's identities as sole supporters of dependent family members and economic migrants in search of work are completely erased by these legal initiatives. Conflating trafficking with migration results in reinforcing the assumption that women and girls need constant male or state protection from harm, are incapable of decision-making or consent and therefore must not be allowed to exercise their rights to movement or to earn a living in the manner they choose. The construction of women who move as victims of a web of criminal networks sits in tension with the counternarrative that regards the movement of labour as part of the globalization process, and the emergence of human trafficking and smuggling networks as the parallel response to the migration phenomenon that (first world) nation-states refuse to address other than as an issue of immigration or criminality.

The dominant narrative is also inscribed within a dominant understanding of family as geographically located in one place, and the assumption that the primary caregivers, women, would not voluntarily seek to venture far from the family unit. This narrative is steeped in a glowing view of history by those who seek to restore the family to the status it enjoyed in some long-lost golden age, and who therefore would support initiatives that keep women at home.

This approach delegitimizes women's movement, while the problem of trafficking, the ostensible purpose of these measures, never gets resolved. Curbing migration does not stop trafficking, but merely drives the activity further underground and makes it more invisible. Borders cannot be impermeable, and stricter immigration measures result in pushing the victims further into situations of violence and abuse. Migrant women and their families are thus pushed into further dependency on an informal and illegal network of agents and rendered even more vulnerable to economic and physical abuse, exploitation and harm.

Legal responses to "trafficking" fail to draw clear conceptual distinctions between migration and trafficking. As a result, migration becomes equated with trafficking, which also means that the number of victims of trafficking becomes equal to the number of those who have migrated voluntarily. This logic operates particularly in the case of adolescent girls and women migrants, rather than men.[8] This practice has resulted in an extremely flawed methodology for conducting surveys on trafficking in "risk-prone" and "affected" districts, for example in various South Asian countries. Absent women or girls are routinely considered tantamount to "missing persons", and therefore as having been trafficked. It is a logic that has resulted in the viewing of all consensual migrant females as trafficked and thus rendering women's cross-border movements as illegitimate.

Women's movement is also conflated with sex work or prostitution by anti-trafficking players, which produces at least two contradictory responses. By collapsing the process with the purpose, the abuse and violence that a woman may experience in the course of transport is equated with the purpose of her journey. And so many anti-trafficking measures are invariably anti-prostitution/sex work measures. Prostitution *per se* as the exclusive purpose of trafficking is an untenable definition, as not all victims are prostitutes and nor have all prostitutes been trafficked. At the same time if women are deemed to have participated in the process of trafficking, they are immediately recast as immoral or criminal, and undeserving of legal protection. The tension between the fact that women from the developing world who cross borders are predominantly victims of traffickers in need of protection and that they are also sexually transgressive is never resolved through trafficking legislation or international initiatives.

Women who cross borders are not afforded the protection or legitimacy accorded to women who practise sex in the privacy of the family or who are victims of sexual violence. Familial ideology operates with dominant sexual ideology to contain and confine women's sexuality and sexual conduct. However, those who participate in the transgression of these norms are rendered exterior and no longer entitled to legal protection. Violence against women who are trafficked is taken up by both progressive and conservative groups working on issues of trafficking in ways that do not challenge dominant constructions of women's sexuality and gender roles. The interventions either reinforce the status of women as victims, or regard them as criminals for participating in the clandestine movement or immoral subjects for transgressing dominant sexual norms.

A woman is received across borders illegally as a victim or legally as a wife and mother. However, her identity as migrant and decision-maker is never acknowledged; this construction is only addressed in the context of sex work or prostitution, in which case she is constructed as a criminal and her breaching of borders regarded as a threat by the "Other" to disrupt the normative family and the nation's security.

These responses affect the rights of women in subaltern families and the legitimacy of their families in a number of ways. The conflation of women's movement and migration with trafficking is reinforced in several different ways in the law and international conventions. As they are primarily treated as having been trafficked, neither the women nor their families can take advantage of the benefits they might receive under the International Convention on the Protection of the Rights of All Migrant Workers and Members of Their Families, 1990 nor the Protocol against the Smuggling of Migrants. The Migrant Workers Convention (MCW) is the only international convention that affords some recognition and substantial rights to migrants and undocumented workers. Its primary purpose is to protect the human rights of legal and illegal migrants and their families, ensure there is no arbitrary interference with the families and protect their rights to liberty and security. The convention came into force in December 2002. One important shift is the adoption of a protocol on human smuggling. It is the first time that smuggling has been treated as distinct from trafficking. Smuggling of migrants addresses a very specific conduct that involves the transportation of women and men, through the provision of money or other material benefit, in order to acquire illegal entry into a country (article 3). At the same time it seeks to protect the rights of the smuggled migrant. One of the concerns of the UN High Commissioner for Human Rights and the International Organization for Migration is that no protections are afforded to women under the trafficking protocol, in contrast to the protections and assistance measures provided under the smuggling protocol. What happens when a state signs one protocol but not the other? A woman could be considered a smuggled migrant under the trafficking protocol because of the wide scope of the definition of trafficking, without being accorded any rights or benefits that accrue under the human smuggling protocol. The issue of providing rights in the form of assistance and protection to trafficked persons was highly contentious during discussion on the trafficking protocol. Ultimately, states simply refused to adopt such measures.

The families are often considered part of the problem, as part of the trafficking chain. The Migrant Workers Convention provides rights to equality and due process to migrant workers and their families, regardless of whether they are documented or undocumented. It also imposes positive obligations on the state to provide housing and other benefits to such persons. Secondly, despite the rights provided under the UN Protocol against the Smuggling of Migrants and the Migrant Workers Convention, neither addresses the obstacles posed by immigration laws and restrictions. Regular, legal and safe migration possibilities have decreased the world over due to restrictive migration and immigration policies of countries of transit and destination. This phenomenon has given rise to a growing market for irregular migration services. Trafficking is an outcome of the need for people to migrate on the one hand and the growth of services in the migration market on the other, including exploitative and violative practices. The legislation fails to recognize and respect women's agency or human rights and the rights of their families in the course of their movement. These initiatives continue to address women as victims and as incapable of choosing to move illegally or for work other than prostitution.

These initiatives fail to recognize that women move in part to seek better economic opportunities to support their families. By casting a woman as a victim, whose consent to move is irrelevant, she is rendered as incapable of decision-making. At the same time, the issue of trafficking is addressed under the Convention on Transnational Organized Crime. Women's movement is addressed within the framework of criminal law, and this in turn treats any actors, including families who facilitate women's movement, as alleged criminals. A further consequence is that by associating trafficking invariably with sexual exploitation, women who move are implicitly suspected of crossing borders for the purposes of sex and in the process their movement is stigmatized. Thus the women, their families and the movement of women are viewed through the lens of criminality and stigma, and the woman herself is rendered both a victim and an immoral subject.

The association of women's victim status with protection reproduces assumptions about women, especially women from developing countries, as incapable of decision-making, as passive and vulnerable. This approach conforms with an earlier approach in equality discourse that views women as in need of protection, naturally weak and incapable of exercising agency, and combines with that which views the "Other" as immutable, as just different. However, this construction is neither fixed nor constant. It is contingent on the crossing of borders and familial ideology. For example, the US Trafficking in Victims Protection Act 2000 affords women limited protection if they are regarded as victims of trafficking. However, if they participate in any way in the facilitation of their illegal movement they are implicated in the trafficking chain and subject to criminal sanctions.[9] If a woman pays for her transport she is regarded as having participated in her trafficking. She is also stigmatized by the fact that the underlying assumption of this legislation is that women are traf-

ficked primarily for sexual purposes. If she is regarded as having participated in her movement, she is also exposed to the assumption that she is
sexually promiscuous, and no longer entitled to the protection of the
criminal law but rather subject to it. This treatment of her agency must
be read against dominant familial ideology, which protects good women
in their private families and regards the marital relationship as the exclusive site of legitimate sexuality.[10]

Anti-trafficking initiatives are infantilizing women, especially third
world women, who are regarded as lacking the capacity to reason or
choose. Women who cross borders are regarded exclusively as victims,
"lured" or "duped" by the "false promises" ostensibly made by traffickers of a better, more prosperous life elsewhere. They also tend to
criminalize women's families, regarding them as part of the trafficking
chain, and do not recognize that women move and are moved partly to
seek out economic opportunities that will provide them with means actually to support their own families. The conflation has had a particularly
adverse effect on women, and the families of women who migrate. It results in painting bright lines between socially acceptable normative familial arrangements and those that are cast as illegal and stigmatized. It
also creates a schizophrenic response to the third world subject – one
that views him/her as a victim in need of rescue and rehabilitation, under-
scoring the anti-trafficking initiatives. And another response reinforces
the fear of the "Other" as a potential threat to the nation's social cohesion or security, intensifying regulation of borders and the scrutiny of the
"Other".

Families that matter

This discussion highlights how the normative family, which is bounded by
the nation-state, is afforded the maximum protection, even at the cost of
the liberty or freedom of the family of the transnational migrant woman.
The discussion reveals how the migrant woman's family has fewer rights,
and at times is subjected to criteria or a punitive regime that is in part
designed to ensure the security and legitimacy of normative familial arrangements. Familial ideology determines access to rights and equal
treatment. Although the features of familial ideology are not the same in
every context and cultural setting, in the context of families crossing borders it is a device used to "Other" the migrant woman's family – the family which seeks to cross borders through a range of mechanisms and for a
variety of reasons. The segmented and incipient nature of this family
means it is not afforded any recognition in law as a family. States remain
reluctant either to confer rights or benefits on this entity in international

law or force it to assimilate and conform to an "everyone else" standard. It is also regarded as an entity to be kept at arm's length, incarcerated or kept out lest it corrupt, contaminate and ultimately destroy the security and freedom of the native family and the culture of the West.

The endeavour here has been to illustrate how the legitimacy/ illegitimacy of the migrant woman is determined by the predominance of the universalist, progressive narrative of human history which is facilitated by those who seek to retrieve past glories and the golden era of family and the nation-state. The discussion illustrates the kind of analysis that needs to be brought to the study of migrant women in a transnational world and reveals the ideological assumptions about women's gender roles and sexuality that are deeply embedded within legal discourse.

Legal interventions in the lives of transnational migrant women have been articulated primarily from the perspective of the host country. The subaltern voices are omitted from these conversations, and yet these are the voices that can assist in untangling the conflations and confusions that are taking place between trafficking, migration and terrorism in the international and domestic legal arenas. The voice of the subaltern must be foregrounded – not as a terrorist, nor as a victim, but as a complex subject whose family is affected by global processes and seeking safe passage across borders.

Contingent legitimacies

The story of the transnational migrant woman must be told in the context of globalization. This subject exposes the need to think about international law and rights in ways that are not confined to the boxes of sovereignty, the nation-state and the autonomous subject of liberal rights discourse. It is an entity that produces a very different narrative about why people move and how to accommodate that movement. As Saskia Sassen has suggested, there is considerable paternizing in the geography of migrations, and major receiving countries tend to get immigrants from their zones of influence.[11] This would explain some of the patterns of migration to the United States and the United Kingdom. It is partly an outcome of the actions of governments' foreign policy and their economic involvement in countries of origin. Earlier colonial patterns also inform current migration patterns, captured in the slogan "We are here, because you were there". The fear of a flood of "Others" is neither grounded in statistics nor a self-evident negative process. The fear of change or survival of one's culture and identity is based on a false assumption that cultures are static and fixed and frozen in time. Yet the colonial encounter is evidence of the fact that a return to a pristine and culturally authentic space is not possible.

The breadth of the challenge posed by transnational migrant women must be sustained at both normative and political levels. They pose a challenge to the nation-state and the fictional boundaries being buttressed in this current moment of globalization. They challenge the normative family by proposing a reconstitution of the familial space and gender roles within that space. And they challenge assumptions about the world's "Others" who are moving, taking advantage of the opportunities afforded by globalization and revealing the vicissitudes of their own complex locations. This project not only benefits the transnational migrant woman, but offers political possibilities to those within the domestic and international arenas who have also been left out of modernist assumptions about progress and a new humanity.

In order for the transnational migrant woman to acquire legitimacy, there is a need to counter the universalizing and linear narrative that is being asserted through the devices of nationalism, the normative family and sovereignty. The core of this response is to address broader transnational processes that affect flows or movements of people and are an integral feature of globalization. And this in turn requires radical rethinking. As long as these issues are not viewed through the complex lens of globalization, market demand and the rights and legitimacy of the migrant subject will remain unaddressed or compromised, and contribute to the growing instability of both the host country and this itinerant population.

The agency of women needs to be foregrounded. A woman remains either a victim in need of rescue from the conniving, manipulative, culturally primitive subaltern family or is herself equated with the demonized "Other". Her complex subjectivity remains unaddressed in the legal and policy approaches being pursued at the national and international levels. Her legitimacy resides primarily in her status as a victim and/or in her role as a mother or wife ascribed to her through the operation of dominant familial ideology. Women's choice or agency remains either non-existent, questionable or tainted. Her choice to move must be distinguished from other situations where her consent is absent or her movement is compelled by strife or conflict.

It is also important to recognize that the strengthening of borders and a policy of repatriation will not stop trafficking, meet a nation's security needs or protect the normative family. Firstly, people will continue to move, illegally if legal means are not available. This process cannot be arrested through stricter border controls or immigration policy. Secondly, as Saskia Sassen has pointed out, there has been a significant reconfiguration of the nation-state in two directions.[12] The first is the re-location of certain attributes of the state on to supranational regimes of authority, such as the World Trade Organization, the European Union or certain human rights codes and institutions. Secondly, there is an increased significance of transnational private actors that is also resulting in the emergence of a transnational legal and illegal regime for cross-border transactions, including labour mobility and exit options for refugees.

In order to address the issue of women's cross-border movements one cannot simply remain confined to the domestic arena, where regulatory enforcement is focused on the individual and the border. Nor can this process be addressed in the international legal arena purely in terms of criminality or trafficking. These responses fail to understand the global context in which such movements are occurring. In order to understand and respond to the relationship between migrant women and the law, it is necessary to address this issue against the broader canvas of trans-nationalism. Transnational movements require a transnational response and analysis – they cannot be caught within older frameworks.

A significant battle over the legitimacy of the migrant subject is being fought in the legal arena. It is a site where contests over the extent of legitimate encroachment on state sovereignty, the legitimacy of border crossings and the players involved are taking place. It is also a site where contestations over the construction of the sexual and familial norms that ought to govern women are being fought out. Law is responding to the cross-border movements from two perspectives – protection and security. Protection has implications specifically for women, resonating with an earlier moment in history when protectionist responses were based on certain gender stereotypes. And security emanates from the desire to return to secure borders, a cohesive society and a defence against the threat posed by these global "Others". Indeed, the already troubled narrative of progress is confounded by those "Others", who desire to participate in that narrative and write the script. This desire marks the point at which liberalism's universal project draws its current line of legitimacy. In the contemporary moment, liberalism has cast the "Other" in opposition to its values, to secure the progressive narrative. It is a project that is exposed as gendered, raced and sexed. Yet in order for liberalism to retain its legitimacy it must retain its distinction and distance from that which it construes as an opponent to liberal values. It is in this search that the "Others" who seek to cross borders are constantly defined as different and/or dangerous.

The examples bring out how law serves as a site of discursive struggle where competing visions of the world are fought out. In the international arena, the view that women's consensual movement should be included within the definition of trafficking has won over the struggle to articulate women's consensual movement within a migration framework. From the position or location of the transnational migrant woman, the struggle must be to modify immigration laws in ways that accommodate her transnational reality. The problems produced through anti-trafficking interventions can be partly alleviated by the expansion of immigration laws that acknowledge and accommodate the entry of people other than those who are part of the highly skilled information technology workforce.

At the same time, legitimacy cannot be secured only by the conferment of legal rights, but rather also through the normative challenge that the transnational migrant woman brings to familial ideology, the porosity of national borders and the emergence of non-state entities as a significant force in the international arena. This conception of legitimacy represents the shift from the mere legitimizing of identity of the transnational migrant to a challenge to injustice and unequal power arrangements. This shift breaks down the binaries, the "us and them", "here and there" distinctions, and enables us to recognize how these oppositions are produced and naturalized through historical power relationships. This challenge also exposes the complex global processes that instigate such movements.

The sovereign state and the sovereign subject are being bared through these challenges posed by the world's constitutive "Others". The liberal state and the liberal subject are based on the idea of fixed borders, with clearly identifiable interests and identities. They are imbued with the power to decide, choose and act autonomously. Yet the challenge of globalization, which brings the challenge of migration and non-state actors to the legitimacy of the borders of the sovereign state and the autonomous subject, indicates otherwise. The complexity of new global formations and the dynamic character of the individual who crosses borders challenge any notion that the state and individual are hermetically sealed or capable of exercising control through self-contained power. The ability to distinguish those who constitute national subjects from those who are alien or foreign is blurred, reflecting the uneasy location of a distinct national entity with distinct borders and a distinct national subject with borders. The legitimizing tools of cohesion, unity and sovereignty become blunt in the face of a more complex and integrated world and global economy.

Taking the anti-trafficking framework and transnational interventions in the legitimacy of border crossings as the focal point, this chapter has argued that the law's claim to legitimacy is premised on a deeper foundation: its assumptions about difference, family and gender. The international and national interact to produce the legal response to this new era of border crossings and the construction of the Other. Yet in the contemporary moment, legitimacy has been defined in and through religious or conservative morality, the war on terror and fears over the disruption of the cultural and social cohesion of the nation.

Women are moving across national, regional and international borders. And they are simultaneously drawing attention to the disparate arenas of power with which we must engage in order to understand the global movement of people and the normative and political significance of the transnational migrant woman.

Notes

1. See Global Commission on Migration, *Global Commission on Migration Report: Migration in an Interconnected World: New Directions for Action*, Geneva: GCM, 2005.
2. See e.g. Katie Willis and Brenda Yeoh, eds, *Gender and Migration*, Cheltenham: Edward Elgar, 2000; Rita James Simon and Caroline Brettell, eds, *International Migration: The Female Experience*, Totowa, NJ: Rowman & Allanheld, 1986; World Bank, *Adjustment in Africa: Reform, Results, and the Road Ahead, A World Bank Policy Research Report*, Washington, D.C.: World Bank, 1994.
3. The statistics on migration flows are not readily available. This is due in part to the lack of a universal methodology, the lack of a common definition amongst countries in respect of determining who is an international migrant, the difficulty in collecting data given the clandestine nature of some forms of migration and a lack of commitment on the part of governments to collect these statistics.
4. See generally "Feminism and Globalization: The Impact of the Global Economy on Women and Feminist Theory", *Indiana Journal of Global Studies* 4(1), 1996; Doreen Marie Indra, ed., *Engendering Forced Migration: Theory and Practice*, Refugee and Forced Migration Studies, Vol. 5, London: Berghahn Books, 1999.
5. The source of these statistics remains unclear and unreliable. The Global Alliance against Traffic in Women undertook a study on behalf of the UN special rapporteur on violence against women, and stated that it was extremely difficult to find reliable statistics on the extent of trafficking that was taking place. There had been no systematic research on this subject, nor was it possible to determine such statistics because of the imprecise nature of the definition of the term "trafficking in women", and so much of this activity had been pushed underground because of the illegal or criminal nature of prostitution and trafficking. See Marjan Wijers and Lin Lap-Chew. *Trafficking in Women. Forced Labour and Slavery-Like Practices in Marriage, Domestic Labour and Prostitution*, Utrecht: Foundation against Trafficking, 1997, p. 15. Statistics are sometimes arbitrarily cited without any back-up research to substantiate the findings. The International Movement against All Forms of Discrimination and Racism (IMADR) prepared a report for the UN Working Group on Contemporary Forms of Slavery stating that over 2 million women and children were trafficked each year, without citing any research or source of the statistics: International Movement against All Forms of Discrimination and Racism, *Strengthening the International Regime to Eliminate the Traffic in Persons and the Exploitation of the Prostitution of Others*, Tokyo: IMADR, 1998. The Human Rights Watch report on trafficking between Nepal and India states that "At least hundreds of thousands, and probably more than a million women and children are employed in Indian brothels." Human Rights Watch, *Rape For Profit: Trafficking of Nepali Girls and Women to India's Brothels*, New York: HRW, 1995, p. 1. Similarly, its report on trafficking between Burma and Thailand states that there are an estimated

800,000 to 2 million prostitutes currently working in Thailand, yet no source for these statistics is provided. Women's Rights Project, Asia Watch, Division of Human Rights Watch, *A Modern Form of Slavery: Trafficking of Burmese Women and Girls into Brothels in Thailand*, New York: HRW, 1993, p. 1. Kamala Kempadoo has stated that there are often extreme variations in the estimates of the number of women in prostitution in Asia, and that even within Bombay figures cited range from 100,000 to 600,000. Kamala Kempadoo, "Introduction: Globalizing Sex Worker's Rights", in Kamala Kempadoo and Jo Doezema, eds, *Global Sex Workers: Rights, Resistance, and Redefinition*, New York: Routledge, 1998, p. 15. Kempadoo questions the veracity of such figures, arguing that such discrepancies would be grounds for questioning the reliability of the research. However, in the context of sex work and prostitution these standards are compromised and the figures are cited without any question. See more generally Beverly Baker-Kelly, "United States Immigration, A Wake Up Call", *Howard Law Journal* 37, 1994, p. 283, who discusses the inadequacy of collecting and processing data on the number of people who cross into the United States, legally or illegally.

6. There are three preliminary points to consider when analysing this issue. One hundred and one countries have signed the protocol to date. Since the UN definition is very recent its impact will only be realized once it begins to be applied and tested. Secondly, the international community has only recently recognized the need to expand the definition of trafficking to include purposes other than prostitution, such as forced labour, forced marriage and slavery-like practices. This is also reflected in the new UN Protocol on Trafficking. Thirdly, an acknowledgement that trafficking is a problem of human rights violation and not an issue of law and order or public morality related to prostitution is also of recent origin.

7. *Human Rights Standards for the Treatment of Trafficked Persons*, Global Alliance against Traffic in Women/Foundation against Trafficking in Women/International Human Rights Law Group, 1999, p. 2, unpublished.

8. This analysis forms the basis of the Protection of Victims of Trafficking Act 2000. For a more detailed analysis of this Act see Ratna Kapur, "Post-colonial Economies of Desire: Legal Representations of the Sexual Subalterns", *Denver University Law Review* 78(4), 2001, pp. 855–885.

9. See Ratna Kapur, *Erotic Justice: Law and the New Politics of Postcolonialism*, London: Glasshouse, Cavendish Press, 2005, ch. 5.

10. Although the Act ostensibly prioritizes concern for the victims, women who cross borders to work in the sex industry and are harmed or experience violence during their travels or are exploited in the course of their work are not a concern. Access to benefits thus becomes partly conditional on a woman's chastity, purity and innocence. The Global Alliance against Traffic in Women and the Dutch Foundation against Trafficking in Women conducted a research project based on questionnaires circulated to groups working directly with "victims" of trafficking: see Wijers and Lap-Chew, note 5 above. Their research reveals that a large majority of the trafficking cases involve women who are in or know they will be going into the sex industry, but are not accurately informed about the conditions of work or the amount of money they will receive. The Act demonstrates how trafficking is being used to justify highly restrictive and punitive policies.

11. Saskia Sassen, *Globalization and Its Discontents: Essays on the New Mobility of People and Money*, New York: New Press, 1998.

12. Ibid., p. 5.

6

Trafficking in women: The role of transnational organized crime

Phil Williams

In recent years the trafficking of women and girls for commercial sex has become a major global problem. Yet there are still some striking parallels with "the white slave trade" at the end of the nineteenth century and the beginning of the twentieth.[1] Then, as now, Russia and Ukraine were among the major source countries, while Western Europe, the United States and Turkey were among the major destinations. Then the trade was facilitated by the expansion of railways, the steamship and the telegraph; now it is facilitated by airline travel, the mass mobility of people and global communications systems such as the telephone and the internet. At the same time there are whole new dimensions of the problem that need to be considered. Women and girls are now trafficked not only from Ukraine and Russia but also from countries as diverse as Nepal, Burma (Myanmar), Bosnia, Romania, the Dominican Republic, Brazil and Nigeria, among others. Moreover, the technological advances that have accompanied and contributed to globalization have increased the efficiency of both legal and illegal markets and significantly reduced transaction costs. Globalization has also facilitated the transshipment process, making it easier and cheaper to link the supply of women for commercial sex with centres of demand. It has provided new opportunities for exploitation that make the trafficking process even more lucrative. The development of the internet, for example, has led to a close connection between trafficking and pornography, with trafficked women sometimes being exploited for internet pornography, either en route or in their destination country.

Trafficking in humans: Social, cultural and political dimensions, Cameron and Newman (eds), United Nations University Press, 2007, ISBN 978-92-808-1146-9

Against this background, this chapter focuses on three dimensions of the phenomenon of trafficking in women and girls for commercial sex, each of which has implications for the development and implementation of effective policy responses. It examines the structure of the market and market dynamics; the criminal networks that connect the various parts of the market; and the facilitating and inhibiting factors that underpin market operations. The balance between facilitators and inhibitors is heavily weighted in favour of the former. By examining all three facets and considering ways in which the market can be disrupted, the networks can be compromised and degraded and the structural balance between facilitators and inhibitors can be tilted in favour of the latter, it is possible to adopt a holistic approach to the development of an effective policy response. The concluding section elucidates – albeit rather briefly – some of the key components of such a response. It is important to emphasize at the outset that the focus is a narrow one – it omits trafficking in men for forced labour, especially on construction sites, as well as trafficking in boys, which is certainly not a trivial problem. The emphasis is strictly on women and girls for prostitution and the main focus is on organized crime, although with discussion of some other levels of criminal involvement in this particular market.

One of the most pernicious and demeaning aspects of trafficking in women and children is that it reduces people to the status of commodities. Understanding this, however, is also an important insight since it suggests that what we are seeing is the operation of a commodity market that is subject to the same kinds of laws, impulses and trends as any other illicit market, whether drugs, nuclear materials, illicit arms, fauna and flora or art and antiquities. This is not intended to be cold or inhumane; it is simply to contend that it is necessary to engage in detached analyses of an emotion-driven subject in order to enhance both our understanding of the problem and our capacity to do something about it. The major players in the market do not take an emotional approach: instead, they trade in human misery and treat women and children as simply more commodities that can be trafficked and sold – and resold – for substantial profits. From the point of view of domestic and transnational criminal organizations or shady entrepreneurs, women and children are a product like any other – except that they are more durable and can be used on a medium- or even long-term basis to make money. A market approach to understanding, therefore, is an appropriate if distasteful one.

Consequently, it is necessary to understand the structure of the market. This requires examining supply and demand, the dimensions of the market, profitability issues and even market trends based on opportunities, cost-benefit calculations and risk considerations. This analysis looks at these issues and seeks to identify the major contours of the market. It also looks briefly at market investments, in effect the costs of entrepreneurship, as well as the profits and what is done with them.

The second part of the analysis focuses on the market participants, with particular emphasis on the supply networks that traffic in women and children. The market for commercial sex depends critically on criminal networks (structural intermediaries) that link the supply and demand sides and bring women and children to places where they are sold into and subsequently enslaved in prostitution. While the nature of the criminals who are involved varies, the trend has been towards greater organization and professionalism. In this section, attention is also given to the way in which traffickers recruit and transport women from source countries to destination countries.

The third part of the chapter focuses on the structural balance between market facilitators and market inhibitors. For criminal markets to function effectively and criminal networks to operate efficiently, the facilitators must outweigh the inhibitors. Consequently, it is necessary to identify both kinds of factors, before considering the ways in which facilitators can be reduced or removed and inhibitors can be expanded. In effect, by identifying and then manipulating facilitators and inhibitors it should be possible to reduce profitability and increase the costs and risks of trafficking. As noted above, the concluding section of the chapter considers briefly some of the ways in which this might be done. Prior to all this, however, it is necessary to identify some of the problems encountered by this kind of analysis.

Problems and complexities of analysis

Numerous problems are encountered in any effort to discuss and analyse the phenomenon of trafficking in women. First is the problem of distinguishing trafficking from alien-smuggling. Indeed, efforts to define the trafficking phenomenon immediately run into the issue of what is voluntary and what is not. Trafficking in women and children overlaps with alien-smuggling but also has certain distinct characteristics that set it apart. Although aliens who are smuggled into the United States or Western Europe often endure enormous and unexpected hardships, the decision to migrate is usually a voluntary one, even if it is based on very few options. In effect the demand comes from the would-be migrants themselves, and those who arrange the transportation and false documents are simply responding to demand from willing customers. With trafficking in women and children, however, the demand tends to come from the other end of the chain, from "legitimate" entrepreneurs requiring cheap or forced labour and unscrupulous businessmen, semi-legitimate enterprises or criminal entrepreneurs seeking a regular supply of participants for the commercial sex trade. As Finckenauer and Schrock note, human trafficking differs from alien-smuggling because of the greater prominence of the elements of coercion and exploitation. "Alien smuggling produces short-term profits. Trafficking, on the other hand, includes long-term exploitation to continue to produce profits. The criminality associated with trafficking usually continues" after the migrants reach their destinations.[2]

Not all cases of women travelling to another country and then engaging in prostitution can be categorized as trafficking. In Murmansk, for example:

> Russian women began taking the bus to a small Norwegian town, where they spent the weekend selling alcohol and souvenirs. Soon they were selling their bodies as well, and bringing home large sums of money. The news of this new enterprise spread among friends and as many as 70 women began boarding the bus each weekend.[3]

This was voluntary prostitution and the women were able to return home at will. Although, given the opportunism of organized crime, it is likely that prostitution in Murmansk subsequently became more organized, more exploitative and more coercive, this was not the case at the outset and this clearly falls outside the scope of the analysis.

Less clear-cut, of course, are situations in which women are trafficked in the full knowledge that they will be engaged in prostitution at their destination. Yet prior knowledge does not necessarily eliminate the element of coercion. On the contrary, women who are trafficked knowingly for prostitution often have the expectation that they will make enough money to live well and send funds back to their families. Instead they find themselves in a form of indentured labour that all too often is more akin to slavery than to traditional forms of prostitution in which the women themselves at least reap significant financial gains. With women who are trafficked, the rewards typically go to others to such a degree that some observers have claimed this marks a fundamental shift in the nature of prostitution. One international aid worker observed: "It's not classic prostitution ... They are not paid. They are never paid. Of the 50 women we have seen, not one has received a single deutschemark. And they are often held in horrendous conditions."[4]

There is also a problem with the standard definition of trafficking in women – the emphasis on its transnational character as a *sine qua non*.

> Trafficking in women occurs when a woman in a country other than her own is exploited by another person against her will and for financial gain. The trafficking element may – cumulatively or separately – consist of: arranging legal or

illegal migration from the country of origin to the country of destination; deceiving victims into prostitution once in the country of destination; or enforcing victims' exploitation through violence, threat of violence or other forms of coercion.[5]

Although this emphasis on the cross-border nature of trafficking is both appropriate and important, there is another dimension to the problem – which occurs at the national level. This does not involve trafficking across national borders, but women being taken from their home environment to another location where they are basically compelled directly (i.e. through intimidation) to become involved in the sex trade. Moreover, in Europe there are cases in which the women continue to be trafficked even after they have arrived in the destination country. Sometime they are sent on to another country; on other occasions they are sold to new owners in the destination country. The same is true in Israel, where women are often sold from one brothel to another. Whether the trafficking is within one nation or across borders, however, it is clear that the financial benefits almost invariably accrue to others rather than to the women themselves.

Another difficulty concerns categorization. Although it is tempting to categorize countries as either countries of origin or countries of destination, the realities are often more complex. The Czech Republic, for example, has been described as being "a point of origin, sale and transit of women". Forty per cent of the female sex trade workers are "foreigners from Ukraine, Bulgaria, Romania and Slovakia", and many of them stay in the country for less than six weeks.[6] Similarly, Turkey is a recipient of women and girls from Romania, Georgia, Russia, Ukraine, Moldova, Armenia, Azerbaijan and Uzbekistan, while also acting as a transshipment country for women from Central Asia, the Middle East, Africa and former Yugoslavia who are destined for other countries in Europe.[7] For its part, Thailand is a recipient of women and girls from Myanmar and a source country for women who are trafficked to Japan.

In the past there was another difficulty, especially when examining the role of organized crime, and that was limited information. In the last few years, however, as the women-trafficking issue has gained greater salience, more details of arrests have emerged, in some cases providing important details of the criminal networks involved and the nature of their operations. It is clear from these reports that organized crime has become very deeply involved in the trafficking business.

The other problem in analysing trafficking in women, of course, is the sheer complexity of the issue. Trafficking in people for commercial sexual exploitation involves fundamental violations of human rights; it is also a gender issue in that it is predominantly – although not exclusively –

women and girls who are victims of trafficking. Yet there is a big debate within feminism. On the one side are those who emphasize a woman's right to choose, and distinguish between free prostitution which does not involve trafficking and forced prostitution. Arrayed in the opposite camp are those who oppose all prostitution on the grounds that women would never willingly choose to be involved. In short, some feminists emphasize the right of women to engage in voluntary prostitution; others contend that all prostitution is the result of a lack of choice or, at the very least, a lack of alternative options.[8] What they tend to agree on, however, is that efforts to treat the trafficking issue as predominantly a problem of organized crime ignore the human rights violations – a tendency that is reflected in the desire of law enforcement to treat women who have been trafficked simply as illegal immigrants and/or potential witnesses to be used against the criminal rather than as victims to be protected from further harm. There is much to this criticism. There are also other dangers in focusing too narrowly on the role of organized crime – including a tendency among some observers to concentrate on large criminal organizations which are among the most obvious perpetrators and to ignore the small operations, the cases in which women are trafficked by friends, boyfriends, fiancés or even family members. A market perspective, at least, suggests that we need to identify the whole range of actors and go beyond the well-known criminal organizations.

The market

Supply and demand

Trafficking dynamics are very simple – women are trafficked from states in transition or developing states to developed countries where the money to be made from prostitution is considerable. This has now been extended into countries and localities in the Balkans and some African countries, where the developed states, acting through the aid and donor communities as well as peacekeeping forces, have established developed-world enclaves that have become major destinations for trafficked women. The extension of trafficking in this way is not surprising. As Soren Christensen, secretary-general of the Nordic Council of Ministers, observed: "modern slave traders are businessmen. They are sensitive to market mechanisms of supply and demand."[9]

The supply side of the market is relatively easily understood. Supply countries are generally states in transition or states with low levels of economic development, high levels of unemployment, limited opportunities, especially for women, in the legal sectors of the economy and significant crime and corruption problems that spill over into many areas, including trafficking in women. Where organized crime is pervasive, it is hardly surprising that it extends into women-trafficking and prostitution. The underlying causes, however, are social and economic. In some countries where family structures have been undermined by poverty, parents sometimes allow their children, especially their daughters, to be taken to work elsewhere, with few questions asked about the form of work or the conditions in which they will find themselves. Even when this does not occur, dysfunctional economies combine with high levels of unemployment, the growing prevalence of divorce, unemployment and discrimination against women, sexual abuse in the workplace and high levels of physical abuse to render intolerable the existing conditions. At the same time there is often a degree of wishful thinking about the possibilities in the West. This was manifest in a 1997 survey of tenth-grade girls in Russia, in which "70 percent responded their career goal was to become 'foreign currency prostitutes'; just 10 years before, respondents to a similar survey said they wanted to become teachers, doctors, cosmonauts, and actresses".[10] For men faced with limited economic opportunities in states in transition, one option has been to become a member of a criminal organization. Women, faced with the same limits, do not generally have this option. Nevertheless, some of them migrate from the legal economy to the illegal economy at home, choosing to become domestic prostitutes. Others prefer to migrate geographically rather than functionally in the hope that there are less unpalatable employment opportunities in other countries. Unfortunately for many of them, they end up in the illegal economy outside the country, forced into prostitution and subject to enormous humiliation, degradation and exploitation.

The other characteristic of many states in transition and developing states is that they are home states for powerful criminal enterprises that exhibit a high degree of sophistication in identifying and exploiting market opportunities. In the case of trafficking in women, this sophistication translates into provision of the necessary documentation, whether real or fraudulent, arrangements for transportation, reception at the destination, maintenance of a cover story and so on. In other words, criminal enterprises have the resources to exploit the opportunities made available to them by social and economic problems. Yet this is not simply a passive response. Recruiters use all sorts of deception methods to expand the supply of women, trading on both the existing conditions and the dreams of a better life. For those women who are deceived the mistake is thinking that the traffickers are facilitators, when in fact they put the women in a position where they can be coerced and exploited.

Most of the demand countries have advanced industrialized or post-industrial economies, high standards of living and substantial levels of disposable income. They also have significant sex industries in which trafficked women usually end up. These can centre around clubs, escort agencies, hotels, bars and red-light districts frequented by men seeking commercial sexual diversions. In thinking about demand, however, there are two distinct levels that have to be separated: demand from those who control the commercial sex trade and provide opportunities for men to buy sex, and demand from the men themselves who use prostitutes. These two levels are mutually reinforcing – and both are exploitative. Consequently, both need to be targeted as part of a comprehensive strategy that attempts to alter the market dynamics.

Scale, scope and profitability of the market

It is evident from all this that trafficking in women for commercial sex is a highly lucrative business. It is also a business in which the entry costs are very low and the barriers to entry are modest. In some cases opportunist individuals will exploit friendships or relationships to traffic a few women; in other cases small-time criminals will use modest proceeds from other crimes to develop small trafficking operations. In all cases, success tends to breed success and deepening involvement in the market.

The value of the market, of course, is extremely difficult to assess with any degree of confidence or certitude. Methodologies for assessment are lacking and there is no agreement on what is to be counted or how it is to be counted. In spite of this there are frequent suggestions that the market is worth anywhere in the region of US$7–12 billion a year. While such figures are always tendentious – and are typically presented with no accompanying explanation of the underlying methodology – neither the range of possibilities nor the upper and lower figures is implausible. And what can be said with some certainty is that the commercial sex market is large and has grown enormously since the end of the Cold War.

There are several reasons why the market is so profitable – for all concerned except the women themselves. For the traffickers, the transportation overheads are generally low, although corruption payments can be significant. For the criminals who control the women once they are in place, prostitution involves continuing enterprises with enduring if replaceable "commodities" that are consumed repeatedly rather than just once. Buying women who are trafficked is a limited once-off investment; the sale of their services continues to generate profits long after the initial outlays have been covered. Moreover, once they are in place the women are usually paid only a pittance, if at all. Finally, in some cases the women can be sold to other brothel-owners, providing yet another accretion of profit in what can be described as a secondary trafficking market. To put it crudely, a trafficked woman involved in commercial sex is a good investment for the person or organization reaping the profits from her activities. It has been estimated, for example, that in Kosovo, where international peacekeepers, NATO officers and development officials add to the demand for commercial sex, a pimp who keeps 15 girls and works them 6 nights a week can easily bring in more than US$250,000 tax-free a month.[11] In the final analysis, therefore, there are few other criminal activities in which the profit-to-cost ratio is so high and in which limited investments can have such large pay-offs.

This, in turn, raises the issue of what is done with the profits. Although there are no reliable and detailed studies of profits from the commercial sex industry, it is likely that the proceeds from trafficking and subsequent controlled prostitution of women fall into four categories.

- Money that is simply spent on the lifestyle the traffickers and pimps want for themselves. It is a myth to think that criminals always launder their proceeds. In the case of some criminal activities, the penalties are so low and the security the criminals enjoy is so high that there is no need for laundering. Consequently, criminals simply enjoy their ill-gotten wealth, with a far more lavish lifestyle than would otherwise be available. Simply spending the money is perhaps most likely with the low-level traffickers and small-time pimps.
- Some of the money is reinvested in the business. It is used for the trafficking of more women, the acquisition of more nightclubs and brothels and so on, as well as the corruption payments that are a key part of the process.
- Some of the proceeds are probably reinvested in other criminal businesses – the money from trafficking and prostitution can be used to finance other criminal activities, including drug trafficking and trafficking in arms.
- Some of the money is laundered so that it is transformed from illegitimate proceeds of crime to legitimate funds that are presented as the profits from legal businesses. The laundering process itself can take many forms. In the Balkans, for example, where most countries still operate through cash-based economies, cash is often smuggled from one part of the region to another, used for real estate and business purchases and construction projects. As government sensitivity to money laundering has grown and more restrictions and safeguards have been put in place, criminals have responded by using or investing their money incrementally in order to avoid triggering suspicious activity reports. In other places the money-laundering process is more sophisticated. It is easiest, of course, when the criminals use legitimate companies as fronts for their illegal activities. Indeed, when the money is presented as legitimate profits the traditional phases of placement, layering and integration that financial institutions and law enforcement

look for are short-circuited. Where Asian organized crime is involved it is possible that an underground banking system or alternative remittance system known as *fie chien* (flying money) is utilized to move and hide the proceeds without leaving a paper trail. In yet other instances the criminals will use lawyers and accountants to put the money through multiple jurisdictions and hide it in offshore financial centres or bank secrecy havens where it will be safe from law enforcement.

In sum, the market in women for commercial sex is large and growing. The demand and supply factors create a synergy that has made this a rapidly expanding and highly vibrant criminal market. In any market, of course, a critical role is played by those individuals and organizations that succeed in bringing together the demand and supply sides of the equation. In the case of prostitution it is those who traffic in women, bringing them from the supply countries to the demand countries, who make the market function effectively. It is essential, therefore, to identify the major types of trafficker.

The trafficking organizations

A typology of traffickers

Although it is tempting to see trafficking in women for commercial sex as something that is dominated and controlled by organized crime, the picture is actually rather more complex. As Finckenauer and Schrock in their analysis of trafficking in women in the United States observe:

> the actors driving this criminal market vary ... Traffickers may be individual entrepreneurs, small "mom and pop" operations, or sophisticated, organized rings. There is little consensus among those who have studied the problem as to the proportions of each of those types; nor with respect to their level of organization and sophistication.[12]

Much the same assessment could be made of the participants in the women- and children-trafficking business at the global level. Indeed, in thinking about the actors in any criminal market, there are those who are criminal already and simply diversify and there are those who are not necessarily involved in crime already but see opportunities that they seize. What follows, therefore, is an attempt to elucidate the major players in this market, recognizing, of course, that the market is highly dynamic with different kinds of entities sometimes working in combination with one another as part of a hybrid trafficking network. Moreover, some actors are so successful that they transform themselves from small groups with limited reach into larger, more powerful and more extensive trafficking organizations. With this in mind, the following typology identifies the most important actors.

- *Opportunistic amateurs.* Perhaps the most pervasive but least important category consists of individuals and small groups of friends. These are generally small-time opportunists and confidence tricksters who, prompted by economic crisis or simple greed and encouraged by friendships with women who can be turned into victims, become traffickers. Instead of describing small criminal groups engaged in the trafficking business as mom-and-pop operations, perhaps it might be better to refer to them as friend-and-fiancé operations. In many cases of trafficking, individual women are inveigled abroad by a friend or boyfriend who promises marriage but is actually intent on either selling his girlfriend to a pimp or exploiting her himself. In either case, the trust that is established is simply a device to lure the woman into a position where she is powerless and can be exploited for profit. Where this is simply opportunist and a one-off case, it will usually exhibit a low level of sophistication. If the trafficking is successful, however, the procurers will tend to repeat it, becoming more adept at a task that, in effect, is small-scale recruiting and trafficking. The result of this is likely to be the emergence of a network of small trafficking groups that resemble some of the patterns identified by the BKA with regard to African drug dealers spreading into Europe and that have "nothing to do with mafia structures. There are neither godfathers nor any hierarchies of note, but instead many small, very flexible groups branching out in all directions, which start and end cooperation as required and set up new groups."[13]
- *Transnational criminal organizations with broad portfolios of activity.* At the other end of the spectrum are broad-based transnational criminal organizations. While some criminal organizations specialize in a narrow range of products and markets, others focus much more broadly. An example of this latter kind of organization is Solntsevo, based in Moscow but with linkages and activities extending into Central Europe and beyond. Characterized by strong leadership and high levels of professionalism, Solntsevo acts as an umbrella organization for over 300 individual crime groups. Not surprisingly, it has a wide diversity of criminal activities and an extremely entrepreneurial approach to any criminal activity that might result in significant profit. A key figure is Semeon Mogilevich, based in Budapest, who is believed to run criminal networks that operate through legitimate, semi-legitimate and simple front companies. The group's control over transportation resources, its capacity to corrupt officials and its transnational links

provide three of the requisites for effective participation in trafficking in women. Moreover, Mogilevich operates a major nightclub in Hungary. There is also speculation that he was linked to several killings in Berlin's red-light district in the early 1990s that were almost certainly about control over the lucrative business in prostitution.

- *Traditional criminal organizations.* Traditional organized crime involvement, especially by Italian mafia organizations, has also been a key factor in the trafficking business and helps in part (although there are other factors too, such as proximity to the Balkans and the emergence of Albanian trafficking organizations) to explain why Italy has become such an important destination for trafficked women. In Asia another traditional criminal organization, the Japanese *yakuza*, has also become deeply involved in the trafficking business. "In the 1970s Japanese sex tours encouraged the Yakuza to follow the excesses of their countrymen across East Asia."[14] As Kaplan and Dubro point out, the *yakuza* did not originally create the conditions that led to the sex tours but it was quick to exploit them, often financing the clubs and trafficking the women overseas.[15] The *yakuza* has also played a major role in trafficking women to Japan itself, luring women with offers of good jobs and then plunging them "into a world of forged passports and faked visas and ultimately into sexual slavery".[16] In other parts of Asia Chinese criminal organizations dominate the commercial sex scene. In Macau during the 1990s, for example, local Chinese criminal organizations or triads were able to maintain control over prostitution in spite of the influx of Russian criminals.[17] Moreover, in China itself:

> the Sun Yee On, 14 K, Big Circle Boys, and Wo On Lok Triads have all repeatedly been linked to smuggling illegal immigrants and prostitution rackets. The American Embassy in London reports that Chinese Triads are the primary traffickers of women and girls from Southeast Asia, South America, and Eastern Europe to Britain. Press reports indicate that Chinese Triads have also worked with Russian organized crime groups in trafficking.[18]

- *Ethnically based trafficking organizations.* Albanian and Kosovo Albanian networks fit this category. They have become critical to the trafficking of heroin from Central Asia to Western Europe, and along with drugs are also involved in trafficking in arms and women. Once the infrastructure, routes and methods (including bribery of officials) are in place, the product itself becomes almost irrelevant. Not surprisingly, contraband of all kinds is smuggled across the Adriatic and groups move from one product line to another with ease and speed as opportunities dictate. There were reports some years ago that some of the Albanian organizations were bringing both people and drugs into Italy, and that when detected or challenged they would simply throw the people overboard to divert their pursuers.

- *Criminal-controlled businesses.* Organized crime infiltration of and control over licit business has become the norm rather than the exception in Russia and other states of the FSU. Import-export companies and criminal-controlled travel agents are particularly useful for trafficking in women. Among the advantages of such companies are their well-established trade links, their affiliations, an existing and seemingly legitimate cover for travel and established financial channels that can be used to move funds and process payments.

The above categorization is neither exhaustive nor rigid. Nor are the categories mutually exclusive. On some occasions various kinds of groups will work together. This is why it is also important to recognize that trafficking networks are dynamic and fluid rather than fixed or static, bringing together different kinds of participants in alliances of convenience. In some cases, where collaboration is harmonious, successful and profitable, it is likely to be repeated. In other instances the network will simply dissolve as the participants move on to other criminal endeavours with other partners. This makes the analytic and intelligence tasks more complex and more formidable, but recognizing it is indispensable to understanding the phenomenon of organized crime involvement in trafficking in women. Moreover, the alliances can come at any stage of the trafficking process: in some instances women will be passed along a chain from group to group; in other cases transnational organizations will simply deliver the women to domestic criminal groups or "businessmen" involved in the commercial sex trade and who own clubs and bars that they use for prostitution. Connections can be forged at the transnational level or between transnational organizations and those who act at the local level. There have been specific cases of Italian organized crime groups in New York and New Jersey, for example, being supplied with women for clubs by Russian criminal networks.[19] None of this should be surprising. As R. Thomas Naylor has argued, inside most criminal markets "one finds operational a myriad of individual entrepreneurs along with 'firms' large and small, all of whom engage in essentially arms-length commercial relations with one another".[20]

If the market is a mixed one, however, the role of organized crime has become increasingly important. There are several characteristics of trafficking operations that are likely to indicate the involvement of organized crime: the groups or networks involved in trafficking in women make extensive use of bribery and corruption to facilitate transshipment; the groups have both the capacity and the propensity to use violence in support of their activities, not simply to keep the women docile and pliant, but to protect their business from rivals or law enforcement agents who attempt to interfere with their activities; the trafficking involves considerable sophistication either in methods of concealment or in methods of circumvention through false documentation; and there are multiple shipments of the women, using well-established routes, methods and facilitators. While some aspects are not unique to organized crime, these indicators provide a useful approach to the issue of organized crime involvement, and certainly go beyond simple assertions that the trade has increasingly become a preserve of organized crime.

Acknowledging that networks can vary in degree of sophistication and organization, geographic scope and reach and the mix of actors, and that some remain atomized and fluid, it is nevertheless very clear that organized criminal networks are playing an increasingly important role in trafficking in women. Organized crime increasingly dominates the supply chain and fulfils a series of functions from the initial recruitment to the exploitation of the women at the other end – in effect acting as both trafficker and pimp. In the mid-1990s it appeared that organized crime was sometimes involved more tangentially, providing protection and coercive support for those who organize the trafficking rather than playing a more central role in trafficking. This has clearly changed. Organized crime is now much more directly involved. The type of organized crime group that is involved, however, varies. In some cases the trafficking network will be created and run by criminal organizations that specialize in the trafficking of women and children; in other instances the criminal organization might do many more things, trafficking in multiple commodities including arms, drugs and people. In some instances the networks will be blatantly criminal, relying on strong-arm tactics and the ability to outrun or corrupt law enforcement; in others the networks might be more subtle, using as cover ostensibly legitimate businesses such as travel agents which engage in some legal activities; still other networks will exhibit a hybrid kind of structure that mixes the blatant and the subtle.

Trafficking networks

Although it used to be fashionable to treat criminal organizations as classic hierarchical structures, in recent years this has changed as many analysts have realized the advantages that accrue to networked organizational structures. Networks are highly flexible and adaptable: they can disperse and reassemble with speed and ease and thereby avoid offering a static and easy target for law enforcement; they can exhibit significant levels of redundancy so that even when attacked and degraded they can regenerate themselves; and they can extend and truncate as needed. One aspect of networks is that they tend not to be preoccupied with organizational form and identity. Achieving their objectives with speed and efficiency takes precedence. This kind of approach encourages important synergies in the criminal world, enabling organizations to work together in ways that are advantageous to all except their victims and those trying to combat their activities.

In the case of trafficking women in Europe, the most important criminal networks are those from Russia and Ukraine, those from the Balkans, particularly Albanian trafficking organizations, and Italian mafia organizations. As suggested above, they are not the only players in the market, but they are almost certainly the most significant. The importance of Russian criminals in transforming the European market in commercial sex is hard to exaggerate. In Finland, for example, prostitution was limited and for the most part non-coercive. Then in the early 1990s Russian criminals moved into Finland and compelled

> almost all of the Finnish prostitutes either to give up their customary livelihood or join their ranks. These criminals read the advertisements put by Finnish prostitutes in the local newspapers, made contact with them, and went to meet them. If the threats they would make had no effect, the women were beaten.[21]

The result was both an expansion and a consolidation of the market in commercial sex in Finland, which is now controlled by 10 major gangs. The leaders of these organizations are based in Estonia or Russia, and local Finns are employed to deal with logistics such as transportation and accommodation for the prostitutes.[22]

Another way in which Russian criminal organizations display considerable ingenuity is in the recruitment process, using women who have themselves been prostitutes to recruit others. In August 2002, for example, police in Dnipropetrovsk caught a group of people who exported women for prostitution abroad via Moscow. In this case the recruiter was herself a Ukrainian prostitute who had gone to Moscow in search of wealthier customers, had met other people in the business and had been sent back to Ukraine to find girls and women to be recruited for sale "into the brothels of the United Arab Emirates. They made 2,000 dollars on each unfortunate girl who wound up in a brothel. This gang managed to ship to this destination more than 15 Ukrainian young women aged between 16 and 30."[23]

If Russian criminal networks were in this market early, they were soon followed by the Albanian mafia clans. Indeed, according to one assessment:

> trafficking in women and forced prostitution seem to have become much more important for Albanian organized crime in 1999, with thousands of women

from Kosovo having fled to Albania during the armed conflict in the region. About 300,000 women from Eastern European countries work as prostitutes in Europe. More and more seem to be "organized" in Albanian networks that are not limited to ethnic Albanian prostitutes, but comprise women from Romania, Bosnia, Moldova, Russia, etc. The pimps often pretend to be Kosovars in order to have the status of a political refugee, even though many of them come from Albania. Some seem to control the "business" from abroad. Belgium, in particular, seems to be the seat of several leaders of the trafficking networks. In 1999, ten people linked to Albanian crime were shot in Brussels.[24]

The other country where Albanian criminal networks are particularly prominent in the women-trafficking business is Italy, where they share control of prostitution with Nigerians. Moreover, whatever their origins:

all the women currently on the streets [of Italy] are slaves. The proof is that the Nigerians, the Albanians, the Romanians and the women from Eastern European countries all have their passports taken away by their pimps. There is not one meter of street in which prostitution is not controlled by criminals ... The Albanians operate in family clans, in "joint ventures" with the Mafia in Eastern Europe and Italy.[25]

Cooperation among criminal organizations is particularly important. As suggested above, a key factor in making Italy such an important destination for trafficked women has been agreement between Albanian criminal organizations and the Camorra and 'Ndrangheta. These criminal associations or alliances have been mutually profitable. Indeed, what is surprising is the lack of competition and conflict among criminal organizations over the trafficking business. One reason for this might well be the expansion of the business. In cases where the market is growing there is usually enough for everyone to have a share of the spoils. In the event that government and law enforcement agencies succeed in reducing the demand and contracting the market, some of this cooperation might well degenerate into more competitive and even violent relationships as organizations, faced with declining revenues, become concerned about their share of the market and increasingly intent on maintaining this share. Unfortunately, indications that this is taking place are very hard to find.

As well as thinking in terms of formal criminal organizations, the trafficking business can also be understood in terms of networks of criminals, with each individual or small group fulfilling certain roles and responsibilities within the network. Moreover, the networks can also include other entities such as legitimate and front companies. As one commentator observed, "The trafficking network includes sellers, guards, numerous modeling and travel agencies, brothel owners, corrupt public officials, and smugglers. Individuals who supply false documents, bribed air and auto transport company workers, etc."[26] This list could easily be extended to include the recruiters who initially identify and approach victims, luring them with false promises and subsequently brutalizing or coercing them. In the case of trafficking through the Balkans it also includes villagers in key border hamlets who know local trails that can avoid checks by border guards and police. The other virtue of the network approach is that it is inherently flexible. In some cases a criminal organization might set up all the infrastructure and arrangements and exert "total control over the process of transporting the 'goods' from the point of departure to the point of delivery".[27] In other instances the organization will control part of the trafficking chain but hand off or contract out other parts to individuals or groups able to bring specialized knowledge or skills to where they are needed.

Trafficking operations

In October 2002 Operation Girasole, a major international effort – led by Italy and coordinated by Europol – to break up women-trafficking operations that brought in over 1 million euros a month, culminated in a series of arrests and asset seizures in several countries.[28] The operation revealed a very successful and sophisticated association of criminal organizations working together in ways that were mutually profitable – if sometimes rather surprising. The network was characterized by a multiplicity of criminal individuals and organizations engaged in high levels of cooperation and making extensive use of front companies and legitimate businesses to facilitate the movement of women and their entry into EU countries.

Whatever the shape and size of the trafficking network or the criminal organizations involved in trafficking women, however, the trafficking process itself has several distinct stages from the initial recruitment of women in source countries to the use of these women as prostitutes in destination countries. In some cases the women continue to be trafficked and are moved from owner to owner and brothel to brothel. These stages can be identified as follows: recruitment, the creation of subservience on the part of the women who are trafficked, the entry into other countries and the process of enslavement in the commercial sex business.

The first stage in the process is recruitment. This is done through a variety of methods, including false advertising of foreign jobs in national and local newspapers, traffickers acting as travel agents, coercion or cooption of legitimate travel agents, the use of face-to-face meetings and in some instances the establishment of close relationships with women who believe they are going abroad to be married. In some cases the women have no idea what they are getting into and are completely duped, travelling abroad in the expectation that they are going to legitimate and reasonably well-paying jobs in the legal economy rather than to sexual slavery or domestic servitude. Sometimes criminal organizations employ female recruiters, since it is easier for them to establish rapport with, and gain the trust of, potential victims of trafficking. In other cases, of course, the recruitment process proves remarkably easy as the women are, in essence, "willing victims". They enter the trafficking process knowingly, albeit with the expectation that, at the end of the process, they will make sufficient money to support themselves and their families. Even in these cases, however, there is still considerable deception, as women who know they are going to another country to be prostitutes are nevertheless given false assurances about living conditions and the expected income they can earn. In short, even what appears to be "voluntary" trafficking usually involves large elements of deception. At the other extreme, of course, the whole process is highly coercive. In the Balkans in particular, reports of women and girls being kidnapped by traffickers are frequent, and in some countries parents are reluctant to let their daughters go outside without some kind of protection. Kidnapping involves coercion and violence from the outset and is usually targeted at girls rather than women.

A second step (and it has to be recognized that there is no single sequence that traffickers invariably follow) is ensuring that the women become subservient to the traffickers en route, and to the pimps and brothel-owners in the destination country. Indeed, even when women are initially recruited through deception and false promises, those who transport them generally resort to violence and intimidation en route or at the destination. Many women who are trafficked are physically, sexually and psychologically abused until they are pliant and unlikely to do anything to interfere with the trafficking process. Nor does coercion end when they are sold or indentured. In many if not most cases the women continue to be brutalized and are repeatedly raped, and their passports confiscated. They are also told that they are illegal immigrants, making them very reluctant to go to the authorities even in the event that they find an opportunity to do this. In addition, their "owners" abuse them directly or employ "guards" to ensure that the women do not try to escape and inflict punishment if they try. These can range from the men who typically provide muscle for organized crime to Nigerian "mamas" who are often associated with forms of witchcraft and exercise psychological rather than physical control over Nigerian women in particular. Whatever form it takes, violence and the threat of violence are among the most distinctive features of trafficking and forced prostitution, as well as important facilitators of global trafficking in women. This was certainly the case with the trafficking activities revealed by Operation Girasole. The women who were trafficked – from Romania, Russia, Ukraine, Poland, Hungary, Bulgaria, Colombia, Somalia and Tunisia – were subjected to high levels of violence both en route and after their arrival in Italy. They were "forced to become prostitutes after being raped by their Albanian 'protectors' who were linked to the Camorra in Naples and the Calabrian Ndrangheta. Girls who fought the system were viciously killed." At least three murders were believed to have occurred.[29]

In short, the trafficking business often involves a variety of other crimes, including both assault and sexual assault or rape. In some cases it also involves the women crossing borders illegally either by circumventing immigration inspections or through the use of false documentation. The false documentation can be used to hide the real age of the victims or simply to provide a false profession or fabricated job offer that assists in the visa process. In the activities uncovered by Operation Girasole, a trafficking infrastructure had been created to assist in the movement of the women to Western Europe. Russian and Ukrainian criminal organizations controlled a network of companies that played a critical role in facilitating the trafficking process. The traffickers operated through "a large number of Ukrainian travel companies in co-operation with partner travel agencies and hotels, mainly based in Austria, Italy, Germany, France and Spain". The criminals and front companies based in Ukraine, along with their associates in Western European travel agencies, facilitated illegal immigration into the European Union by means of Schengen visas that were fraudulently obtained. For their part, "the tourist agencies had the girls arrive by regular bus trips and with tourist visas" while the complicit hoteliers came up with false reservations.[30] Moreover, this "closely woven collusive network" extended beyond the travel agents and hoteliers to encompass people who facilitated the acquisition of residence visas and permits by providing forged documents for certifying attendance at university courses, arranging marriages of convenience or devising similar schemes.[31] This was reflected in the arrests, which included not only the usual suspects such as nightclub managers and madams, but also lawyers, complicit hotel-keepers and a university professor in Rome.

The other dimension of the trafficking process, which often starts en route but becomes dominant after the women have arrived at their destination, is the process of enslavement, including the continuous and systematic financial exploitation of the women. As one report on the trafficking network unearthed by Girasole noted: "the young women were provided with false passports bought by the gang for a few hundred thousand lire, but which they [the women] were forced to pay 8–10 million lire for by means of their 'job' in the clubs. Nothing was free for the 'sex slaves': they paid out 50,000 lire per night to sleep squashed together in concentration camp-style apartments."[32] A fee was even charged for the trip from their houses to the nightclubs. In some cases the women were subsequently moved from one EU country to another. Once again this is neither surprising nor unique, as there are many reports of trafficked women in Israel and elsewhere being sold from one brothel to another. Not only does this reduce women and girls to the status of commodities, but the elements of coercion and violence transform much of the commercial sex industry into a contemporary form of slavery. Unfortunately, it is likely to prove even more difficult to eradicate than earlier forms of slavery. One reason for this is discussed in the next section, which deals with facilitators and inhibitors.

Facilitators and inhibitors

In assessing those factors that facilitate and those that inhibit the global trafficking of women for commercial sex, the most striking point is the asymmetry in favour of the former: there are many facilitating factors and very few inhibitors of any significance.

Facilitators

State weaknesses in source countries

States in transition and developing states generally suffer from capacity gaps and functional holes that can readily be exploited by organized crime. In this respect it can hardly be overemphasized that many states in transition lack the framework of laws, regulations and enforcement mechanisms to prevent trafficking in women. These states also offer congenial low-risk environments that provide attractive home bases or safe havens for transnational criminal organizations. Although some organized crime figures are prosecuted, many leading criminals are able to act with impunity simply because of the limitations of the legal system and the paucity of enforcement mechanisms. Such conditions often exist not only in source countries but also in transshipment countries – which are numerous.

Multiple transshipment countries

Another facilitator is that there are invariably multiple transshipment countries and multiple routes for traffickers and the women they traffic. Richard Friman has argued that most transshipment countries exhibit two major characteristics: ease of transit and access to target.[33] In Central Europe, which is the gateway to the European Union, ease of transit reflects the same kinds of state weakness as are evident in the source countries. Indeed, in the Balkans in particular – which have become both transshipment and destination countries – state structures are, in many cases, less effective than those in the former Soviet Union. Consequently, transshipment is easy. So too is access. Central Europe offers multiple points of access to the European Union – both across land borders and across the Adriatic. Once access to the European Union has been achieved there is considerable mobility and few serious checks. Getting into the United States is more difficult, particularly after 11 September and the efforts to combat terrorism. Yet there are still opportunities to come in directly with good-quality counterfeit documents, or to come in with the help of alien-smuggling groups across the Mexican-US border. Another way in is through Canada, which itself has had a number of cases of women being trafficked from Asia for work in the commercial sex trade in cities such as Vancouver and Toronto.

The political-criminal nexus

A major problem in many source and transshipment countries is the existence of what Roy Godson termed the political-criminal nexus, a symbiosis of crime and politics that is mutually advantageous.[34] The political-criminal nexus and the corruption that goes with it represent a triumph of individual interests over collective good, and private profits over public order and well-being. Indeed, the nexus allows criminals to operate not only with little fear from law enforcement but also with a safe haven in the event that their transnational criminal activities elicit tough reactions from other governments. For politicians it offers a reciprocal relationship that can provide financial political support, personal financial advantage and sometimes even a willingness to coerce or eliminate political opponents. In such circumstances the state itself is either unable or unwilling to uphold the security of its citizens, protect their rights and ensure their safety.

At the very least, efforts to stop organized crime in general and trafficking women in particular typically fail to generate much political support. Indeed, it is possible to identify several reactions on the part of the political élite to trafficking in women and children. The first kind of reaction is acquiescence or apathy, where they simply fail to take the problem seriously and take no action that might interfere with it – either because of indifference or because other problems appear more urgent and important. According to Mariana Peterdel, director of the Romanian-based aid organization Salvati Copii, this is the situation in Moldova where "even the highest ranking officials ... condone the trade in women and children because the economic crisis means the state cannot take care of the population".[35] A second and even more disturbing possibility is connivance, where the political élites accept bribes in the form of money or sexual favours. Revelations about the deputy state prosecutor in Montenegro suggest an important degree of connivance in the trafficking of women on the part of the political élite in that country. A third possibility is official collusion in the trafficking business. The investigations in Russia undertaken by Global Survival Network during the 1990s, for example, "revealed serious allegations of government complicity in the business, including allegations that the Russian Ministry of Foreign Affairs was falsifying passports to get underage girls out of the country".[36] Indeed, it is highly likely that, in various countries, corrupt officials assist in provision of passports, visas, work permits and any other documentation that is required. In this area of criminal activity, as with so many other forms of trafficking, corruption is a critical lubricant and allows criminal organizations to operate efficiently and with minimum interference.

Police corruption

The same phenomenon of corruption (albeit at lower level) and the same kinds of attitudes to trafficking are also evident in police forces. Although there are honest police who genuinely seek to help women who are trafficked and used for prostitution, all too often the police are facilitators rather than inhibitors. Stories are legion about women being held in sexual servitude, escaping and going to the police, only to be handed back to the pimps, brothel-owners or other organized criminals who control them. In other cases they are mistreated as badly by those with whom they seek protection as they were by the traffickers. A Moldovan woman, for example, who "tried to flee the clutches of the sex trafficking mafia three times ... had the misfortune to turn for help to policemen who had contacts with her powerful bosses and who immediately handed her back to them".[37] In some countries connivance and collusion are all too prevalent. In Bosnia, for example:

> "trafficked women reported ... that their employers sometimes forced them to provide free sexual services to local police officers. In a handful of cases, Bosnian police actively participated in trafficking, either as part owners or employees of the clubs, or by procuring false documents for traffickers. Trafficking victims, terrified of retaliation by traffickers, feared reporting the abuse to law enforcement authorities. Eager to fan that fear, employers routinely claimed that they counted police officers among their friends.[38]

Even some members of the International Police Task Force (IPTF) in Bosnia had visited or bought prostitutes. As one report noted, "trafficking of people into Bosnia continued unabated in 2002, as did the corruption that allowed it to flourish".[39] In October of that year 11 local police officers were fired either for using sexual services in nightclubs or informing the bar-owners of forthcoming raids. A UN spokeswoman commented that the conduct of these policemen revealed "not only their lack of respect for victims of human trafficking but also their total disregard for the role of police in upholding law and order".[40]

Widespread public connivance

Even if the police are vigilant, they face an uphill battle. In border villages in the Balkans, for example, the villagers typically help traffickers avoid the police and military checkpoints and continue their journeys. Yet in many respects even this is merely another example of connivance that in some countries (Myanmar is a good example) starts with families selling their daughters and continues with travel agents and hoteliers working closely with traffickers to ensure that the women arrive at their destination with minimum interference.

Globalization and technology

Trafficking in women has also been facilitated by several facets of globalization. The ease of travel, whether for business, tourism or even legal migration, makes it difficult to distinguish women and girls who are being trafficked from normal vacationers or business travellers. Immigration officials generally have a limited time to clear planes or boats and, as with smuggling, the ability to embed illegal activities within legal and normal activities makes detection very difficult. The other component of globalization that is useful for trafficking organizations is the internet, which can be used for anything from advertising foreign bride schemes to pornography sites to arranging assignments with prostitutes. In June 2004, for example, 25 people were arrested in Slovakia and the Czech Republic for selling women into prostitution. They had reportedly tricked as many as 230 women into signing up for a "modelling agency" which then offered the women as prostitutes on the internet to clients in various European countries and the United States.[41] Although the members of this particular group were arrested, the internet typically provides criminals with enormous opportunities for anonymous transactions that in turn make them difficult to identify, let alone catch.

Diaspora and migrant networks

An important facilitator for many transnational criminal activities is the existence of migrant communities in developed countries. These communities can provide recruitment, cover and safe havens for criminals. The role of Turkish and Kurdish networks in drug trafficking in Western Europe through the 1990s and to the present is a case in point. The same phenomenon is evident in the women-trafficking business. Russian migration to Western Europe, Israel and the United States facilitates the trafficking business. So too does the Albanian diaspora into several countries in Western Europe. Indeed, "the Albanians and the Russians have set up enough networks of contacts across several countries to be able to organize large-scale trafficking. Through these networks, the girls are moved from one town to another and from one country to another."[42] The Nigerian diaspora also facilitates trafficking in drugs and women. Nigerian networks that operate throughout Western Europe are frequently active in drug trafficking; in terms of trafficking in women, as suggested above, they are especially important in Italy. Chinese ethnic networks have also been important in facilitating various aspects of Chinese organized crime, including trafficking in women. It can even be argued that organized crime has almost invariably followed the Chinese diaspora. Significantly, "Malaysian police and non-governmental organizations believe that ethnic Chinese criminal syndicates are behind most of the trafficking in their country".[43] Moreover, "trafficked women are usually fed into an extensive system of Chinese owned lounges, nightclubs, and brothels that exist throughout much of Asia", especially in countries where ethnic Chinese have significant communities.[44]

The low risks of trafficking

Another major facilitator of trafficking in women for commercial sex is that it is a very low-risk activity. The reasons for this are twofold. In many countries there are few serious laws against trafficking in women. Moreover, even when a legal framework designed to combat trafficking is in place, a large gap usually exists between the law and its implementation. Enforcement is generally poor. Even when this is not the case, penalties are modest to say the least. Men arrested for trafficking are usually treated as if they committed a misdemeanour; in very few cases do their crimes elicit punishment truly commensurate with the nature of the offences. Part of the reason for this is the traditional tendency to treat prostitutes as criminals, not victims, and a concern over illegal immigration that again militates against the women being treated as victims – especially if they have been brought into a country illegally or overstayed the permitted time for visiting. When women are encouraged to testify against their tormentors this also puts them at risk, as few countries have witness protection programmes, and even those which do often fail to extend them to the victims of trafficking. What makes all this a particular dereliction of duty by law enforcement and criminal justice agencies is the high rate of very serious violence inflicted on many trafficking victims. According to some reports, significant numbers of Nigerian and Albanian women and girls have been killed for trying to get off the streets and out of organized prostitution.[45]

Uncertainty about ownership of the problem

The problem with many transnational phenomena is that they are so ubiquitous that they tend to be everyone's problem. The corollary of shared ownership is that no one has primary responsibility for combating the problem. Moreover, there is a tendency to "pass the buck" and emphasize that the problem is caused by someone else. In the current debate in Europe on organized crime and corruption in general, and trafficking in women in particular, the focus on Russian organized crime and the Balkans obscures the harsh reality that the market for commercial sex is in Western European countries. The same is true in Japan and the United States, where the main focus also tends to be on the supplier countries.

Variability in combating trafficking

Trafficking is not only a low-risk activity, it is also an activity in which the risks are unevenly distributed. As well as increasing risks, therefore, these risks also need to be distributed more evenly.[46] This requires efforts to harmonize legislation and impose similar and much harsher penalties. Until such conditions are established, organized crime will continue to operate with little interference. As one observer noted, organized crime is "very experienced in exploiting loopholes in national legislation and national employment practices".[47] Moreover, "crime is becoming much more sophisticated in the way it operates and traditional approaches to law enforcement are not sufficient".[48] Unfortunately, much still has to be done to create inhibitors which can come even close to offsetting or neutralizing the facilitators.

Inhibitors

To argue that the inhibitors on trafficking in women are weak is not to suggest they are non-existent. Indeed, throughout the 1990s, as the trafficking problem received more attention, efforts were made to develop or create inhibitors that would make the business more dangerous for organized crime in terms of the risks of both detection and punishment. Moreover, efforts were also made to transform the image of women who were trafficked from that of perpetrator to that of victim. Even so, the list of inhibitors to trafficking in women is much shorter than the list of facilitators. The market in women for commercial sex has had few serious obstacles. Law enforcement has tended to be complacent and give it a low priority. Legislators have exhibited outrage, but have rarely passed laws imposing penalties commensurate with the kinds of brutal crimes that are typically involved in the trafficking process. And even many countries that bemoaned the human rights abuses have done little to target the abusers. Nevertheless, there are some signs that the market is becoming slightly less risk-free and that efforts are being made to create an anti-trafficking regime. There are even some law enforcement successes that suggest the criminals involved in this activity can no longer count on operating with impunity.

Among the things that have changed for the better since the trafficking problem became apparent in the early 1990s is the degree of public and government awareness. This can be attributed in large part to the coalescence of interest of human rights groups on the one side and women's issues groups on the other. This alliance of convenience created a far more effective advocacy network than either kind of NGO could have created acting alone. Another component was the overlap with NGOs focused on reducing child sexual abuse, including exploitation of children for commercial sex. The organization End Child Prostitution in Asian Tourism, for example, was a major participant in sharpening global awareness of the issue and organizing the Stockholm World Congress on the Commercial Sexual Exploitation of Children. It was a natural extension from this to express concern and outrage over the trafficking of women as well as children.

If the NGO community has succeeded in placing the issue of trafficking women firmly on the international agenda, and even on the agendas of many national governments, it has also taken the lead in attempts to shift law enforcement attitudes towards the women involved from treating them as criminals to treating them as victims. This transformation, however, is far from complete, and in many countries there is still a tendency to focus on trafficked women as perpetrators of crime. The other problem is that in many countries and regions there is a lack of trust between the NGO community and law enforcement. This is certainly the case in the Balkans, for example, where women have escaped from their captors and sought help from the police, only to be further mistreated by the police before being handed back to the brothel-owners, pimps and organized crime members who control them. The kind of corruption discussed under facilitators is also an impediment to the creation of more effective inhibitors that could result from a true partnership between law enforcement agencies and NGOs. Indeed, the NGOs often have sources of information about the trafficking organizations that could be really useful to law enforcement agencies whose members have resisted the blandishments of the traffickers to become part of their payroll. Unfortunately, efforts to turn this information into actionable intelligence for law enforcement could all too easily be neutralized by corrupt policemen, who are able to warn the traffickers of impending actions directed against them. Even so, some NGOs have been able to provide safe havens for victims of trafficking and also take steps in the process of reintegrating these women into society.

Another plus is that the United Nations has also focused on the close link between organized crime and trafficking women. This is reflected in the Protocol to Prevent, Suppress and Punish Trafficking in Persons that supplements the Convention on Organized Transnational Crime unveiled at Palermo in December 2000. In essence the protocol seeks to "prevent and combat" trafficking in persons, especially women and children, and to facilitate international cooperation against such trafficking while also encouraging measures to assist the victims of trafficking. Even prior to the protocol the UN Office on Drugs and Crime in March 1999 launched the Global Programme against Trafficking in Human Beings. In effect this programme is an information-sharing mechanism that seeks to illuminate trafficking methods and develop and diffuse "best practices" that can assist in attacking the criminal organizations involved in trafficking women. Technical cooperation to strengthen state capacity is also a crucial component of the programme.

If the United Nations has taken important initiatives against trafficking women, so has the US government. In recent years the US State Department, following the precedent of its annual International Narcotics Control Strategy Report, has produced a yearly report evaluating national efforts to combat trafficking in persons. Authorized by the Trafficking Victims Protection Act of 2000 and the Reauthorization Act of 2003, the State Department evaluation distinguishes between Tier 1 countries whose governments fully comply with the Act's minimum standards, Tier 2 countries which do not fully comply but are making significant efforts to do so and Tier 3 countries which are failing both to comply and to make significant efforts to do so. In 2004 a subcategory was added which placed some states on a Tier 2 watch list. In some cases at least this reflected a failure to make good on promises that had been made in prior years. It also suggests a political reluctance to drop some states into Tier 3, where they might be subject to the withholding of non-humanitarian, non-trade-related assistance.

Welcome as this effort is, it is certainly not a guarantee that other governments will be compelled to introduce serious measures against trafficking. The sanctions incurred for Tier 3 status are relatively mild, and for at least some of the governments involved reputational harm is not a serious issue. Moreover, as of 14 June 2004 only 92 governments had signed the Protocol to Prevent, Suppress and Punish Trafficking in Persons, and only 45 had ratified it. Although this might reflect procedural constraints rather than substantive reservations, the numbers alone suggest that much still remains to be done in mobilizing the international community to adopt a common approach to the trafficking problem.

While it is clear that national and international responses have improved significantly since the mid-1990s (in that more states have passed laws to criminalize trafficking in women), many gaps remain. Moreover, in this area as with money laundering, a real problem is cosmetic conformity where governments are concerned with meeting the formal standards but do not engage in significant actions to deal with the problem. There have been some arrests and convictions for trafficking in women – something that was rare in the mid-1990s. Arrests have taken place in countries as diverse as China, Nigeria, Portugal and Indonesia, and it is clear that some major trafficking organizations have been disrupted. If the environment in which traffickers operate is not quite as congenial as it was a few years ago, however, progress should not be exaggerated. The successes represent no more than a drop in the bucket given the scale of the problem. Moreover, what remain to be seen are the kinds of penalties imposed on those who have been arrested, the lengths of prison sentences and the extent to which imprisonment is accompanied by asset seizure and forfeiture. Indeed, a more punitive approach needs to be developed in an attempt to strengthen the inhibitors on criminal organizations which seek to operate in the market. The concluding section develops this theme more fully.

Conclusions

The preceding analysis has sought to identify the market structure that has led to a major upsurge in the trafficking of women, the criminal networks that play a major role in connecting the supply and demand sides of the market and the facilitators that allow the market and networks to function effectively. What also emerges from this analysis is the relative paucity of inhibitors. There is no real deterrent to trafficking: the risks remain low and are greatly outweighed by the gains. For criminals – whether individual and simply opportunist, or organized and highly coercive – it is a rational economic decision to enter and stay in this market. The aim, therefore, must be to change this calculation – both to create serious risks and to distribute them in such a way that the safe havens for the traffickers are removed. To the extent feasible, therefore, it is important to engage law enforcement agencies in Russia and the Eastern and Central European countries in an increasing number of joint operations such as Girasole. The problem with Girasole, however, was that the extensive arrests made in Western Europe were not mirrored by similar actions in Eastern Europe and the former Soviet Union. The implication is that it is sometimes necessary to recognize the risks in cooperative engagement, given the pervasiveness of corruption in states in transition and states in the developing world. Acknowledging this, however, there are still things that can be done, especially increasing the penalties for those who are convicted of trafficking, and using asset-seizure and asset-forfeiture laws to combat trafficking networks. This can start with the nightclubs and other premises used by the criminals for prostitution, and extend to all property of convicted traffickers. Taking the profit out of the crime is not a complete answer, but is an important component of a more comprehensive approach.

Following on from this, and given the major role that is now played by organized crime in trafficking in women and children, the adoption of classic law enforcement weapons to fight organized crime – electronic surveillance, infiltration of the organization, the use of controlled deliveries and other undercover operations – is essential. The adoption and use of US racketeering-influenced corrupt organizations (RICO) types of legislation or laws prohibiting criminal association enable law enforcement to attack criminal structures and go after high-level criminals rather than simply the rank and file. When combined with asset forfeiture these kinds of statutes provide law enforcement with a much more potent arsenal than has typically been available. At the same time it is worth emphasizing that – as Girasole revealed – the networks are often highly distributed, and therefore difficult to attack as there is no obvious centre of gravity. One clear point of vulnerability, though, is the intersection of the underworld and the upper world, something that is exemplified in the use of travel agencies and hotels and embodied even more in the networks of facilitation created by the political-criminal nexus. Going after the links between criminals and their protectors, whether in government or the police, is critical to combating organized crime in general and, as we have seen, has considerable relevance to attacking trafficking in women.

The other aspect of risk creation is that it has to be extended to the customers. The changed nature of prostitution makes those who visit prostitutes and use their services wholly complicit in the trafficking and exploitation processes. This is not a victimless crime, and the customers need to recognize that they are a large part of the problem.

It is at this point that the law enforcement component intersects and overlaps with other parts of what has to be a holistic strategy. Part of this is education, which has to be directed both at the women who are potential victims of trafficking and at the customers who are the ultimate reason for the trafficking. Along with education is empowerment. Repressive and indeed punitive strategies against the traffickers need to be combined with both sensitive and empowering approaches to the victims of trafficking. Witness protection measures and special treatment of victims in terms of immigration are important measures that need to be introduced.

In the final analysis, the trafficking of women and children for commercial sex is a symptom of the growing disorder and breakdown of governance – globally, regionally and nationally – that has characterized many parts of the world since the end of the Cold War. The implication is that it is a problem which is going to get worse before it gets better. The experience of the 1990s reveals very clearly that unless more measures can be taken to reduce the role of organized crime, trafficking in women will continue to expand. The experience of the early years of the twenty-first century has done little to alter this conclusion.

Notes

1. Edward J. Bristow, *Prostitution and Prejudice: The Jewish Fight against White Slavery 1870–1939*, New York: Schocken Books, 1983.
2. James Finckenauer and Jennifer Schrock, *Human Trafficking: A Growing Criminal Market in the U.S.*, Washington, D.C.: International Center, National Institute of Justice, 2001, available at www.ojp.usdoj.gov/nij/international/ht.html.
3. Mikhailina Karina, "The Myth of 'Pretty Woman'. Russian Women Are Victims of Illegal Trafficking", 23 March 1999, available at http://veracity.univpubs.american.edu/weeklypast/032399/story_1.htm.
4. Peter Finn, "A New Torture Visits Kosovo: Imported Sex Slaves", *Washington Post*, 30 April 2000, quoted on www.KFORmyas.com.
5. International Organization for Migration, *Trafficking and Prostitution: The Growing Exploitation of Migrant Women from Central and Eastern Europe*, Geneva: IOM, 1995, available at www.old.iom.int/documents/publication/en/mip_traff_women_eng.pdf, p. 7.
6. Kazi Stastna, "Taxing the Professionals", *Central Europe Review* 1(22), 22 November 1999.
7. US Department of State, *Human Rights Report for Turkey: Trafficking in Persons*, Washington, D.C.: US Department of State, 2005.
8. For a useful discussion of the debate see Chris Corrin, "Local Particularities – International Generalities: Traffic in Women in Central and South Eastern Europe", paper presented at European Consortium for Political Research, Copenhagen, 14–19 April 2000, unpublished.
9. Quoted in Grace Sung, "Ready Buyers Fuel Thriving Slave Trade in Europe", *Straits Times* (Singapore), 23 September 2002.
10. Lyubov Vertinskaya, quoted in Karina, note 3 above.
11. Martin A. Lee, "Women and Children for Sale: The Globalization of Sexual Slavery", *San Francisco Bay Guardian*, 5 March 2001, available at www.hartford-hwp.com/archives/63/111.html.
12. Finckenauer and Schrock, note 2 above.
13. Heike Vowinkel, "Mafia Without Godfather – A West African Network Conquers the German Drugs Market. The Federal Office of Criminal Investigation Is Unable To Make Out its Structures", *Hamburg Welt am Sonntag*, 26 January 2003, p. 12.

14. David E. Kaplan and Alex Dubro, *Yakuza: Japan's Criminal Underworld*, Berkeley: University of California Press, 2003, p. 233.
15. Ibid. p. 236.
16. Ibid. p. 238.
17. Bertil Lintner, *Blood Brothers: The Criminal Underworld of Asia*, New York: Palgrave Macmillan, 1993, pp. 85–89.
18. Amy O'Neill Richard, *International Trafficking in Women to the United States: A Contemporary Manifestation of Slavery and Organized Crime*, Center for the Study of Intelligence, 1999, available at www.vawnet.org/Intersections/OtherViolenceTypes/Trafficking/ciatraffic.pdf. See Appendix II: International Organized Crime and its Involvement in Trafficking Women and Children Abroad.
19. Ibid.
20. R. Thomas Naylor, "From Cold War to Crime War: The Search for a New National Security Threat", *Transnational Organized Crime* 1(4), 1995, pp. 37–56 at p. 43.
21. Ari Lahdenmaki, "Prostitution Procurement Rings Divide Finland in Perfect Harmony", *Helsingin Sanomat*, 27 October 2002.
22. Ibid.
23. *Kiev Holos Ukrayiny*, "Women-trafficking Group Arrested in Eastern Ukraine", *Kiev Holos Ukrayiny*, 14 August 2002.
24. Ralf Mutschke, assistant director of Interpol's Criminal Intelligence Directorate, testimony before the House Subcommittee on Crime, 23 December 2000.
25. Ibid.
26. Lada Glybina, "Black Traffic", *Uchitel'skaya Gazeta* [Moscow], 18 September 2001.
27. Ibid.
28. Francesco Grignetti, "Large-Scale Trafficking of Slave Girls From East – Traffic Between Russian Mafia and Albanian Clans – 80 Arrested", *Turin La Stampa*, 3 October 2002, p. 11.
29. Ibid.
30. Ibid.
31. Ibid.
32. Flavio Haver, "'Sex Slave' Trade: 100 Arrests", *Milan Corriere della Sera*, 10 April 2001, p. 14.
33. H. Richard Friman, "Just Passing Through: Transit States and the Dynamics of Illicit Transshipment", *Transnational Organized Crime* 1(1), 1995, pp. 65–83.
34. For an example of Godson's analysis of this phenomenon see Roy Godson, "The Political-Criminal Nexus and Global Security", *Asia Times*, 19 June 2002.
35. Quoted in Lee, note 11 above.
36. Gillian Caldwell, Steven Galster and Nadia Steinzor, *Crime & Servitude: An Exposé of the Traffic in Women for Prostitution from the Newly Independent States*, Washington, D.C.: Global Survival Network, 1997.
37. Budo Simonovic, "Fifty Girls Have Disappeared", *Belgrade Politika*, 8 December 2002, p. A6.
38. "NGO: B-H Failed to Confront Corruption, State Complicity in Women Trafficking", *Sarajevo ONASA*, 1335 GMT, 26 November 2002.
39. Quoted in "Human Rights Watch Report Reviews Developments in Bosnia", *Sarajevo ONASA*, 1555 GMT, 15 January 2003.
40. "UN Sacks 11 Bosnian Policemen for Involvement in Sex Slave Trade", *Sarajevo ONASA*, 1458 GMT, 17 October 2002.
41. Pavol Stracansky, "25 Arrests in East Europe Spotlight Sex Trafficking", *IPS-Inter Press*, 13 July 2004.

42. Council of Europe, Parliamentary Assembly Report by Committee on Equal Opportunities for Women and Men, Rapporteur Ruby-Gaby Vermot-Mangold, "Violence against Women in Europe", Document No. 8667, 15 March 2000, available at http://assembly.coe.int/Main.asp?link=/Documents/WorkingDocs/Doc00/EDOC8667.htm.
43. Richard, note 18 above, p. 66.
44. Ibid.
45. Marian Douglas, "International Trafficking in Black Women 'La Africana' and 'La Mulata' Out in the World: African Women and Women of African Descent", April 2001, available at www.lolapress.org/elec2/artenglish/doug_e.htm.
46. The author is grateful to Ernesto Savona for this observation.
47. Bernardo Mariani, quoted in "Think Tanks Take on Trafficking in Europe", *United Press International*, 14 December 2002.
48. Ibid.

Part II
Regional experiences

7

The fight against trafficking in human beings from the European perspective

Helga Konrad

If one uses the unveiling of the UN Protocol to Prevent, Punish and Suppress Trafficking in Persons, Especially Women and Children as the starting point for the modern era of confronting human trafficking, then trafficking in human beings has now received concerted international attention for at least four years. This was when broad enactment of new anti-trafficking laws started, funding for anti-trafficking projects and programmes began to flow and more governments, organizations and individuals dedicated increasing attention to this problem. More and more actors have been getting involved in the fight against human trafficking. At the same time, a continuing stream of commentators, researchers and analysts are attempting to inform people about the problem.

Yet, in spite of all this attention, there does not seem to be evidence of a substantial reduction in human trafficking, which is exactly what all these activities are or are meant to be about.

Why – after years of work – has human trafficking remained undiminished? Some significant answers may be found if we test the assumptions on which we have been conducting the fight. We will not make meaningful headway against the traffickers nor provide the lifeline needed for the victims of trafficking until we confront these issues directly and explicitly.

National security versus human security

It is universally recognized, and has been forcefully and repeatedly proclaimed by government officials in countries around the world, that

Trafficking in humans: Social, cultural and political dimensions, Cameron and Newman (eds), United Nations University Press, 2007, ISBN 978-92-808-1146-9

human trafficking is a serious crime and human rights violation. There is also broad agreement that it is a multidisciplinary issue, requiring counteraction by a range of governmental and non-governmental actors to be effective. Yet most countries organize their response to trafficking in persons in a rather narrow way, based almost exclusively upon prevailing notions of national security, national sovereignty and border control.

When we look into the practice of many European countries it becomes quite obvious that the protection of the fundamental rights of victims of trafficking takes second place to the promotion of state interests. Governments very often see the battle against illegal immigration as their first priority, while pretending to fight human trafficking. Thus victims of trafficking run the risk of being treated as illegal immigrants and immediately deported to their countries of origin. And even when victims are allowed to stay temporarily, support for them depends on whether they are useful to the prosecution of the traffickers and willing to cooperate with law enforcement authorities. As a result, victims are often instrumentalized in the interests of the prosecution. Again, state interests take precedence over the right of victims to protection of their physical and mental integrity.

The European Union and many destination countries in general put the emphasis on preventing irregular immigration and fighting asylum abuse. Concentration on border controls, deterrence and immediate repatriation of trafficked persons is frequently the beginning of a vicious circle. Studies confirm that up to 50 per cent of those immediately deported are reintroduced into the criminal cycle or recycled. Instead of realizing that such measures are shortsighted, it is stubbornly held that they are effective means of self-protection serving the interests of state security; but in fact it has been established that not even 30 per cent of all trafficked persons are discovered, because they are prevented from seeking help by fear of deportation and of being caught in the machinery of law and order of a foreign country. Offering an extended stay in the country to trafficked people is not only called for from the human security perspective, but would also be a major contribution in the interest of national security, since trafficked people would be more inclined to support the prosecution of the traffickers and help disrupt their networks by cooperating with the authorities and possibly testifying in court.

If we want to be effective in diminishing human trafficking, it must not be seen primarily or exclusively from the perspective of national security; fighting human trafficking must not be seen only as a fight against illegal migration. It is first and foremost a violation of human rights. Therefore it is indispensable to raise awareness of the fact that trafficking in human beings is both a security issue and a human rights concern, and that it is not a question of "either/or". Both issues must be tackled together if we wish to be successful in the fight against human trafficking.

It is part of this national security approach to focus on border control efforts in the attempt to address human trafficking. And it is true that the UN Protocol calls upon states to strengthen border and security measures: by obliging commercial carriers to check passenger travel documents; by ensuring that travel documents are difficult to misuse, falsify, alter or replace; by safeguarding issuance of genuine travel documents; and by verifying travel documents as genuine on request.

Properly trained and vigilant border officials certainly have an important role to play in a comprehensive approach to fighting human trafficking, but for a number of reasons – which will be given below – they cannot be the sole or even the principal element of an effective national strategy against human trafficking. Very few cases of trafficking are identifiable and identified at the border, because very often, when crossing the border, people are not yet aware of the fate in store for them: being trapped into enslavement by traffickers and their accomplices. Experience reveals that most future victims cross borders legally and only later do they become illegal migrants by overstaying their visas. Often the traffickers simply arrange for the women to travel on their own, using legal travel documents which will be confiscated upon arrival abroad by traffickers or their middlemen. So the standard response of many states, which is to reinforce anti-fraud measures, making travel documents and identification procedures ever more sophisticated and training border guards to spot false documents, may be important in discovering illegal entrants into the country, but fails to address the essential part of human trafficking meaningfully and effectively.

At the border, the criminal actor typically is facilitating the transportation and (illegal) crossing of potential victims. Disrupting the border crossing will thus not disrupt the overall trafficking scheme. At best it merely inconveniences or removes a driver or smuggler temporarily from the equation. Their role, although forming part of the trafficking chain, is not the most decisive part in the continuum. Moreover, putting the emphasis on border control neglects the growing phenomenon of internal trafficking.

It is the smuggling of people that border guards and authorities try to prevent, but these efforts do not target the very substance of human trafficking, which is characterized by deception, coercion and exploitation. Smuggling people across borders may be considered to be a crime against the sovereignty of a state, but human trafficking is a serious crime and a human rights violation directed against a person. This "protect the borders" approach – styled and practised as the one and only solution – is ineffective as the main operational focus of a country's anti-trafficking effort.

There are a number of good reasons for strengthening a country's border controls, but it does not hit human trafficking at its core.

What is needed is a shift in perspective. If countries, individually and collectively, want to be effective in diminishing human trafficking, fighting it must not be seen primarily or exclusively from the perspective of national security, the main interest of which is to prevent illegal immigration. Although laid down in international standards and the expressed political will of many countries, this insight is hardly reflected in practical measures and approaches.

We have to recognize that human trafficking cannot be managed by measures of exclusion and control only. The emphasis on control, deterrence and immediate repatriation of victims of trafficking is often the beginning of a vicious circle.

We must be aware of the fact that state policies, which primarily tend towards measures of self-protection as opposed to a more comprehensive approach to the issue, are counterproductive and therefore part of the problem – and EU member states and the European Union as a whole, as the main destination area in Europe, have to play a vital role in this context.

Smuggling versus human trafficking

The continuing confusion over smuggling versus human trafficking and the fact that human trafficking is continually used interchangeably with smuggling is an important point to raise. Although the UN Protocols on Trafficking in Persons and on Smuggling are very clear about the definition, the concept of trafficking in persons is still being confused with other concepts, especially with smuggling of migrants.

While trafficking in human beings may share common characteristics with alien-smuggling and illegal immigration, we must be aware that it has its own distinctive features and dynamics, involving particularly grievous human rights abuses which demand specific and appropriate responses. Some of the victims may well have accepted the services of smugglers to get to a foreign country, or may have crossed borders illegally; but the fact that they are deprived of their freedom, that they are put into slavery-like situations, creates a clear distinction. Trafficking in human beings is distinctly different from human smuggling or illegal migration, and as such requires specialized measures for its investigation, prosecution and prevention. The smuggling of people, while often undertaken in dangerous or degrading conditions, implies the consent of those smuggled. Victims of trafficking, on the other hand, have either never consented or any initial consent has been rendered meaningless by the deceptive, coercive or abusive actions of the traffickers and their middlemen. Smuggling in general ends with the arrival of the people smuggled at their destination; whereas human trafficking involves the ongoing exploitation of victims in order to generate illicit profits for the criminals. Smuggling is always transnational, whereas human trafficking may also be internal, with victims being moved from one place to another within the same country.

In accordance with the UN Protocol, smuggling of people means effecting the illegal entry of a person into a foreign country for the purpose of financial or other material benefit.

Migration versus human trafficking

It is true that the movement of people, voluntary or forced, presents multiple aspects, implications and dilemmas for states. The development of appropriate policy and management responses to this challenge by governments has become a fundamental issue for many countries around the globe, and it also impacts on interstate relations more than ever before.

In the past two decades industrialized countries in particular have registered record numbers of migrants. According to the estimates of international organizations, more than 150 million people – in other words every fiftieth person – live as migrants outside their countries of origin. Compared with the world population this number is relatively small, accounting for about 2.5 per cent of the population worldwide. (This figure may fluctuate by some millions, as statistics are either not standardized or non-existent.)

Prior to 9/11 the discussion on migrants focused on issues such as adjusting their numbers to labour market requirements, the integration of migrants and multiculturalism. Nowadays the focus is increasingly on security and, for some time to come, migration is likely to be perceived through the magnifying glass of the fight against terrorism. In recent years the number of migrants using irregular ways of travel and entering countries without permits has steadily risen. Moreover, the speed of migratory movements has increased, more and more countries have been involved as both countries of destination and of origin and migration is becoming increasingly feminized. Recently, intergovernmental cooperation in the field of migration management has focused primarily on stepping up border controls and preventing irregular migration and illegal immigration by concluding readmission and repatriation agreements and

other restrictive measures, and the trend towards establishing a link between irregular migration and international crime is rising. This is where
the concept of national security comes into play, which frequently and
uncontestedly implies that states assume the right to determine who is
permitted to enter the country and who is removed from it. The fact that
migration is more and more often linked with organized crime impacts
negatively on the attempts made to fight trafficking in human beings.
Nowadays it is widely known that most of the potential victims of trafficking leave their countries "voluntarily", as it were, to find work and earn
money as migrants abroad. (As few as 10 per cent of those trafficked are
forced to leave/kidnapped.) It is from the fact that these people are frequently perceived as illegal migrants, and often work illegally, that criminal organizations – exploiting the demand for low-cost, unprotected
labour and commercial sex – derive their immense profits. As a rule, migrants in general and illegal migrants in particular are at the mercy of the
traffickers and their accomplices, who ruthlessly exploit the total lack of
social and legal protection. Instead of being provided with appropriate
protection and assistance – one of the main points of discussion is temporary residence for trafficked persons – the victims of trafficking are usually expelled/deported as soon as possible and returned to their home
countries. This attitude is also influenced by the assumption that the offer
of temporary residence would attract more migrants and be abused.
Since most Western European governments are concentrating on the
fight against illegal immigration, trafficked persons run the risk of being
categorized as illegal immigrants and frequently criminals, and of being
immediately deported to their home countries.

Close analysis goes to show that in practice there is a danger that state
interests – which are primarily to control migration and put the emphasis
on criminal prosecution – run counter to the needs and rights of the
victims of trafficking. Far too often the defenceless victims of cynical
traffickers are still regarded as perpetrators and are criminalized and
deported before their true circumstances have been investigated. The
women know that as "illegal aliens" the best treatment they can hope
for is deportation, unless they are treated as undocumented/illegal immigrants and simply turned away by border officials. Practical experience
demonstrates that immigration responses to the complex problem of human trafficking are almost always inadequate.

The main point to be made about migration policy and human trafficking is simple: there are lots of hypotheses about restrictive versus open
migration policies and their relationship to human trafficking, but there
is little certainty. In the face of migration restrictions it seems logical
that individuals must rely on others to help them, and some of these
turn out to be traffickers. On the other hand, it is almost universally rec-

ognized that the opening of the borders of the former Soviet Union contributed greatly to human trafficking of residents from that part of the world and to the ease with which traffickers move their victims without detection. Now one sees human traffickers taking advantage of Schengen visa travel and other techniques in order to move their routes towards paths of least resistance or scrutiny. This suggests that they manipulate eased migration policies to further their criminal purposes. The conclusions at this point must be that, first of all, there is no evidentiary basis for determining conclusively the correlation between a particular migration policy and human trafficking. It is obvious that the arguments over open versus restrictive borders are typically used to serve the agendas of particular advocates regarding migration policy. Secondly, human traffickers do not seem to care very much about different immigration policies. One sees human trafficking move easily where borders are relatively open, such as within the European Union, and also moving without much trouble through areas where there are restrictive immigration policies. According to Europol, more than 3,000 mafia organizations with up to 30,000 activists operate within the boundary-free Europe.

Owing to the fact that most industrialized countries wish to restrict immigration to the absolute minimum and seem to compete for the "most restrictive asylum regulations", the choice left to the majority of migrants is illegal or irregular migration. Where regular channels for migration are closed or too difficult to move through, space will be created for abusive practices, including human trafficking. And where the desperate need for work meets the pull of the labour market, the traffickers and their accomplices are the link between demand and the exploited people who can satisfy it.

Unlike the movement of goods and capital, the movement of labour still raises sensitive political and sociological issues, although more and more countries are beginning to realize that they will need migrant workers to be able to maintain current growth levels and respond to demographic changes.

Experts believe that even a marginal liberalization of international labour flows could create gains for the world economy far larger than prospective gains from trade negotiations.

But the fact that human trafficking has emerged as a global theme, setting migration in a framework of combating organized crime and criminality and subordinating human rights protection to control and anti-crime measures, has unfortunately had extremely negative impacts on how such trafficking is approached and on the protection of victims of trafficking.

Migrants in general – and irregular migrants in particular – are most vulnerable and may easily become victims of trafficking. Many of them work under very exploitative conditions: without health services, un-aware of their rights, subject to physical and mental abuse, underpaid, or wages withheld by recruiting agents. Traffickers take advantage and exploit the lack of social and legal protection.

But, of course, an illegal migrant worker is not the same as a trafficking victim. And human trafficking clearly is not migration, economic or otherwise. Human trafficking involves violent criminal enterprises, op-portunistically targeting those who can be easily separated from home, family and friends in order to move them to unfamiliar surroundings for the purpose of trapping them in sexual exploitation or forced and bonded labour.

Trafficking victims are subjected to force or coercion at some point: either when they are recruited, during transport or on entry into and dur-ing work. However, there are forms of coercion in recruitment and em-ployment that can be difficult to detect. Besides physical restraints, there can also be restraints which are less overt, such as confiscation of papers, non-payment of wages, induced indebtedness or threats to denounce ir-regular migrant workers to authorities if they do not accept working con-ditions. In contrast to this, the traffickers make a hefty profit. They make money from the desperate worker who is seeking to move. They take a cut on services provided in arranging travel, accommodation, reception and other daily costs, charged to the worker. They take a cut of the money paid for the labour. And, if all goes wrong and the worker is found to be in a foreign country and working illegally, the traffickers and their collaborators are unlikely to be prosecuted. While the worker will generally be locked up or deported, the traffickers and their collabo-rators are most likely to go undetected, because the victim will fear repri-sal against him/herself or his/her family if he/she gives information to the authorities.

In practice it seems to be very difficult to prosecute those responsible. This is true for the employers and contractors, the recruiting and trans-porting agents, etc. The current trend seems to be towards increasing penalties for the hiring of "illegal" migrant workers.

In this context particularly close scrutiny is called for, because although migrant workers often come to a foreign country with valid, government-issued work permits, they may nevertheless fall victim to traffickers. They may be bound to a single employer, to whom the workers' passports are handed over by the state authorities, and the moment the employment is terminated for whatever reason (underpayment, no payment, violence, bankruptcy or corruption of the employer, etc.) they will lose their legal status. This automatically deprives them of their right to stay in the coun-try and look for alternative employment. They may be forced to conform to illegal and abusive employment terms under threat of dismissal, followed by loss of legal status and possible arrest. Although in most countries the law forbids the charging of mediation fees to workers, workers are nevertheless charged enormous fees and may even have to put up their homes as collateral in order to fulfil their work contract. The debts incurred by workers in this way may reach such huge amounts that they can never hope to pay them back. By failing to enforce existing laws, quite a few states provide the infrastructure for human trafficking.

Law enforcement versus human rights approach

It goes without saying that law enforcement has a major role to play in the fight against human trafficking.

Currently, victims of trafficking are identified almost exclusively by police officers. It depends on the insight of these officers into the problem whether people are recognized as victims or not, and whether victims of trafficking are correctly treated. And it depends on them whether a case will be followed up by the prosecutor or not, as it is for them to question the victims and prepare the files.

These facts already highlight some of the main areas of concern in the fight against human trafficking. It is a persistent problem that victims of trafficking are tracked down almost exclusively by the police – instead of being able to resort to a network of points of contact and support services without running the risk of being immediately caught in the law and order mechanisms of a foreign country.

Although in recent years things have changed slightly, many – too many – victims of trafficking are still seen as perpetrators and are criminalized. Frequently, they are still taken to detention centres instead of to shelters – with some shelters actually being run like detention centres – and are deported before circumstances have been thoroughly investigated.

Most of the victims of trafficking are usually not able to speak the local language; they have no money, no papers and are under constant threat. It is thus of the utmost importance to make sure that these victims get access to the local state authorities, such as the police.

There is still a trend among the police towards an interrogation strategy which tries to take the person interrogated by surprise. It is argued that a statement given immediately after arrest is true and unfalsified, because the people concerned are not given the chance to think over their statements or monitor their behaviour.

In contrast to this, NGOs which are service providers for victims of trafficking have found that victims need a period for recovery and recuperation from their traumatic experience and for developing trust in foreign authorities and institutions. Frequently they do not see themselves initially as victims of a crime, and it takes time and a lot of talking before they are able to grasp their situation. Furthermore, victims of trafficking very often have been warned by their traffickers not to trust anyone, least of all the police. Sometimes victims are ashamed of what they were forced to do – for example to work as prostitutes – and even condemn themselves. This is why NGOs and international organizations believe that victims will come up with the full truth only over time. It is only on the basis of longer contacts and regular talks that victims are willing to tell their stories and even to testify and finally to uphold their statements.

The lesson we can learn from this is that, because of this element of uncertainty, identification of victims of trafficking should not be left exclusively to the police. It should rather be jointly undertaken by the police and NGOs.

In many countries there is a lack of structured and systematic cooperation between law enforcement officers and those who run victim protection centres. Their mutual distrust is rooted in their different objectives and often the reluctance of both parties to communicate with each other. This is a great disservice to trafficked victims. Although cooperation between law enforcement and NGOs has improved, it is still unsatisfactory; equally, the cooperation between police and prosecution/judiciary leaves much to be desired.

According to an Interpol survey, in more than 40 per cent of countries no special policing techniques are employed in the investigation of human trafficking. This brings out in clear relief the urgent need for investigative efforts by the police to be tuned to the victims' well-being and for law enforcement agents to be sensitized to special techniques – such as non-threatening interrogation techniques – when working with victims. They must be familiarized with victims' needs and also with victims' limits.

We must overcome the remnants of the outdated view that the rights and needs of trafficking victims are inimical to effective law enforcement. This is shortsighted and will ultimately undermine law enforcement efforts. We must realize that it is impractical and ultimately unacceptable to disaggregate the notion of law enforcement from assisting and protecting victims of this crime. Since trafficking victims currently are the primary source of witnesses for the prosecution, a victim-centred approach by law enforcement is not only consistent but logical if law enforcement objectives are to be achieved.

Another problem is the sole focus on testimonial evidence given by victims acting as witnesses. This is another issue that needs discussing, because a prosecution that builds exclusively on testimonial evidence by victim-witnesses is the least successful. Other forms of evidence are indispensable and must be fitted together like a mosaic. From practice it is known that often the credibility of victims depends on the investigator's and prosecutor's insight derived from other sources of information.

Law enforcement must go after the network itself, from the start in the countries of origin to the end-users in the countries of destination. It must seek to disrupt the chain of human trafficking from beginning to end by targeting the perpetrators along the entire continuum. This includes investigating and going after the financial assets of the network, the lifeblood of organized criminal enterprises. This is a crucial alternative source of evidence. The police have to target the financial records of the organized human trafficking enterprises and the locations where they are kept – which is generally not behind a bar. The focus on raiding bars and brothels cannot be the only answer to the problem and will not disrupt trafficking networks.

The tendency to view human trafficking primarily or exclusively as a security issue has detrimental implications for the rights and needs of trafficking victims. It does tend to draw attention away from a victim-centred approach towards a strict and almost exclusive law enforcement strategy. This is not appropriate. Moreover, an exclusive law enforcement perspective cannot work, since there still needs to be reliance on the victims to cooperate against the traffickers.

On the other hand, the legal tools that are used by law enforcement against organized crime are rarely utilized in human trafficking cases – such things as wire-taps, tracking the financial assets of the criminal enterprise, addressing the crime from beginning to end, long-term undercover investigations and/or surveillance, etc.

Widespread training holds a large part of the answer to the continuing need for spreading understanding. What is called for is thorough training of law enforcement officers, both front-line police and special investigators, and of prosecutors and judges. Training must have a curriculum and teach new skill-sets over several days based on a victim-centred approach. Training needs also to be provided for border and consular officials, government officials in key positions, etc.

The education of all those who need to be reached is an enormous undertaking, but it is the only measure that will work. This, then, needs to be a rigorously organized effort based upon a specific strategy of who will be trained, when and by whom. Team teaching by law enforcement officers and NGO representatives as service providers for the victims has proved highly effective and adds a new quality to education and training.

Another factor designed to diminish the conceptual confusion over definitions is the process of criminal law reform engaged in by individual countries. When countries wrestle with the practical distinctions required to distinguish legally between smuggling, illegal immigration, exploitation of prostitution and human trafficking and various other crimes, they find it necessary to refine and clarify these distinctions. This impacts not only on criminal law provision but also on measures for providing, *inter alia*, assistance and victim/witness protection. The differences between human trafficking, smuggling and illegal immigration again reveal themselves when countries must determine which benefits they will provide to human trafficking victims that they will not provide to smuggled persons or illegal immigrants, and why.

The human trafficking laws enacted and implemented must be comprehensive to match the multidisciplinary character of the horrible crime and human rights violation of human trafficking. All of this will influence the understanding in this field. Those involved in investigating and enforcing the laws refer to what the law says. That is why human trafficking requires its own set of enacted laws.

UN Protocol versus European Convention

It goes without saying that the UN Protocol on Trafficking in Persons represents a major step forward when it comes to the definition of human trafficking as well as to the prosecution of the perpetrators and the protection of victims' rights.

It is true to say that the definition is not perfect. But this was a political necessity to gain agreement to a document that represents a major achievement. While imperfect, the definition is a serviceable framework for countries to start and spur the process of developing new laws for addressing human trafficking. The existing problems are by no means fatal to the document or to the anti-trafficking work proceeding around the world. Issues can be addressed as we go forward in enacting and implementing these new laws and the activities that surround them.

However, one has to be aware that the Palermo Protocol is the outcome of a process based on a law enforcement perspective. This is both a strength and a weakness. It is a strength because it means that law enforcement authorities of countries around the world have agreed on the need to provide protection and assistance to victims of human trafficking. It is a weakness in the sense that it was never intended to address fully victims' needs or governmental responsibility for addressing these needs. It is the absolute minimum required to provide for the safety and care of trafficking victims. The protocol provides the agreement and political impetus needed by countries to take the required anti-trafficking steps. However, the process of drafting and implementing human trafficking laws goes forward as part of a larger process of people working on this issue.

On the other hand, it is apparent from the wording that victims' rights are generally granted in a non-committal and conditional manner – in a "soft" manner. Practically every single right is granted only conditionally, using phrases such as "in appropriate cases", "to the extent possible", "if permissible under domestic law", "each state party shall consider" or "shall take into account" or "shall endeavor". In the last analysis, the text of the protocol does not contain any binding, stringent obligations for signatory states to take effective measures to assist and protect victims of trafficking.

This might be another reason why states do not really feel responsible for victim assistance and protection. One must admit that the victim protection measures in the Palermo Protocol are not entirely sufficient. However, the protocol is only the substrata of assistance and protection that needs to be provided, and it includes a fairly good, if basic and general, list of what is needed – shelter, medical care, legal representation, not treating the human trafficking victim as a criminal, etc.

Despite increased attention at the political level, few states have taken adequate measures to protect individuals from trafficking and its related human rights abuses, or to provide effective assistance or remedies to victims. It is the practice of most destination countries, even when victims are allowed to stay temporarily, to make support to them dependent on their willingness to cooperate with law enforcement authorities and on their supposed usefulness to the prosecution.

Unfortunately the EU Council Directive "on the residence permits issued to third-country nationals who are victims of trafficking" also intends to grant an extended stay only to those willing to cooperate with the competent authorities. In most Western European countries such cooperation is the precondition for support programmes to be accessible by the victims. The conditions safeguarding against the abuse of residence permits, which are contained in the directive, testify to the reluctance of states to provide assistance and protection to victims.

It is questionable whether the European Convention against Human Trafficking – which is currently being drafted – would essentially change this situation, and it goes without saying that a European convention would be meaningful only if it stood up with more determination – as it were without ifs and buts – for the rights of victims of trafficking.

The status and protection of the victims deserve particular attention. States must play a crucial role in the fight against human trafficking, especially when it comes to the treatment of victims. For victims to be able to free themselves from relationships of violence and life contexts in which they are permanently threatened by violence, they need comprehensive social and economic support, but also legal assistance. Effective empowerment starts with the granting of a strong legal status. The total lack of such status is exploited by the traffickers.

The legalization of the status of a trafficked person is a crucial element in any effective victim and witness protection strategy, and may help to assist a much greater number of trafficked persons who would normally not dare to seek refuge for fear of deportation. A secure, safe legal status for victims is the prerequisite for support programmes to reach them. A central issue in this context is the right of (temporary or permanent) residence for victims in the transit and destination countries. The granting of a residence permit would signal to victims that the state on whose territory they find themselves sides with them without reservations. In addition, it would disrupt the so-called recycling of the victims of trafficking – since it is well known that up to 50 per cent of those immediately repatriated are retrafficked. After a reflection period – which would give the (potential) victims time to stabilize their situation, recover physically, medically and psychologically and reorientate themselves, and would also allow the authorities to establish whether somebody is a victim of trafficking or not – the state should grant a temporary residence permit for at least six months. The temporary permit should be renewable for one year, with the possibility that victims may be allowed to remain permanently.

The temporary residence permit would also present an instrument for enhancing the prosecution of traffickers and organized crime, as it offers trafficked persons time to decide on making a complaint to the police, on cooperating with the investigating authorities and eventually on testifying in proceedings. Even if the victim decides not to testify against the traffickers, the authorities will still have vital information on traffickers' strategies, practices and networks. Ideally, legal residence status should be granted irrespective of the victims' ability or willingness to testify in criminal proceedings. The legal status of residence should also imply access of victims to the labour market as well as the right to state welfare benefits and crime victims' compensation.

Furthermore, the status of victims of trafficking in criminal proceedings deserves particular attention. Frequently victims suffer from severe trauma. To expose them or force them too early to confront the traumatizing experience may cause additional trauma. The victims must therefore not be instrumentalized in the interests of state criminal prosecution. They must have the right to refuse to testify, and if they agree to testify they should be able to do so in a non-confrontational environment. In any case, the process of testifying against the trafficker must not revictimize a victim, but should be an empowering, positive experience.

To start with, one should therefore make sure that victims really want to testify against traffickers and are not just submitting to police pressure. Victims have to be informed about the implications of testifying before they make a statement. Whether they are prepared to become witnesses will depend to a great extent on the capacity and willingness of states to protect and support them.

In practice, however, many states do not even provide the most basic protection for victims who participate in proceedings. Many countries do not allow witnesses to remain in the country during the proceedings, but summon them back without giving a thought to the financial burdens involved or to the safety of the witnesses and those close to them.

Effective victim-witness protection does not end at the conclusion of a trial, of course. Research has indicated that in countries of origin women and their families are more or less totally unprotected against threats or violence. Thus another right should be that of family reunification, which is frequently the only way to ensure the security of the closest relatives of trafficking victims.

On the other hand there is a risk of victims being excluded from criminal proceedings, thereby negating the serious injustice they have suffered at the hands of the perpetrators. State authorities should not obstruct victims of trafficking from participation and make criminal proceedings exclusively their own business. Victims should be given the possibility to present and describe the injustice they have suffered and to witness that the perpetrators are held to account for their deeds.

Victims of trafficking versus criminals

So far there has been no effective cooperation across borders. Foreign ministries are not communicating with one another on the issue of trafficking in persons. There is no systematic method of following up on the fates of repatriated victims of trafficking. There is no evidence that governments in the source countries take clear responsibility for the protection of their nationals upon their return home. On the contrary, in many countries women are arrested upon repatriation or branded as deviants or criminals. Such actions prevent the successful reintegration of these "survivors" of trafficking into their communities. They have little chance of re-establishing a normal life in the fold of their families. Very often families will not take them back, and if they do it is rarely for long. Generally the repatriated women have few prospects back in their home countries. Often they face distressing stigmatization both from their families and from society. Given the scope of the trafficking problem and the limited resources for addressing reintegration, most victims of trafficking receive little or no assistance. Once a trafficked person is repatriated there is no communication between the governments to ensure that those responsible for the trafficking in the country of origin are brought to justice or to ensure the protection of the victims.

States must play a crucial role in changing the perception of victims of this crime. This will have to start with governments themselves recognizing them as victims, and with the way they treat them. This will happen when countries establish the status and protection of such people as consistent with being victims of crime and not criminals.

A particular and problematic issue arises from the interrelation between various laws, more specifically between the laws on trafficking in human beings and the legislation on immigration. According to the experience of different countries, it is essential for the prosecution that victims report to the police and act as witnesses, even if other means of investigation, such as electronic surveillance (phone tapping), financial investigation etc., have been used. But since crossing borders illegally is a crime in most countries, victims of trafficking will be prosecuted for being illegal aliens. This is a serious obstacle to a successful prosecution of traffickers, because it impedes and prevents the cooperation between the victim and the police or the prosecutor. Moreover, some countries consider the illegal crossing of foreign state borders by their own citizens a criminal offence. In general this is a special rule of extraterritoriality and applies to a limited range of very serious crimes, such as terrorism, corruption committed by national public officials abusing their power etc., but some countries apply it also to victims of human trafficking. If one of their own nationals has illegally crossed the borders of a country of transit or destination as a victim of trafficking, he/she will be prosecuted for this crime upon being voluntarily or involuntarily returned or repatriated. Though the struggle against human trafficking is connected with the struggle against illegal migration, it should be clearly understood by the competent authorities that only the traffickers should be prosecuted for illegal border crossing, and not the victims of trafficking.

Admittedly it is not easy to decide whom to consider as a victim of trafficking at an early stage of investigation, especially if the person concerned migrated because of a misrepresentation of the real purpose by the traffickers, e.g. the promise of a regular job in the country of destination. Nevertheless, the competent authorities ought to investigate every case of illegal border crossing to find out if there is a case of trafficking behind it. This could be a way of improving the effective prosecution of human traffickers.

In the course of being trafficked it may happen that trafficked victims will commit acts, with or without intent, which can amount to administrative offences or crimes; for instance crossing a state border without, or with forged, documents, etc. A victim may actually be identified as such while committing such an offence or crime. The practice of non-prosecution if the victim reports to the police and acts as a witness, thereby facilitating the arrest of a trafficker and/or his middlemen, should be extended to any kind of assistance in the prosecution at any stage of the criminal investigation.

States should ensure that victims of trafficking are not subject to criminal or administrative liability and sanction for acts arising from the trafficking situation. This will prevent trauma and promote recovery and social reintegration of the victims. Governments must therefore refrain from immediately expelling potential victims of trafficking due to their unlawful entry into the country and their irregular residence and/or labour status.

Although attention at the political level has increased, few states have come to see it as their responsibility to protect individuals from trafficking and its related human rights abuses and to provide effective assistance and remedies to victims. States and their governments bear primary responsibility for the implementation of measures to combat human trafficking, and they have to ensure that they comply with their international obligations under human rights norms, namely to respect and protect the rights of individuals.

There is a role for everyone in working together on this problem, but the ultimate responsibility for responding appropriately and effectively lies with governments. Each government must accept this role of responsibility and accountability if progress is to be made in the fight against human trafficking.

Despite significant progress in the creation of institutionalized governmental mechanisms in many countries, an assessment in South-Eastern Europe has shown (but the author believes the same would apply to almost all regions in the world) that there is little evidence of governmental ownership, especially when it comes to assisting and protecting victims of trafficking. Notwithstanding the extensive coverage of this issue in conferences and by the media, most countries have in practice failed to give it the time and attention it deserves. An objective look at what is needed to confront this problem reveals that anti-trafficking work demands full-time attention. Yet there are few full-time government officials assigned to cope with the wide range of anti-trafficking work.

Instead, responsibility for the implementation of anti-trafficking measures – especially in countries where financial support from donor countries is expected – is increasingly shifted by governments to international organizations. This has immense implications. Governments frequently withdraw to the sidelines when it comes to facing the problem head on and becoming practically involved in this fight. But international organizations can never do all that is necessary. After all, it involves the protection of the human rights of citizens, which is a fundamental responsibility of the state.

Multidimensionality versus one-dimensionality

Trafficking in persons is a very complex problem. There are numerous contributing factors which have to be analysed and taken into account if we wish to crack down on human trafficking and find sustainable solutions: the unequal economic development of different countries; unemployment and few job opportunities in many countries of origin, but also inequality and discrimination on the basis of sex and race and gender-based violence in our societies; the prevailing market mechanisms; the patriarchal structures in the source and destination countries; the demand side including the promotion of sex tourism in many countries of the world; the mindsets of men (the "men are men" attitude), etc. Human trafficking has links to migration (legal and illegal), to the smuggling of people, to other criminal activities and, last but not least, to organized transnational crime.

The realization that human trafficking involves a chain of criminal behaviour and activities is fundamental to addressing it effectively. No appropriate response – in terms of either law enforcement or victim assistance objectives – to human trafficking is possible unless this is clearly understood and all actions are designed to deal with these facts.

Human trafficking cannot be captured in a single "snapshot"; it is better characterized as a series of actions unfolding like a "movie". This is to say that it does not happen within a discrete moment in time and then it is over, nor does it happen in one place. It is not perpetrated only in the country of destination, where the victim is discovered. It is much rather a chain – or series – of criminal offences and human rights violations, starting in the country of origin and extending over time and across countries of transit into countries of destination. Even internal trafficking involves a series of crimes and human rights violations that extend over time.

Realizing that human trafficking is a chain of criminal activities explains why law enforcement must cooperate across borders and must engage in proactive rather than reactive investigation. It explains why a strategy based upon lining up "deterrence" at the borders is not adequate.

While it has almost become a cliché that human trafficking is a transnational crime, the problem is that virtually no one actually addresses it as such. There are hardly any investigations of human trafficking that link up the criminal activity in the countries of origin with the criminals in the countries of destination. There is hardly any institutionalized and concerted follow-up of victims once they have been returned to their countries of origin.

From the above it is evident that, in search of an easy answer, repeated attempts have been made to reduce a highly complex and multidimensional problem to a simplistic, often one-dimensional issue. All those who work on this problem in practice have come to realize the breathtaking intricacy of this puzzle. Therefore, the efforts of certain people and organizations who are trying to reduce this multitude of dimensions to a single aspect with which they are familiar or in which they are particularly interested need to be resisted. They see trafficking in persons either solely as a problem of illegal migration, or solely as a labour market issue, or solely as a demand-driven problem, or solely as a problem of organized crime. This is a tunnel vision that completely misjudges the complexity of human trafficking and is not designed to lead to a desirable outcome.

A change in the working assumptions and an improvement in the effectiveness of all programmes and measures will largely depend on making policy-makers, donors and others understand the "why". Unless they understand the why, they will not be convinced of the how or the what. They will not understand how to use the available tools properly, which measures to take in which situation, which approach to take to the victims and how to treat them correctly.

We must find the means to make people internalize the reality of modern manifestations of slavery; we must make them "see" the problem and understand it. In the end, this is what will ensure that we make the right choices and find the right path to combating this crime effectively.

If we wish to diminish human trafficking, there is equal need for short-term and long-term measures. Short-term measures, such as the immediate and urgent need to assist and protect the victims, will only have the desired effect if they are based on serious research into the root causes of trafficking. On the one hand, the countermeasures have to be quick-acting. On the other hand, it is necessary to raise and address the issue of the structural roots of human trafficking – namely the global inequalities in the distribution of jobs, resources and wealth. We have no alternative but to engage with the root causes, no matter how complex, difficult and forbidding they may be. Anti-trafficking initiatives must offer real prospects of escaping from the cycle of poverty, abuse and exploitation.

As human trafficking is becoming increasingly internationalized and complex, the flow of information must be speeded up. Coordination on all aspects in the fight against human trafficking and absolute cooperation on everything are indispensable if we wish to be successful. Only if we all join forces and intensify and coordinate our efforts will we be able to master this challenge. We must demonstrate that cooperation can work in practice, and that cooperation must be worldwide.

8

Human trafficking in East and South-East Asia: Searching for structural factors

Maruja M. B. Asis

Asia has been a theatre of increasing and diverse international migrations in the last three decades. Large numbers of people are migrating for various reasons: migration for permanent residence in the traditional countries of settlement – the United States, Canada, Australia and New Zealand; refugee migrations; forced migrations; temporary migrations of workers and the highly skilled; student migrations; and marriage migrations. Since the 1970s a large part of international migration has occurred *within* the region.

Of the world's 191 million international migrants, some 53.3 million are in Asia, making it the second-largest region hosting international migrants after Europe, which hosts 64.1 million.[1] In addition, Asia is home to 7.8 million refugees out of a worldwide total of 13.5 million.[2] What these statistics do not reflect are the huge numbers of unauthorized migrants as well as the suspected large numbers of men, women and children who are trafficked. Although there are legal channels in place, the scale of unauthorized migration in Asia is significant. In South-East Asia, for some time about one-third of an estimated 6 million people who were working outside their countries of birth were in an unauthorized situation. In Malaysia and Thailand there are more unauthorized than legal migrant workers. The massive repatriation drive in Malaysia in 2004–2005 and the reform of Thailand's registration system in 2004 reduced the share of unauthorized migrants, although it remains to be seen whether this decline is temporary or long term. In East Asia, Japan and Taiwan have been relatively successful in checking unauthorized

Trafficking in humans: Social, cultural and political dimensions, Cameron and Newman (eds), United Nations University Press, 2007, ISBN 978-92-808-1146-9

migration, while South Korea has been dealing with a huge population of unauthorized migrant workers since it became a labour-importing country in the 1990s. The introduction of the employment permit system in 2004 is expected to reduce unauthorized migration and provide more protection to migrant workers. Estimates of human trafficking in the region suggest that the phenomenon is also alarmingly significant.[3] East and South-East Asia are, in fact, often cited among the hotspots of trafficking, either as origin, transit or destination locations. The clandestine or illicit conduct of unauthorized migration and human trafficking renders it difficult to come up with more precise or verifiable estimates. Amidst the debates and unsettled questions about these phenomena, the realization of the human rights abuses experienced by unauthorized migrants and those who are trafficked provides a common ground to curb these inhumane practices. When the scale or magnitude is considerable, the call to action assumes even greater urgency.

Since the 1980s the renewed international attention given to the issue of trafficking in women for sexual exploitation (which later expanded into human trafficking for various purposes) has resulted in a proliferation of programmes and activities devoted to counter-trafficking efforts.[4] Other factors which contributed to the (re)discovery of trafficking are global trends, notably the increase in international migration, the influence of the feminist movement, the spread of AIDS, child labour, prostitution and sex tourism. Alongside these developments was a shift in the focus of trafficking (mostly for prostitution) from European and American women to women in Asia, Latin America and, recently, East Europe.[5] Research on human trafficking also increased attempts to understand its causes and consequences better, and has provided guidance in designing policies and programmes to combat it.

In line with the focus of this project, this chapter examines the structural factors underlying human trafficking in East and South-East Asia.[6] It approaches this objective by considering trafficking as part of the accelerating, expanding and diversifying international migrations taking place in the Asian region. There could be other ways in which unauthorized migration and trafficking can be framed. In part, the continuing debate on these subjects is related to the different ways of approaching the phenomenon, i.e. as an issue of migration, labour, health, national security or human rights. This chapter examines trafficking mainly through the lens of migration, largely because mobility is intrinsic to it, with the acknowledgement that migration in general, and trafficking in particular, crosscut other issues.

Furthermore, under conditions of globalization, present migrations (including trafficking) are affected by factors that simultaneously push, facilitate and impede the movement of people across international borders.

The displacing impact of globalization in developing countries results in increased economic dislocation. In the face of volatile or fragile national economies, families and households turn to overseas migration as a strategy to meet their needs. The facilitative processes come from improved communications and transportation that not only promote the movement of people (as well as ideas, goods, technology and capital) across borders, but also enable migrants to maintain linkages to their countries of destination and origin; a possibility that has transformed migrants into "transnationals" who can play a vital part in the creation of "transnational communities".[7] Greater access to more information about economic opportunities and lifestyles in other countries – of the potential good life, so to speak – has also contributed to openness about the idea of migration. Moreover, through these transnational linkages migrants and their social networks provide information and resources that contribute to further migration.[8] States, however, do not allow the free movement of people. The migration-generating aspects of globalization are thus checked by the continuing power of states to regulate the entry, residence and economic activities of non-nationals in their territories. In limiting the legal channels of migration, these state-driven regulations and measures inadvertently lead to more unauthorized migration, including trafficking. In this situation, marked by emigration pressures and/or possibilities on the one hand and demand for migrants on the other (although this may not be formally recognized by state policies), transnational networks, recruiters, immigration consultants and other intermediaries intervene to facilitate migration. When migration occurs through unauthorized or trafficking channels, migrants bear the costs and other adverse consequences.

Having described the big picture that frames the phenomenon of human trafficking, this chapter will now:

- propose a framework examining the origins and development of human trafficking
- examine the patterns of trafficking in East and South-East Asia in terms of what they imply about the structural factors of human trafficking
- examine the approaches of regional initiatives aimed at curbing trafficking.

Analysing human trafficking

In the migration literature trafficking as a type of population movement did not warrant a specific label and discussion until quite recently. The increasing recognition of the abusive conditions to which migrants are subjected introduced the categories of legal versus unauthorized migration,[9] a typology which privileges the power of the state to define who, how and how many non-nationals may enter, reside and participate in its national territory. Unauthorized migration refers to "any population movement that violates legal migration regimes ... as a departure from the migration norms of the countries of origin, transit and destination".[10] Defined from the perspective and interests of the state, the state is the "aggrieved" (or unknowing) party in unauthorized migration. The effectiveness of the state to control its borders is called into question in trafficking, but it is the trafficked person who is the aggrieved party and whose rights have been violated. The possibility that the state – through its policies, regulations and offices – could also contribute to unauthorized migration or trafficking is rarely considered or not at all.

When discussions about trafficking resurfaced in the 1980s and 1990s, trafficking was understood as distinct from legal migration and was thus conceived under the general rubric of unauthorized migration.[11] However, the tendency to lump unauthorized migration and trafficking together can be misleading; at times, migration and trafficking are even used interchangeably. Such sweeping and haphazard conceptualization causes confusion. To classify all migrants (including unauthorized migrants) as trafficked persons grossly ignores the different realities underpinning these different migration regimes. At the same time, disregarding the parallels would not be constructive either, particularly if the objective is to look for structural causes. In reality there are overlaps and shifts from one migration regime to another.

A study of unauthorized migration in South-East Asia viewed human trafficking as a specific type of unauthorized migration which is distinctive because of the greater degree of abuse and exploitation of trafficked persons.[12] The crucial difference between unauthorized migration and trafficking is the abuse and exploitation that are universal characteristics in human trafficking, but which may or may not accompany unauthorized migration. The existence of abuse is central in the definition of trafficking according to the Protocol to Prevent, Suppress and Punish Trafficking in Persons, Especially Women and Children (hereafter referred to as the Trafficking Protocol).

Figure 8.1 summarizes the macro variables, proximate variables, intermediaries and channels operating in *both* origin and destination countries. A combination of these factors may result in either regular or unauthorized migration.[13] Although there are some references to trafficking, the original formulation of the framework was intended to explain the factors and processes that lead to legal versus unauthorized migration. The framework is premised on the following concepts.

• Regular migration and unauthorized migration are part of the same migration system. Hence, if we consider the determinants and the intervening factors, the same factors would apply to both legal and unau-

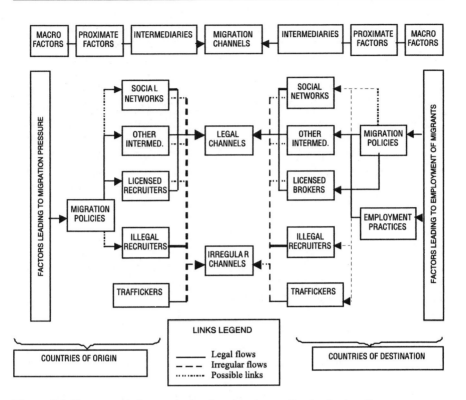

Figure 8.1 Framework for analysing legal and unauthorized migrations
Source: Graziano Battistella and Maruja M. B. Asis, eds, *Unauthorized Migration in Southeast Asia*, Quezon City: Scalabrini Migration Center, 2003, p. 14.

thorized migrations. Where the two differ is in the access of migrants to either legal or unauthorized channels – those who have more access to legal channels go through regular migration; those who do not end up using unauthorized channels.

- Since migration is a transnational phenomenon, conditions and processes in the countries of *both* origin and destination must be considered. If there are supply-related determinants in the origin country, what are the corresponding demand-related determinants at the destination? What kinds of migration policies in the origin and destination countries facilitate migration through which channels? Who are the migration intermediaries in the origin and destination countries? Emigration pressures or aspirations in the origin country may compel people to migrate, but if there is no corresponding demand for migrant workers in the destination country, migration will not be realized. Supply factors in the origin country, demand factors in the destination country, migration policies in the origin and destination countries and access to legal or unauthorized intermediaries in the origin and destination countries are conditions that impinge on a migrant ending up in either legal or unauthorized channels of migration.

- A migrant's legal status – i.e. as legal or unauthorized – is not fixed. In reality migrants may slip into a regular or unauthorized status depending on external conditions, such as migration policies or working conditions.[14] For example, a legal migrant worker can turn into an unauthorized migrant worker if he or she runs away from his/her employer or sponsor. Or an unauthorized migrant may adjust his or her status to that of a legal migrant where a regularization exercise or an amnesty is offered.

Extending the framework

It is proposed to extend the framework outlined in figure 8.1 by examining trafficking in relation to legal and unauthorized migration. This approach offers the possibility of identifying factors, actors and phases or moments in the migratory process that may be common or distinct to legal migration, unauthorized migration or human trafficking.

Considering supply-side factors and processes, the determinants that generate legal and unauthorized migration in the countries of origin – emigration pressures created by lack of economic opportunities, population pressure, political factors or emigration aspirations brought about by more information of opportunities outside – apply to trafficking as well. There could be a difference. Although poverty is generally perceived as a push factor for migration, it is not a sufficient condition for migration. As suggested by research findings, the poor are not the ones who migrate because migration requires resources.[15] In trafficking, however, the poor can be specifically targeted by traffickers because of their vulnerability. Studies have documented that traffickers time their recruitment of migrants for when families are economically vulnerable and their pitch of better opportunities elsewhere is well received.[16] Unlike legal or unauthorized migration, wherein migrants have to pay for the services of intermediaries, traffickers either pay the victim's family or do not charge a fee when they offer promises of a better life. Later, victims realize that the advance money (as well as transportation costs, meals and accommodations) has to be repaid, trapping them in debt bondage.[17]

As preconditions for migration (including trafficking), the macro factors described above may directly or indirectly affect migration. The indirect effects will have to operate through proximate variables, of which migration policies are an important part. If migration policies in the origin and destination countries provide avenues for legal migration, unauthorized migration and trafficking are likely to be reduced.

The demand-side factors or processes in the destination countries are also similar across the different migration regimes. If there are emigration pressures operating in the countries of origin, demographic and economic factors create the demand for migrants in the more developed countries of destination. If migration policies are not congruent with the demand for migrant workers, this discrepancy could result in unauthorized migration or trafficking. Demand is actually more critical in migration than supply-side factors. It is the unmet demand for migrant workers in the destination countries, combined with the large pool of potential migrants in many countries of origin and the interventions of intermediaries (both legal and unauthorized, including traffickers), that promotes unauthorized migration, including trafficking. While unauthorized migration largely addresses labour shortage in the destination countries, trafficking not only addresses some of this but also responds to other shortages – e.g. shortage in brides, shortage in babies and shortage in organs.

As in legal and unauthorized migrations, various actors and institutions participate as intermediaries in trafficking. The role of the migration industry (recruitment agencies, brokers and their related businesses which have a formal structure) in Asian migration has been described as unique to the region. These players emerge to connect workers and employers in this vast and diverse setting. While there are legitimate agencies which must apply for a licence to operate and are regulated by governments, there are illegal entities, including smugglers, traffickers and syndicates, whose operations fall outside government regulation. There are also legal or licensed agencies which engage in irregular practices, and which may also interface with the various illegal entities. The participation of intermediaries in the migration industry has increased the costs of migration for migrants. The costs are not only financial but also increased vulnerabilities and risks to migrants when intermediaries launch them into unauthorized or trafficking routes.

In extending the framework to human trafficking, it is useful to view migration in phases or moments. As noted earlier, the notion of the migrant as "legal" at *all* points of the migration process – from exit in the origin country to entry, residence and engagement in economic activity in the destination – and its converse, the migrant as "unauthorized" or "trafficked" at *all* points, are just subsets of the migrant population. Migrants may move from one regime to another, but when it comes to trafficked persons their limited mobility and rights may restrict the possibility of securing legal status compared to unauthorized migrants. What is important to recognize here is that not all trafficked persons were necessarily trafficked when they started their migration history (some may have started out as legal migrants, but became trafficked persons at some point). Conversely, even if migrants were not trafficked and even if they were legal migrants, their conditions may have trafficking elements. The framework will have to address the consequences for migrants, as this is important in clarifying the ambiguities and possible overlaps between trafficking and migration. A consideration of the consequences will also shift the perspective to the conditions of migrants, particularly the common sources of vulnerabilities migrants face across the different migration regimes.

A legal migration regime primarily means compliance with state regulations on the exit, entry, residence and work of migrants – but it stops short of regulating their working and living conditions. Where migration regulations are concerned, the state is very much felt, but when the focus shifts to migrants' rights, the state somehow recedes to the background. This rights gap has given rise to abusive conditions attendant to migration, including legal migration. Migrants can thus be placed in a hierarchy in terms of the protection of basic rights: legal migrants are generally better protected, unauthorized migrants are less protected and trafficked persons are generally most vulnerable. Furthermore, between unauthorized migrants and trafficked persons, states view the former as immigration violators (who must be punished) and the latter as victims (who must be protected). In the Asian context, the premise of legal migration does not guarantee safe working and living conditions for migrants. Although legal migration entails state regulations, these regulations are focused on controlling migrants and keeping migration temporary. Migrants are admitted to the receiving country as workers; as workers who cannot change sector or employer, or when they do, they become unauthorized migrant workers. State regulations on the migration industry and employers are weak or absent, which opens a plethora of abuses and violations that can be committed against migrants. Thus, even if a worker were a legal migrant, his or her recruitment (e.g. use of fraud and deception) and working and living conditions may have trafficking elements. Some of the common violations which suggest elements of trafficking are withholding of information on actual wages, work and conditions, withholding of passports (which puts migrant workers under the greater control of their employers), contract substitution (which is fraudulent and deceptive) and difficult working conditions (long working hours, delayed payment or non-payment of wages, physical abuse, sexual abuse – conditions which resemble slavery or servitude). *Legal* women migrants in the domestic work and entertainment sectors are particularly vulnerable to these trafficking-like conditions because these sectors are generally not covered by labour laws or policies are poorly enforced.

Unauthorized migrant workers generally earn less, do not enjoy benefits and do not have access to redress and grievance. According to unauthorized migrants, they do not feel free to move about for fear they will be apprehended and repatriated. Again, in the case of unauthorized migration, trafficking elements are present in terms of the abusive and exploitative conditions experienced by migrants. Although unauthorized migrant workers experience much insecurity, they have some freedoms compared to trafficked persons.[18] The latter are subjected to more control, intimidation and exploitation than unauthorized migrants. Isolation and confinement in the case of some trafficked persons (e.g. those trafficked for prostitution in brothels) cut them off from support systems and services.

To sum up, there are parallels across the different migration regimes in terms of root causes, preconditions and intermediaries. The framework attempts to explain how migrants are channelled into different migration regimes, which is an important part of the puzzle. To be able to address trafficking adequately, the framework needs to incorporate the consequences for migrants as they go through the different stages (pre-migration, travel, arrival, post-arrival and repatriation) under different migration regimes. Accounting for consequences is critical because it helps clarify the ambiguities and parallels between migration and trafficking. Gender dimensions, governance issues, the participation of non-state actors and the specification of how factors and processes operate at different levels must also be considered in extending the framework to account for trafficking as well.

Human trafficking in East and South-East Asia

Identified as a "hotspot" of trafficking, there has been a surge of research on trafficking in the Asian region, particularly South-East Asia, generating considerable information on the scale and routes of trafficking, the *modus operandi* of traffickers, the profile of victims and purposes for which they are recruited and transported, based on accounts provided by trafficked persons. Thorough reviews of data and research on trafficking in South-East and East Asia have been undertaken by Piper and Lee, respectively.[19] A recent article by Marshall also provides an informative summary of the state of trafficking research in the region.[20] Derks, Henke and Vanna examined a decade of research of trafficking in persons in Cambodia.[21] These are the sources of the summary description provided below.

In South-East Asia the Mekong region – Burma (Myanmar), Cambodia, Laos, Thailand, Viet Nam and Yunnan in China – has received the most research and advocacy attention. Of this cluster, Thailand is the destination of most countries of origin in the subregion, and is a transit and destination country for migrants from other regions. Thailand is also a country of origin of women trafficked for prostitution to Japan and Western countries. Cambodia is a country of origin in relation to Thailand; at the same time it is a destination of women and children from Viet Nam who are trafficked for prostitution. Women from Viet Nam have also been trafficked to China for marriage.[22] Trafficked persons to Thailand are mostly women and children from Burma, Cambodia, Laos and Yunnan, mainly for the purpose of forced prostitution or domestic work. Children are trafficked for begging; there are also some reports of children being trafficked for adoption. Although men have not figured in studies on trafficking, work on unauthorized migration and general migration suggests that men may be in traffic-like situations in the fishing industry; men and women may also be trafficked for forced labour in sweatshops, plantations and construction.

Trafficking research in the Malay peninsula has not been as intense as in the Mekong region. Indonesia and the Philippines are classified mostly as countries of origin of trafficked persons, but since most migrants from these countries are migrant workers, trafficking involves mostly cases of labour exploitation, particularly among domestic workers. The case of entertainers from the Philippines is discussed in more detail in a separate section. Concerns about the well-being of Filipino women participating in international marriages urged the Philippines to pass the 1990 Anti-Mail Order Bride Law which prohibits the operation of mail-order services and similar practices in the Philippines. This was later revised to include the operations of internet-based services, which are considered trafficking under the 2003 Anti-Trafficking in Persons Act. Malaysia's involvement with trafficking is discussed in relation to unauthorized migration and the traffic-like conditions of unauthorized migrants (and even legal migrants, too). Reports of foreign women – from China and neighbouring countries – apprehended for prostitution hints at some trafficking activities. The city-state of Singapore has managed to control unauthorized migration, but the government's *laissez-faire* attitude towards foreign domestic workers has resulted in harsh conditions reminiscent of those experienced by trafficked persons – no days off, debt bondage and long working hours, among others.[23]

In East Asia, Japan's recruitment of entertainers has been at the centre of most discussions on human trafficking. The legal framework for admitting entertainers to Japan has been seen by critics as veiled prostitution. The heavy involvement of organized crime in Japan's sex industry has fanned concerns of women being forced into prostitution as well as the direct involvement of organized crime in the trafficking of women for prostitution. The Philippines is one of a few select countries with which Japan has an agreement to recruit entertainers legally. Many women from other countries are trafficked to Japan. In Korea the trafficking of women is also linked to the sex industry. As in Japan, the legal channel to enter Korea as an entertainer does not provide protection for workers. In response to the shortage of brides, agencies and marriage brokers (including internet-based companies) have emerged to find foreign brides for men based in the rural areas. Taiwan used to be a major source country of women trafficked to Japan, but the pattern stopped when its economy improved. Concerns about trafficking in Taiwan have less to do with the sex sector as the working and living conditions of migrant workers in general, and those in the domestic work and care-giving sectors in particular. International marriages have increased significantly in Taiwan, and some elements of trafficking may be involved in bringing in foreign brides, mostly from Viet Nam. Among the countries in the subregion, China alone is classified as a country of origin. Since China's entry into international migration from the late 1970s, irregular migration/trafficking has touched off concerns of an impending wave of such migration/trafficking from this demographic giant. According to Skeldon, one must consider that international migration is highly localized, mostly originating from Guangdong, Zhegiang and Fujian.[24] In particular, much irregular migration originates from Changle and Fuzhou cities in Fujian province. More data are needed to ascertain the "threat" of massive irregular migration/trafficking from China.

Despite the growth of the research literature on trafficking, some fundamental problems remain. Attempts to quantify the phenomenon have not met with much success. There is also the continuing problem of identifying trafficked persons, which is the starting point in designing interventions to curb the practice.[25] Trafficking research has been funding-driven, i.e. it developed to meet the information needs of funding and implementing agencies for developing counter-trafficking interventions. When the implementing agency is also the one carrying out the research, the research process may be compromised. The action-oriented thrust of many research projects has slowed down the development of concepts and approaches that would clarify the nature and dynamics of trafficking. The association of trafficking with women and children has been perpetuated in part by the focus of trafficking research on these groups. A study of migrant workers in different sectors may not only uncover trafficking in men and boys but could also enhance a gender analysis of trafficking across different labour markets or sectors.

The site of trafficking research thus far has been mostly in countries of origin, which also draws much more attention to supply-side factors and processes. Further research will have to address demand-side factors and processes, inasmuch as the exploitation of trafficked persons (and migrants in general) takes place in the destination countries.

Estimates of trafficking

For all the research efforts that have been undertaken, accurate basic information on trafficking – i.e. volume and basic demographic profiles of trafficked persons – is elusive.[26] Estimates are not lacking, but they are as variable (and wild) as the sources which produce them. The UNESCO regional office in Bangkok initiated a statistics project which aimed to collate data on trafficking and document their sources. The latter task is important because often there are no explanations about how these estimates were derived. The numbers are usually presented as aggregate estimates which do not provide indications of domestic versus international trafficking, nor the gender and age profile of those who have been trafficked. The dangers of this practice are described by the UNESCO Trafficking Statistics Project as follows:

> Numbers take on a life of their own, gaining acceptance through repetition, often with little inquiry into their derivations. Journalists, bowing to the pressures of editors, demand numbers, any numbers. Organizations feel compelled to supply them, lending false precisions and spurious authority to many reports.[27]

An examination of worldwide estimates of the annual flow of people trafficked from 1999 to 2003 revealed varying numbers by source. At one point there were an estimated 4 million people who had been trafficked.[28] For 2002–2006 the US State Department's *Trafficking in Persons* reports provide widely quoted statistics on trafficked persons (i.e. severe cases of trafficking, such as sexual exploitation). The figures are as follows: 2002 – 700,000–4 million; 2003 – 800,000–900,000; and from 2004 to 2006 the numbers went down to 600,000–800,000.[29] Trafficked women and children in South-East Asia are estimated at 200,000–225,000, which is about a third of the low end (600,000) of trafficked persons worldwide. Women and children from South-East Asia comprise 60 per cent – 30,000 – of those trafficked to the United States; most of the trafficking, however, is within the region.[30]

While there is a great deal of global attention to international trafficking and huge resources have been mobilized into anti-trafficking interventions, little has been said or done about internal trafficking. One issue that needs to be clarified is the extent of international versus domestic trafficking. Less than 3 per cent of the world's population live outside their countries of birth, hence the overwhelming majority of the world's people do not cross international borders. Much more mobility takes place within national borders, especially short-term movements. It follows that quite possibly there is more internal than international trafficking, and yet domestic trafficking does not merit as much attention.

Where are the trafficked men and children?

Although the purposes of trafficking are no longer confined to prostitution and/or sexual exploitation, most studies report that these are still the major purposes. Not surprisingly, women and children (often the data do not distinguish between the two) are usually profiled as trafficked persons. Methodological considerations, particularly the selection of respondents, are crucial in this regard. If respondents were interviewed from shelters, most likely these are victims who have been rescued, and they may fit a certain profile. Likewise, a focus on the sex sector is likely to identify more women (and children as well) than men as trafficked persons.

If men are relatively absent from trafficking studies, they are very much part of the picture in unauthorized migration. In South-East Asia, for example, unauthorized migrants from the Philippines were equally divided between men and women;[31] those from Indonesia tended to be mostly men;[32] and Burmese migrants to Thailand were mostly men in an inland province and mostly women in a border province.[33] In Thailand, while there are many reports pointing to the trafficking of Burmese women and girls, men are frequently referred to as unauthorized migrants. Similarly, in Indonesia women and girls are trafficked, but men are "just" unauthorized migrants. Trafficked men seem to figure more in trafficking from China. Questions must be asked. What accounts for the persisting representation of women in trafficking and of men in unauthorized migration? To what extent are these representations influenced by gendered views of migration – i.e. of women as "passive" migrants and "victims" and of men as "autonomous" migrants and actors/agents?

While the trafficking of children is generally accepted as significant in volume, estimates are not readily available. Because most estimates rarely provide breakdowns by gender and age, there are few statistics on trafficked children. The tendency to report the trafficking of children *and* women jointly may have unfortunate consequences. The intent may be to underscore the greater vulnerabilities faced by women and children, but it can also perpetuate a view of women as children while children do not receive due attention. The International Labour Organization's International Programme to Eliminate Child Labour has contributed to increasing awareness of the possibility that a significant part of child labour (across various work sectors, not just the sex industry) may involve trafficked children. For example, in the Philippines, according to an NGO, more migrant children (including those who had been trafficked) are in forced or hazardous labour conditions than in prostitution.[34]

Who are the traffickers?

A mapping out of the origin, transit and destination points of trafficking in East and South-East Asia reveals that a large part involves individuals and networks in this human trade, more like "cottage industries", as Phil Marshall described the situation in the Mekong region.[35] References to organized crime come up in East Asia (specifically the *yakuza*'s hold over the sex industry) or when long-distance international migration is involved (e.g. the case of Chinese trafficked to Western countries).

Cottage industry traffickers

Based on patterns of regular and unauthorized migrations, it is reasonable to suggest that cross-border flows are dominant in trafficking in the region. In four-country research on unauthorized migration in South-East Asia, findings underscored that with the exception of the Philippines,[36] most unauthorized migration takes place within the region, and specifically between contiguous areas.[37] Note, for example, the large numbers of Indonesian migrants in Malaysia and of Burmese migrants in Thailand.[38] Likewise, in South Korea the largest numbers of unauthorized migrants are ethnic Koreans from China.

As mentioned earlier, cross-border trafficking is intense in the Mekong region, with Thailand as the major destination of women, children and men trafficked from Burma, Cambodia, Laos, Viet Nam and Yunnan (China). In peninsular South-East Asia, Malaysia, Singapore and Brunei are the major destinations of migrants, mostly coming from neighbouring South-East Asian countries and some from South Asia. While unauthorized migration and trafficking are relatively under control in Singapore and Brunei, Malaysia grapples with a large population of unauthorized migrants. Currently there are some 2.0–2.4 million migrants in Malaysia, of whom at least half are unauthorized. The public discussion about migration in Malaysia centres on unauthorized migration, mostly pertaining to Indonesians in west Malaysia and to Filipinos and Indonesians in east Malaysia. If there is discussion about trafficking, it is usually associated with prostitution. It is possible that some unauthorized migration is actually trafficking.[39] The reported conditions of migrant workers, both authorized and unauthorized, have trafficking elements, except that they are discussed in terms of "migrant worker problems" rather than trafficking. In East Asia cross-border trafficking is also significant in the areas adjoining Viet Nam and China. Much cross-border unauthorized migration, and possibly trafficking, occurs through the movement of ethnic Koreans from China to South Korea.

History and geography underpin these cross-border flows. The long history of migration in the border areas and their proximity to each other – between Burma and Thailand, Yunnan (China) and Thailand, Indonesia and Malaysia, Western Mindanao (Philippines) and Sabah (east Malaysia), Viet Nam and Cambodia, Viet Nam and China and the border areas of China and Korea – lend themselves to the circulation of people. Proximity is also more than just geographical. In many cases these areas also share a history and culture that pre-date the rise of nation-states and national borders.

In these areas there are well-placed and long-established networks spanning the borders. These transnational (or transborder) networks include family members and friends, former migrants, transport-related personnel (i.e. bus drivers, conductors and porters; shipping personnel), border police and officials, local crime syndicates and local government officials. Those who engage in trafficking are not regarded as traffickers by potential migrants, but rather as people providing assistance. Again, the distinction between unauthorized migration and trafficking in the border areas is blurred. Some of those who are reported to be trafficked may actually be migrants who crossed to the other side of the border without any travel or work documents.

The migration industry and organized crime

Unlike cross-border flows, interregional migration most likely involves the participation of more formal organizations (such as recruitment agencies, travel agencies, immigration consultants, etc.) and/or transnational organized crime groups.[40] While travel documents may be avoided in cross-border flows, they are necessary in international migrations that span long distances. This is where the migration industry (both legal and illegal), traffickers and smugglers enter the picture as "facilitators" – i.e. as suppliers of forged or fraudulent documents, as escorts for migrants or trafficked persons or in arranging travel routes that would not invite the scrutiny of state authorities. There could also be collusion between legal establishments and illegal entities in these operations.

Beyond exit and entry requirements, the post-migration scenario includes other phases and other actors or institutions which can expose migrants to abuse and exploitation: the workplace, employers, husbands, law enforcers, etc. When organized crime groups are involved, their control over migrants can be encompassing, as cases of Fujian Chinese trafficked to Western countries highlight. The distance and the sometimes circuitous routes entailed in transporting migrants expose them to the control of various characters in the smuggling/trafficking chain – snakeheads, transporters, guides, enforcers, support personnel, safe-house operators, collectors.[41] Organized crime, the *yakuza*, has been implicated in the legal migration of foreign entertainers to Japan; its role is believed to be greater in unauthorized migration and trafficking in women.

The involvement of the state

The role of the state in trafficking is not readily evident. In East and South-East Asia "managing" migration generally does not extend to protecting the rights of migrant workers. This hands-off policy with respect to migrants' rights does not promote safe and orderly conditions for migrants, and instead breeds abuse and exploitation that can be qualified as trafficking. The policy also suggests that the legal avenues for migration do not guarantee decent working and living conditions for migrants.

The legal migration of entertainers is an example that implicates the state as a player in the trafficking of women (who make up the great majority of entertainers). The entertainment market is very specific to Japan and South Korea (other destination countries do not issue work permits to entertainers). These two countries have increasingly turned to other countries to meet the demand for women workers in this sector.[42] The demand is met through both legal and unauthorized channels, including trafficking.[43] Legal entertainers to Japan are mostly from the Philippines. As agreed by the two countries, entertainers (officially known in the Philippines as overseas performing artists) are admitted to Japan as guest artists on a three-month contract, which can be extended to six months. This has been going on since the late 1970s. Until recently, annual deployment to Japan has been in the vicinity of 70,000, of whom the great majority are entertainers.[44] While Japan has a policy of not admitting less-skilled workers, it is open to the migration of professionals and the highly skilled (which includes entertainers). For its part, the Philippines introduced a system of screening Japan-bound entertainers. To professionalize the industry and separate the legitimate entertainers from non-entertainers (i.e. those who get into the sex industry), aspiring entertainers must go through 90 days of training and pass a test before they can be issued with an artist's record book. However, despite these processes and the mantle of legal migration, Filipino entertainers in Japan do not perform but rather work in bars as hostesses. The line between plain hostessing and prostitution is sometimes very thin. The pressures to engage in prostitution are strong, with such practices as the *dohan* (dates) or the quotas imposed on the women to bring in a certain number of customers. Women's passports are taken from them, they are guarded and their salaries are not given until they have completed their contracts. This is to ensure that they do not run away or change clubs. Reports of violence and a slip into prostitution are not uncommon.[45]

In 2004 the Japanese government introduced several measures to address the recruitment of women entertainers. The long-running criticism and protest by domestic and international groups against this practice gained momentum when the US State Department's *Trafficking in Persons Report in 2004* placed Japan on the Tier 2 watchlist.[46] By December 2004 the Interministerial Liaison Committee, after consultations in the Philippines and Thailand, came up with an action plan to combat trafficking in persons. A stricter policy for the issuance of entertainers' visas was enforced in 2005. The policy required two years of study in the performing arts or two years' experience outside Japan; this requirement did away with the artist's record book specified by the Philippine government. The impact of this new policy on the volume of migration from the Philippines is highly remarkable. In 2004 deployment of Filipino workers to Japan stood at 74,480; in 2005 the numbers went down to 42,586, or a 43 per cent decline compared to 2004. It is too early to tell whether this decline will continue in the long haul. It is also possible that more restrictions will diminish the volume of legal migration but will increase unauthorized migration, including trafficking.[47]

The migration of entertainers to South Korea started in the 1990s and is much smaller in scale than that to Japan. The Philippines and Russia are the two major source countries for entertainers, who enter Korea via E6 visas. According to reports, there is a high degree of deception and fraud in the recruitment of women. As in Japan, women are under surveillance by club owners. Their passports are taken from them, they survive on a meagre meal allowance, they work long hours and there are many reports of women being forced into prostitution.[48] In part the trafficking of Filipino women to South Korea is linked to the presence of US military bases there.

The involvement of governments in legal entertainer migration implicates them in the trafficking chain. It also raises the question of whether legal or unauthorized migration and trafficking really makes a difference in the protection of women workers in this sector. Trafficking of women in the sex-related industry may be "obvious" and the connection between trafficking and abuse may be appreciated more easily. However, this association can lead to assumptions that all women in the entertainment sector have been trafficked and are abused. Furthermore, the abuse and exploitation of other migrant workers in other sectors, including legal ones, may be obscured and not recognized as forced labour or servitude.

Regional initiatives and responses

Unauthorized migration and trafficking (especially trafficking) have provided a launching pad for regional discussions on migration. The economic crisis of 1997 highlighted the magnitude of unauthorized migration in Asia and was instrumental in starting regional discussions on migration. Some steps towards this started with the Manila Process and the Asia-Pacific Consultation, but action was mostly informal. The momentum for regional discussion picked up with a conference on irregular migration and trafficking in Bangkok in 1999, which drew up a regional plan of action to combat unauthorized migration and trafficking in the region. This was followed by the Asian Regional Initiative against Trafficking, or ARIAT, in 2000 (jointly organized by the United States and the Philippines), and the Bali Meeting in 2002 (jointly organized by Australia and Indonesia). Governments are willing to cooperate and to discuss unauthorized migration and trafficking, but are extremely reticent about discussing legal migration. The issue of national security and the threat of international terrorism, a fallout from the 9/11 attacks, provided the rallying points to step up the discussions on unauthorized migration and trafficking. The plans of action that have been identified in these discussions typically focus on border control, data-sharing and a to-do list of programmes and activities directed at the "3Ps and 1R" – prevention of trafficking (mainly through information-education programmes), protection of trafficking victims, prosecution of traffickers and repatriation of victims of trafficking.

NGOs, networks and international organizations have been active in counter-trafficking efforts. The early anti-trafficking work of NGOs was focused on prostitution and sexual exploitation, with women and children as the primary targets of these efforts – examples are the Coalition against Trafficking in Women (CATW), ECPAT International (End Child Prostitution in Asian Tourism) and Save the Children. The Global Alliance against Traffic in Women (GAATW), an umbrella organization of women's community-based groups around the world, also focuses on trafficked women and girls. Sex tourism was and continues to be a major component of anti-trafficking advocacy. In the 1990s the issue of trafficking became intertwined with migration (because trafficked persons cross national borders), human rights, health (particularly in relation to HIV/AIDS) and child labour (which coincided with the International Labour Organization's focus on the elimination of child labour). UN agencies – UNICEF, UNESCO, the UNHCR, UNIFEM, ESCAP and the ILO – and the International Organization for Migration have been active in research, advocacy and supporting anti-trafficking programmes.

South-East Asia has been the focus of these activities, especially the

Mekong subregion. Many of these initiatives were introduced in the 1990s. In East Asia, China is about the only country where various anti-trafficking programmes have been introduced (Yunnan has been incorporated in the Mekong subregion programmes). Domestic NGOs, including faith-based organizations, in Hong Kong, Japan, South Korea and Taiwan are working on or cooperating with anti-trafficking efforts. In South Korea, for example, many local NGOs provide services to women and children in international marriages and advocate for policy changes.

In East and South-East Asia notable progress has been made in the area of legislation. Thailand, the Philippines, South Korea and Burma have passed anti-trafficking laws. Thailand had passed such laws – the Prostitution Prevention and Suppression Act B.E. 2536 (1996) and the Measures in Prevention and Suppression of Trafficking in Women and Children Act B.E. 2540 (1997) – prior to its ratification of the Trafficking Protocol. The Philippines enacted the Anti-Trafficking in Persons Act (Republic Act 9208) in 2003. South Korea's 2004 Act on the Punishment of Intermediating in the Sex Trade and Associated Acts specifically prohibits trafficking in persons, including debt bondage and related practices. In 2005 Burma passed the Anti-Trafficking in Persons Law, which bans human trafficking and provides for life imprisonment for traffickers. The enactment of anti-trafficking laws is a major step in defining trafficking as a crime, protecting victims and punishing traffickers. However, not all these laws are comprehensive – e.g. Burma's anti-trafficking law is strong on trafficking for prostitution but is silent on trafficking for forced labour. Where anti-trafficking laws have not been enacted, governments employ relevant provisions in existing laws (penal code, child welfare/protection, labour, immigration) to aid victims and prosecute traffickers. For example, Cambodia's law on Suppression of the Kidnapping, Trafficking and Exploitation of Human Beings (1996) has been used in anti-trafficking investigations while the draft law is still under review by the National Assembly. To date, Cambodia and Indonesia have draft anti-trafficking laws which have yet to be passed. Government efforts to enact anti-trafficking laws can be interpreted as one of the impacts of the Trafficking Protocol. Four countries in the region have ratified the protocol – Burma, Laos, the Philippines and Thailand – and four more have signed it – Japan, South Korea, Cambodia and Indonesia. The same number had also ratified the Smuggling Protocol: Cambodia, Laos, Malaysia and the Philippines (table 8.1). The region's scorecard in ratifying and signing the Trafficking Protocol compares favourably with its record in ratifying other international instruments on forced labour and children's rights, and is better than its ratification record with respect to the Migrant Workers Convention, which was ratified by the Philippines and Timor Leste and signed by Indonesia.[49]

Table 8.1 Status of ratification of trafficking and migration instruments

	Trafficking Protocol	Smuggling Protocol	Migrant Workers	Child Labour	Forced Labour	Child Prostitution and Pornography	Children in Armed Conflict
East Asia							
People's Republic of China				X	X	S	
Japan	S			X	X	X	X
Mongolia					X	X	X
Republic of Korea	S			X	X	X	
North Korea					X	X	X
South-East Asia							
Burma	X(a)						
Brunei Darussalam					X		
Cambodia	S	X		X	X	X	X
Indonesia	S		S	X	X	S	S
Laos	X(a)	X		X	X		
Malaysia		X			X		
Philippines	X	X	X	X	X	X	X
Singapore				X	X		X
Thailand	X			X		X(a)	X(a)
Timor Leste			X			X(a)	X(a)
Viet Nam				X		X	X

Notes

"S" signifies signature only, which is a preliminary step to ratification, whereby a state agrees to be legally bound by the terms of a particular convention; "X" signifies ratification, whereby a state agrees to be legally bound by the terms of a particular convention; and "X(a)" signifies accession to the instrument, which implies that a state has ratified a convention, the convention's standards are incorporated into national law and the country becomes a state party to the convention.

The instruments are: Protocol to Prevent, Suppress and Punish Trafficking in Persons, Especially Women and Children and Protocol against the Smuggling of Migrants by Land, Sea and Air (both protocols are supplements to the 2000 UN Convention against Transnational Organized Crime); UN Convention on the Rights of All Migrant Workers and Members of Their Families; ILO Convention No. 182, Elimination of Worst Forms of Child Labour; ILO Convention No. 29, Forced Labour; Optional Protocol to the Convention on the Rights of the Child on the Sale of Children, Child Prostitution and Child Pornography; and Optional Protocol to the Convention on the Rights of the Child in Armed Conflict.

Source: Data on the ratification of the UN Migrant Workers Convention are from UN Department of Economic and Social Affairs, Population Division, *International Migration 2006*, New York: UNDESA, 2006, available at www.unpopulation.org.; the rest are from US State Department, *Trafficking in Persons Report 2006*, Washington, D.C.: US State Department.

What is next?

The global attention directed at trafficking has definitely created some awareness about it, but more awareness and educational campaigns are needed to go beyond a simplistic appreciation of such a complex phenomenon. Thanks to the initiative and support of international organizations, governments in the region are taking concrete steps to support the global campaign to combat trafficking. More significantly, discussions on trafficking and how to counter it have been elevated to the bilateral and regional levels, a remarkable development in a region where a supranational approach to migration is in its early stages.

The momentum of bilateral and regional discussions on trafficking must be sustained. The action plans that have been drafted in various meetings can serve as a benchmark in assessing what has been done, what needs to be done and lessons learned from past practices and approaches. These discussions can also be expanded to include reflections on trafficking in relation to unauthorized migration and legal migration. These three modalities of human mobility must be seen as part of one migration system, which calls for a more integrated approach. In other words, a segmented and separate approach to trafficking, unauthorized migration and legal migration is likely to be counterproductive.

It is high time to devote more attention to the demand side of factors and processes of trafficking. For a long time many of the efforts at curbing trafficking emphasized preventive measures, typically awareness campaigns that discourage migration. Instead of solely focusing on stopping the flow of people at the very source, the conditions at the other end of the migration equation have to be addressed. Marshall has noted that the approach and message of trafficking awareness have changed – rather than discouraging migration, the message of more recent campaigns provides information on the legal and safe channels of migration.[50] This will make sense if states in the origin and destination countries will commit themselves to expanding the legal channels of migration and making available support services to migrants, particularly in destination countries where migrant workers are considered people of a lesser kind than nationals. The protection and promotion of the rights of migrants, regardless of their migration status, will have to be a necessary component to manage migration.

Notes

1. United Nations, *International Migration and Development: Report of the Secretary-General*, 60th Session, agenda item 54(c), "Globalization and interdependence: International migration and development", New York: United Nations, 2006, p. 12.

2. Estimated by the UN Population Division, available at http//esa.un.org/migration/ p2k0data.asp.

3. The distinctions as well as the overlaps between unauthorized migration and human trafficking are discussed in a separate section. Estimates of unauthorized migration and human trafficking usually do not qualify to what extent the figures include cases of unauthorized migration or trafficking.

4. International counter-trafficking efforts date back to the first international conference on trafficking of women held in Paris in 1895. A summary of developments and landmarks in this area is discussed in Lynellyn D. Long, "Anthropological Perspectives on the Trafficking of Women for Sexual Exploitation", *International Migration* 42(1): 19–22.

5. International Organization for Migration, *Combating Trafficking in South-East Asia: A Review of Policy and Programme Responses*, IOM Migration Research Series No. 2, Geneva: IOM, 2000.

6. The countries/areas under consideration are China, Hong Kong, Japan, South Korea and Taiwan in East Asia; Brunei, Burma (Myanmar), Cambodia, Indonesia, Laos, Malaysia, the Philippines, Singapore, Thailand and Viet Nam in South-East Asia.

7. For example, see Stephen Castles, "Migration and Community Formation under Conditions of Globalization", *International Migration Review* 36(140): 1143–1168. Transnational communities have been described as "globalization from below" as opposed to "globalization from above" (the globalization that involves multinational corporations, the movement of capital, etc.).

8. Social networks help explain the persistence of migration flows, even after the original reasons for migration no longer hold. After migration has acquired some history, it gains acceptance and support, and networks and institutions develop to support it. The facilitative role of networks in sustaining migration can be seen in the continuing flows of people despite state restrictions. The greater proportion of unauthorized to legal Indonesian migrants in Malaysia illustrates this. The role of networks in sustaining migration is also demonstrated by findings from a recent study which show that increasingly migrants are relying on their networks – mostly family members and friends – rather than intermediaries to provide information on how to migrate and how to secure jobs in Malaysia. Rianto Adi, "Irregular Migration from Indonesia", in Graziano Battistella and Maruja M. B. Asis, eds, *Unauthorized Migration in Southeast Asia*, Quezon City: Scalabrini Migration Center, 2003.

9. The term "illegal migration" tends to criminalize the migration violations committed by migrants, and obscures the fact that migrants can be victimized by other actors and institutions involved in the migration process, such as intermediaries, employers or states and their representatives/instrumentalities.

10. Migration norms pertain to the exit regulations of the country of origin, and conditions of entry, residence and economic activity of the countries of transit and/or destination. Based on this definition, smuggling, the facilitation of unauthorized entry into another country, is a form of unauthorized migration. Other forms of unauthorized migration in East and South-East Asia are use of a non-working visa to enter a country and then working (and overstaying), overstaying, running away from the employer or sponsor and undocumented migration (not having travel and/or work documents). The last one is common in cross-border flows. See Graziano Battistella and Maruja M. B. Asis, eds, *Unauthorized Migration in Southeast Asia*, Quezon City: Scalabrini Migration Center, 2003.

11. The renewed attention to trafficking coincided with the increasing participation of women in international migration. By the 1980s women were becoming visible as labour

migrants in East and South-East Asia. The concentration of women migrants in domestic work and entertainment, however, raised concerns about the risks and vulnerabilities of female migration. These concerns perhaps may have shaped the representation of female migration as "trafficking" while men engage in "labour migration".

12. Battistella and Asis, note 10 above, pp. 11–13.
13. Ibid. As noted earlier, the study focused on unauthorized migration and tried to maintain a distinction between unauthorized migration and trafficking. However, the experiences of abuse and exploitation by some of the respondents in the country studies reflect traffic-like conditions. It is interesting to note that trafficking has received a great deal of research and advocacy attention compared to unauthorized migration.
14. Graziano Battistella and Maruja M. B. Asis, "Irregular Migration: The Underside of the Global Migrations of Filipinos", in Battistella and Asis, ibid., p. 63.
15. In the initial stages migration is selective of those with more resources – i.e. those with access to funds, information and social capital – but over time, as migration becomes more widespread and more information about it becomes easily available, it becomes less selective. In the Asian context migration does require resources because, among others, recruitment agencies charge job applicants a "placement fee", a service fee for matching them with employers. Marshall presents some cautionary notes on poverty as a "root cause" of trafficking: Phil Marshall, "Raising Our Own Awareness: Getting to Grips with Trafficking in Persons and Related Problems in South-East Asia and Beyond", Asia-Pacific Population Journal 20(3): 143–163 at 150–151.
16. Muhadjir Darwin, Anna Marie Wattie and Susi Eja Yuarsi, eds, Living on the Edges: Cross-Border Mobility and Sexual Exploitation in the Greater Southeast Asia Sub-Region, Yogyakarta: Center for Population and Policy Studies, Gadjah Mada University, 2004, p. 250.
17. In some instances traffickers do not offer anything to the victims or their families – e.g. cases of abduction or kidnapping. On the other hand, reports of migrants paying money to smugglers seem to suggest that "trafficking" targets are not limited to the poor. Although smuggling and trafficking have distinctive characteristics, in reality smuggled persons, despite entering into a consensual transaction with human smugglers, may experience traffic-like conditions in transit and the at the point of destination. Chin details the dangers – beatings, rapes, deaths – that trafficked persons, both men and women alike (although women are fewer), are subjected to while in transit or in safe houses: Ko-Lin Chin, Smuggled Chinese: Clandestine Immigration to the United States, Philadelphia: Temple University Press, 1999.
18. Indonesian migrants in Malaysia, for example, have formed communities or enclaves, drawing vital support from their networks – see Diana Wong and Teuku Afrizal Teuku Anwar, "Migran Gelap: Irregular Migrants in Malaysia's Shadow Economy", in Battistella and Asis, note 10 above. In Thailand unauthorized migrant workers may be joined by their families – see Amorntip Amarapibal, Allan Beesey and Andreas Germershausen, "Irregular Immigration into Thailand", in Battistella and Asis, note 10 above. While unauthorized migrants generally acknowledged that they would be better off if they were in an authorized situation, they also noted they have the freedom to change employers or jobs when better opportunities arise – see Battistella and Asis, note 10 above.
19. June J. H. Lee, "Human Trafficking in East Asia: Current Trends, Data Collection and Knowledge Gaps", International Migration 43(1/2): 165–201; Nicola Piper, "A Problem By a Different Name? A Review of Research on Trafficking in South-East Asia and Oceania", International Migration 43(1/2): 203–233.
20. Marshall, note 15 above.

21. Annuska Derks, Roger Henke and Ly Vanna, *The Review of a Decade of Trafficking in Persons in Cambodia*, Asia Foundation, available at www.asiafoundation.org.pdf/ CB_TIPreview.pdf.
22. There are concerns that international marriages involving women from Viet Nam and men from Taiwan and Korea may have involved the trafficking of women, particularly because marriage brokers in Viet Nam and Korea are actively involved in arranging such marriages for a fee.
23. See Human Rights Watch, *Maid to Order: Ending Abuse of Migrant Domestic Workers in Singapore*, 2005, available at http://hrw.org/reports/2005/singapore1205/5.htm.
24. Ron Skeldon, *Myths and Realities of Chinese Irregular Migration*, IOM Migration Research Series No. 1, Geneva: IOM, 2000.
25. Marshall, note 15 above, p. 156.
26. Lee, note 19 above; Piper, note 19 above; Marshall, note 15 above.
27. Available at www.unescobkk.org/culture/trafficking/ev.asp?ev+833&id=89&pr=86.
28. Available at www.unescobkk.org/fileadm/user_upload/culture/Trafficking/project/ Graph_Worldwide_Sept_2-4.pdf.
29. Liz Kelly, "'You Can Find Anything You Want': A Critical Reflection on Research on Trafficking in Persons within and into Europe", *International Migration* 43(1/2): 239; US Department of State, *Trafficking in Persons Report 2006*, Washington, D.C.: US State Department, 2006.
30. International Organization for Migration, *Combating Trafficking in South-East Asia: A Review of Policy and Programme Responses*, IOM Migration Research Series No. 2, Geneva: IOM, 2000, p. 16.
31. Battistella and Asis, note 10 above.
32. Adi, note 8 above; Wong and Teuku Afrizal, note 18 above.
33. Amarapibal, Beesey and Germerhausen, note 18 above.
34. Interview by the author, April 2004. More information on migrant children and trafficking in women and children in the Philippines is available at www.visayanforum.org.
35. Marshall, note 15 above.
36. As a country of origin, legal and unauthorized migrants from the Philippines migrate beyond South-East Asia and Asia. See Battistella and Asis, note 10 above.
37. Battistella and Asis, note 10 above. Given this pattern, Wong and Teuku Afrizal, note 18 above, suggested that it would be more appropriate to consider these cross-border population flows as regional rather than international migration.
38. Legal migration shows the same pattern – the great majority of legal migrant workers in Malaysia are Indonesians; the rest are Bangladeshis and Filipinos. Similarly in Thailand, most registered migrant workers are Burmese – the rest are Cambodians and Laotians.
39. If abuse and exploitation were the criteria, many unauthorized migrants would be considered trafficked persons.
40. Social networks continue to play a role in interregional migration or more long-distance international migration, mostly by providing information, resources (e.g. money to finance the move) and promises of assistance upon arrival in the destination.
41. Ko-Lin Chin, "The Social Organization of Chinese Human Smuggling", in David Kyle and Rey Koslowski, eds, *Global Human Smuggling: Comparative Perspectives*, Baltimore: Johns Hopkins University Press, 2001. In June 2000 the world was shocked by the report of 58 Chinese nationals who died of suffocation while they were being smuggled into the United Kingdom. The event came to be known as the Dover tragedy, a stark reminder of the dangers of irregular migration.
42. The migration of "exotic dancers" to Canada also implicates the government, similar to the migration of entertainers to Japan and South Korea.

43. Thailand has a huge sex industry, but foreign women in this sector came to the country via unauthorized migration or trafficking.
44. Japan has been one of the top 10 destinations of overseas Filipino workers. It is one of the most highly feminized destinations as entertainers are largely made up of women. There are many other foreign women in Japan's entertainment sector, but they are either in an unauthorized situation or are trafficked into Japan.
45. Nobuki Fujimoto, "Trafficking in Persons and the Filipino Entertainers in Japan", *FOCUS Asia-Pacific News* 43, March 2006, available at www.hurights.org.jp/asiapacific/043-05.html.
46. US State Department, *Trafficking in Persons Report 2004*, Washington, D.C.: US State Department, available at www.state.gov/g/tip/rls/tiprpt/2004/.
47. In addition to tougher requirements for the issuance of entertainer's visas, beginning 1 June 2006, the Japanese government imposed more requirements for employers of foreign entertainers – they must not have been involved in illegal employment or falsified immigration documents in the last five years, and they must have records of at least three years showing that they have paid foreign entertainers at least ¥200,000/month: Fujimoto, note 45 above.
48. Lee, note 18 above.
49. Data on the status of anti-trafficking laws and ratification of the Trafficking Protocol are based on information available as of 31 August 2006. Sources consulted include www.humantrafficking.org and US Department of State, note 29 above.
50. Marshall, note 15 above.

9

Human trafficking in Latin America in the context of international migration

Gabriela Rodríguez Pizarro

Human trafficking from the perspective of the UN Commission on Human Rights special rapporteur on the human rights of migrants

In 1999 the UN Commission on Human Rights nominated a special rapporteur on the human rights of migrants (HRC res. 1999/44), with the mandate to examine the necessary means for overcoming obstacles to the full and effective protection of the human rights of all migrants.

Since then, and in conformity with this mandate, the special rapporteur solicits and receives information from all pertinent sources on human right violations of migrants, wherever they occur; formulates recommendations in order to impede and remedy these situations; promotes the application of standing legislation on the subject; and recommends activities and applicable measures for the elimination of these violations against migrants.

In addition, visits have been made *in situ* when there are situations that should be investigated about a particular country. Denunciations are received of alleged violations against the human rights of migrant workers. The special rapporteur presents annual reports to the UN Commission on Human Rights in Geneva and the General Assembly in New York, and also presents rapports of her official visits to different countries[1] and the denouncements or allegations that have taken root during the year. Characteristics of those migrants who are especially exposed to violations

Trafficking in humans: Social, cultural and political dimensions, Cameron and Newman (eds), United Nations University Press, 2007, ISBN 978-92-808-1146-9

of their human rights and of situations that produce grave human rights abuses have been identified.

In the resolution from which this mandate originated and developed, bilateral and regional negotiations are recommended. These recommendations have begun to address the return and reinsertion of migrants who do not possess documents or are migrating under irregular administrative conditions. The HRC also mandated the establishment of criteria, strategies and recommendations for the promotion and application of policies in favour of the protection of the human rights of migrants.

Latin American countries possess similar characteristics in the context of international migration and trafficking in persons. Many of them are countries of origin, transit and destination of migrants. There are strong migratory movements in the South American regions, for example, as well as in the Andean regions. Peru, Bolivia, Ecuador and Colombia are countries characterized by an important movement of their population to different countries of the world. An important migratory movement to countries of the North characterizes Central America, but there are also a large number of Nicaraguans in Costa Rica, which responds to historically bi-national migratory phenomena. The countries in the North with the largest quantity of Latin American migrants are the United States, Canada, Spain and Italy. From a regional standpoint the countries of destination for South American migrants are Brazil, Chile and Argentina. Central American countries are countries of origin, transit and destination of migration. Costa Rica, besides being a country of origin for migration to the North, is eminent in the reception of Nicaraguan migrants and Colombian asylum-seekers, as well as a large number of irregular migrants.

The different resolutions from the UN Commission on Human Rights[2] recommend that the special rapporteur, as an independent expert of the United Nations, assumes as part of her mandate responsibility for trafficking in persons within the framework of international migration. Since the beginning of the work of the special rapporteur, the phenomenon of human trafficking has become one of the principal subjects of focus, manifested by some of the most atrocious human rights violations.

The conceptual framework used by the mandate is based on the UN Convention against Transnational Organized Crime and its Protocol to Prevent, Suppress and Punish Trafficking in Persons, Especially Women and Children. This protocol creates a definition globally recognizing human trafficking, which allows victims to be identified without ambiguities. Hence it includes an extensive number of offences linked to trafficking in persons. It also establishes global legislation in order to prevent such trafficking and persecute and prosecute those responsible, as well as ensure the protection of their victims. The author maintains that the protocol takes into account a human rights dimension, which is indispensable for the effective protection of victims of trafficking.

All victims of trafficking have rights to this protection, not only those who want to demonstrate they have been forced. In accordance with the dispositions of this protocol, in is not necessary that victims cross a national border in order to be considered victims of trafficking, since the key element in the process is exploitation. Nevertheless, the author has observed a large number of victims of the crime of trafficking in persons who have been registered in a country other than their country of origin.

With the adoption of this protocol, the victims of trafficking are not considered delinquent subjects to be penalized or subsequently deported. The protocol makes it very clear that they are victims of a crime. In Latin America governments have recently ratified the protocols against trafficking and smuggling,[3] but the lack of national laws still presents difficulties in the protection of trafficking victims and they are generally regarded as delinquents.

The author believes trafficking in persons is a category within which three elements are uncovered:
- first, the relationship between the capture, transfer and hosting or receiving of persons
- second, the use of threats, force, abduction, fraud, deceit or other kinds of coercion, resulting in abuse of power or a situation of vulnerability
- third, the end objective is to exploit, whether sexually through prostitution or other kinds of sexual exploitation, or through forced labour and services, slavery or practices analogous to slavery, servitude or extraction of organs.

Trafficking produces practices such as servitude due to debt, forced labour, slavery-like labour conditions, forced prostitution and other forms of sexual exploitation. All of these constitute violations of fundamental human rights, such as the right to dignity and the security of persons, the right to fair and favourable working conditions, the right not to be subjected to slavery or servitude, the right to health and the right to equality.

The mandate has focused on addressing migrants' rights from the perspective that trafficking in persons is not only considered a form of forced migration and a violation of the human rights of migrants, but is also a transnational crime which states have the duty to eradicate. Furthermore, there is a link between trafficking in persons and smuggling of migrants. In Latin America national borders are areas in which migrants involved in smuggling become vulnerable to trafficking.

Structural and proximate variables of human trafficking in Latin America

Trafficking in persons constitutes one of today's most degrading and abusive violations of human rights. The phenomenon of trafficking responds to structural variables and proximate variables, which should be taken into account to achieve an adequate understanding of the phenomenon and consequently an effective and responsible approach.

Structural variables

The structural variables of human trafficking in Latin America are the variables historically focusing on human rights in general and the human rights of international migrants in particular. In the communities of origin in the southern part of South America, the Andean region, Central America, Mexico and the Caribbean, these variables relate to the social and economic exclusion of minorities, national economic underdevelopment, extremely poverty, gender inequality, intrafamily violence, lack of development at the local level, discrimination, xenophobia, impunity, corruption, unemployment and, more recently, transnational organized crime and the lack of control over recruiting agencies.

According to the Economic Commission for Latin America and the Caribbean, it is estimated that approximately 700,000 to 2 million women and children are trafficked each year across international borders. The analysis of these facts observes, with unease, the use of irregular channels of migration of women and unaccompanied minors. Women and children from underdeveloped countries are particularly susceptible to networks of trafficking. The lack of access for women and children to opportunities such as social security, education, health and decent employment reveals the disadvantaged situation of these persons in Latin America.

The structural variables of trafficking in Latin America are related to the historical processes of poverty, economic crises, state dependence on developed countries and scarce opportunities for human development in the local and national spheres. Corruption and the proliferation of networks of transnational organized crime are compounded by the structural variables, which have very powerful economic ramifications. In addition, in South America the internal conflict in Colombia is the cause of massive exits of migrants to bordering countries, Central America, the Caribbean and the United States. In countries where there is internal conflict, almost all citizens exiting the country should be refugees; however, Colombian government statistics show only a limited number of refugees exiting the country in relation to the large number of migrants exiting the country. This suggests that there are many Colombian citizens who are unregistered or in irregular conditions, which has serious implications for the vulnerability of trafficked populations in Latin America.

In Latin American countries the regularization and restriction of migrants' passage through borders are directly related to the numerous women and minors, looking for better life conditions, who cross the borders by irregular or clandestine channels. In the countries of origin, especially in communities with a lack of development options, there is an important presence of traffickers who present the communities with more options and better life conditions. To facilitate the clandestine crossing of borders, migrants pay large sums of money or mortgage their goods and those of their family in the country of origin; very often they are deceived or subjected to debts, which further aids the facilitation and expansion of trafficking in persons.

The main Latin American countries of origin for migration are the Dominican Republic, Mexico, El Salvador, Nicaragua, Guatemala, Honduras, Peru, Brazil, Colombia, Ecuador and Bolivia. In the last five years there has been an increase in the number of women who migrate to the United States, the European Union and Japan as domestic workers, nurses to care for the elderly and some as "entertainers". Men usually migrate alone; they work in construction, agriculture and as hotel-keepers.

Argentina in particular is a country of reception of migrant workers. The bad conditions of Bolivian workers are known in this country. Young Peruvians have been reported in Chile. Similarly, there are many Peruvians in an irregular administrative situation. In Chile young Peruvian migrants work as domestic workers; and there is increasing information on victims of trafficking in erotic clubs in northern Chile.

Peruvian men in Chile are offered work at the Plaza de Armas, a public park in Santiago. This situation is very worrying, since the relationship gives employers absolute power without giving workers any entitlements to social security.

The phenomena of trafficking in persons and smuggling of migrants have only recently been linked to each other. In Latin America migrants who are deceived in order to cross a national border are left unprotected at the other side and are consequently easy targets for the networks of traffickers or smugglers; these provide migrants with hope, as guarantors transporting migrants and promising commercial development, employment or education in the origin countries and local communities.

The law in some Latin American countries punishes as criminal offences or administrative infractions irregular entry, entry without valid documents or engaging in prostitution, including forced prostitution. Victims of trafficking are thus often detained and deported without regard for their victimization and without consideration for the risks they may be exposed to if returned to their country of origin.[4] Colombian, Ecuadorian and Peruvian victims of trafficking have been encountered in detention centres in Italy, Spain and Japan. The author has observed that smuggling may increase the risk of trafficking. Migrants who have recourse to the services of smugglers may find themselves in a position of extreme vulnerability owing to their irregular situation, the debt they may incur in their countries of origin and the impunity with which trafficking and smuggling networks often operate. At times their undocumented status puts them in a situation where contracts are changed or they are forced into degrading and humiliating jobs, often in conditions amounting to slavery. As a result they go from being irregular migrants to being victims of trafficking. In official visits to Mexico, Ecuador, Peru and Colombia, communities of women alone, grandparents with children and men alone have been observed.

Equally worrying is how networks of human traffickers abuse the families of victim migrants. Frequently migrants who cross borders thanks to the services of criminal gangs are subdued in the places of origin by debts that neither they nor their families can pay. The informal networks of lenders benefit, in that many migrants in countries of origin have no formal means of obtaining credit and lenders therefore charge migrants a very high rate of interest (especially cases in Ecuador, Peru, Costa Rica, Mexico and the Dominican Republic).

Networks of transnational organized crime take advantage of the necessities of migrant workers in the countries of destination and the lack of opportunities in the countries of origin, and dedicate themselves to deceiving, intimidating and creating slaved dependency by exploiting the vulnerable position of undocumented migrants. In Latin America national laws penalize undocumented migrants, but are more forbearing with those who participate in networks of trafficking in persons, thus an environment is created that is especially propitious for deceit and exploitation. Victims of trafficking have been found in detention centres for migrants in irregular administrative conditions. Unaccompanied minors travel by means of smugglers, and therefore are easy victims of trafficking.

The needs of migrants and their difficulties in finding work under regular conditions make them easy targets for networks of trafficking in persons, especially when there exists impunity in favour of these networks.

Migration under irregular administrative conditions not only exposes migrants to abuses during the journey, but also determines their rights in the country of destination. Businesses, employers and contractors exploit migrants, paying them inferior wages to those they would pay a foreigner under regular conditions or a national. Moreover, the profits gained by the labour of these migrants are enhanced by a failure to meet social obligations. The clandestine character of these workers and the lack of labour contracts allow the employers to impose abusive work schedules under unacceptable working conditions which put the mental and physical health of migrant workers at risk.

The clandestine character of their employees also offers businesses, employers and contractors without scruples the possibility to threaten migrants with denouncement of their irregular situation in the receiving country, leading to exploitation, forced work and trafficking. In fear of being detained and/or deported, irregular migrants will accept the worst work conditions; they may even end up under conditions of slavery.

Unaccompanied minors who are involved in smuggling networks are clearly victims of trafficking in persons. These minors do not have support from their communities of origin. During a visit to Peru about 300.000 minors without documentation were observed[5] in regions of massive displacement due to internal conflict with the terrorist group Sendero Luminoso. There are problems of basic documentation in Bolivia and Ecuador. In some Latin American countries basic documentation such as identity cards began only 10 years ago. This phenomenon of lack of documentation in the countries of origin and unsuitable identity registration exposes migrant people involved with smugglers to serious risks. In some cases the travel documents are falsified. Even in cases of legal documents (passports), the source documents (identity cards, birth certificates) are easily falsified. This means that false birth certificates can be utilized to gain a legal passport.

Proximate variables

The proximate variables of the phenomenon of trafficking in Latin America are linked to the lack of adequate legislation in the countries of origin, transit and destination, lack of information, lack of documentation, criminalization of victims, impunity of agents of trafficking and unfamiliarity with principal international obligations which countries in Latin America have ratified.

The lack of familiarity with juridical means of emigrating and the risks involved with irregular migration, such as lack of documentation, contributes to the likelihood that migrants fall into the hands of networks which traffic persons. Restrictive and selective migration policies and corruption leave migrants without options other than to cross borders irregularly with the help of criminal networks. In the majority of cases victims of trafficking in persons migrate under inhumane conditions. Many incidents have been reported of the death of migrants when attempting to cross borders through irregular channels (for example the Mexico-US border, from the Dominican Republic to Puerto Rico, from Cuba to Miami and from Ecuador to Central America and Mexico).

Women victims of trafficking are even more vulnerable to abuse. After being deceived in their home countries, they are frequently forced to undertake humiliating work and on some occasions even forced prostitution in the countries of destination. However, as cited in the report submitted to the UN Commission on Human Rights in 2004:

> The Special Rapporteur considers it important to understand that sex work and trafficking do not always go hand-in-hand. As indicated in the definition given in the Protocol, trafficking does not imply only sex work, but can also cover forced or enslaving labour that is not the prostitution of others. Besides, it must be understood that sex work may be a voluntary choice of employment.[6]

This is the case of Colombians, Ecuadorians, Brazilians and Dominicans migrating to Japan, Spain, the Netherlands and the United States.

In Ecuador the practice of *coyotaje*, or illicit traffic of migrants by surface, sea and air, creates acute conditions of vulnerability for the Ecuadorians who leave their country. Moreover, emigrating by irregular means through the system of *coyotaje* is considered the norm, illustrated by trafficking of young and indigenous people from Ecuador, Guatemala and Peru. According to reliable sources, young adults in Ecuador are offered employment in Japan as Spanish instructors or domestic workers. They are transported by boat to Japan, where they are subjected to slavery-like working conditions in the sex industry.

There is much concern regarding the existing networks which sexually exploit minors, taking advantage of unaccompanied minors who arrive at the borders or are deported. The available information concerning the situation of migrant women and minors is alarming: traffickers sexually abuse such migrants as a method of payment. The difficulty in trying to escape from the hands of traffickers, the scarce political protection and the risk of being detained thereafter or unfamiliarity with the language mean that many people opt not to denounce these abuses.

In the origin communities (for example in Ecuador, Peru, Mexico, Honduras and the Dominican Republic), families of migrants who have gone missing suffer, worrying that their relatives have disappeared in the countries of transit. It is extremely difficult to locate migrants who use irregular channels of migration, due to them travelling under false identities of which even their own relatives are unaware. In some cases migrants are detained, judged and sentenced under different names and nationalities than their own, which prevents their families from ever finding them again.

Migrants are tired of the working conditions in their countries of origin, and are thus easily deceived by traffickers and fraudulent recruitment agencies promising them a more dignified future and easy means of making money abroad. Once convinced, migrants are generally transported through irregular channels, without receiving information on a completely unfamiliar destination country – the language, the rules of law, the cultural codes. In these countries, traffickers make the migrants vulnerable; meanwhile these dangerous networks of criminals are treated as common delinquents.

It is particularly troubling that in some countries the business of trafficking in persons remains unpunished and is supported by the participation and corruption of some public officials. It is also troubling that certain countries, such as Panama and Japan, grant special visas to women contracted abroad to work as "animators" or "artists" (entertainers). These permits can also benefit trafficking of women for forced prostitution.

In the struggle against trafficking in persons and in the protection of victims, consular support is vital. By support is meant visits to migrants deprived of their liberty, legal assistance, attendance in situations of accident or health problems and medical or psychological assistance. Nevertheless, it has been possible to observe that embassy and consulate employees often do not have enough resources for the adequate support of their nationals, and in the case of victims of trafficking there is a tendency to classify victims as guilty. This is the case with victims of forced prostitution.

Consular services of Latin American countries are constrained by lack of money (Ecuador, Peru) and do not adequately protect their nationals when they are victims of trafficking; they do not regularly visit, nor provide legal aid from the country of origin. As an example of good practice, in the last few years Mexico has improved access to services and consular protection available to its victims of trafficking.

The victims of trafficking feel trapped between the threats of their exploiters and their irregular administrative condition in the country of reception. This situation means that many victims cannot or dare not denounce the abuses to which they are subjected. And the agents of trafficking not only impose on victims, they also impose on the families of victims. In light of the high vulnerability of migrants to trafficking and their fear of denouncing abuses, the adoption of measures which would guarantee that victims of trafficking are not penalized for their illegal entry into the country and receive adequate protection against possible reprisal due to the involvement of criminal networks is indispensable. Although Mexico has started to support its citizens in the United States and Canada, migrants are still working under slavery-like conditions. The adoption of these protective measures is vital to counter the vulnerability of this group due to fearing the consequences of denouncing abuses.

In many countries (for example Ecuador, Mexico, the border between Mexico and the United States, Canada and Peru) victims of trafficking are penalized for their illegal entrance to or residence in the country. In the majority of cases they are boarded in *ad hoc* centres and afterwards expelled without any guarantee on the security of their repatriation. In many countries the necessary political will to adopt solid measures and legislation to fight against human trafficking and degrading and slavery-like work does not exist.

It is important to reiterate that in Latin America migrant women are of special concern in addressing (the plight of) trafficking in persons. Women in the sex trade generally find themselves exposed to threats, humiliations, physical violence, rape and other sexual abuses, deprivation of their liberties and forced and degrading labour. Also worrying is the case of unaccompanied minors, who are highly vulnerable to trafficking in persons, whether it is to make them work under slavery-like conditions, subject them to sexual exploitation, make them participate in armed conflicts or trade with their organs. It is equally worrying to observe racial discrimination and xenophobia, which accompanies trafficking in persons. There is information on Latin American women victims of trafficking in Mexico, Iran and EU countries such as Italy, Spain, the Netherlands, Belgium, Germany and France. Latin American women are taken to Asia, the United States, Europe, etc. Recently there have been cases of women from Russia, Romania and Eritrea in Latin America, some of whom are victims of trafficking, in administrative detention as irregular migrants.

Dichotomies and tensions with respect to trafficking

Trafficking in persons is related to human and national security, migration management, internal armed conflict and transnational organized crime. All these interactions are interconnected and involved in the discriminatory practices that perpetuate the vulnerability and victimization of persons migrating through irregular channels.

Trafficking in persons with regard to human and national security

The human rights of all persons ought be respected according to the UN Universal Declaration of Human Rights. For this reason, policies that are centred on human security or the security of borders must not undermine human rights during the entire process of migration. Consequently, "security" cannot be used as a pretext when abused victims of trafficking in the predicament of administratively irregular migration are discriminated against.

Thus the protection of human rights of migrants is directly connected to the management of migration, an issue that cannot remain isolated from its context. Neither is it incompatible with sovereignty, which states exercise in order to control their borders and the entrance of people into their territory. States have the sovereign right to regulate entry, length of stay, movement, asylum, refuge and immigration policy; however, this policy must be in accordance with international human rights obligations. Moreover, human security is fundamental, and the right of persons to a dignified and just life does not contradict it.

In Canada there are victims of trafficking from China and the Philippines. Confusion in the implementation of the armour-plating of borders has been observed. This armour-plating is not enough: the situation also requires the coordination of policies, juridical aspects and concrete practices to protect victims of trafficking.

Trafficking in persons and migration management

One has to be very careful with polarizing the vision of human rights and the control of borders. Both factors are important to have in mind during the whole process of migration management. This is as valid for states as for civil society in general. The dichotomy obstructs the protection of victims of human rights abuses; the authorities on migration need to comprehend the phenomena of trafficking in persons and smuggling of migrants in an international context.

It is important to make a distinction between the fight against trafficking in persons and restrictive policies of migration. In addition to being discriminatory, restrictive migration policies only strengthen the use of irregular channels of migration and consequently increase the possibilities of people falling into the hands of trafficking agents.

Trafficking in persons and transnational organized crime

There are a range of difficulties in associating the issue of international terrorism with the phenomenon of migration. One must recognize the strong responsibility that exists to combat terrorism in all its forms and at the same time emphasize the importance of protecting the rights which characterize free and democratic societies.

Many Latin American countries have recently ratified the Convention against Transnational Organized crime and its protocols, but still need to ameliorate their national laws with the ratified international instruments. Moreover, they still have minors trafficked by the clandestine networks.

Terrorism is certainly a major concern, but better intelligence, international community mobilization and exchange of information can coordinate efforts without further victimizing and abusing migrants who have no connection to terrorism. This has been written in the rapports to the UN Commission on Human Rights since the end of 2001.

On several occasions requests have been made not to consider migrants as a category of persons whose rights can be made vulnerable for the simple reason that they are not nationals. Neither can one permit the use of discriminatory policies towards migrants due to their country of origin; states should observe their international obligations in the context of human rights, in particular those pertaining to the non-derogatory rights of all human beings.

It is well known that trafficking in persons violates human rights, such as the rights to free movement, adequate documentation, mental and physical health and education, among others. All this affects victims, turning them into passive subjects, frightened and dependent.

Trafficking in persons and internal armed conflict

In countries of Latin American with internal armed conflict, especially Colombia, we see how armed groups on the margin of the law recruit children and adolescents in order to turn them into soldiers. Many are deceived with false promises, and single parents are even offered money. This is a crime of trafficking in persons. There are few if any formal mechanisms specifically designed to aid these child victims of trafficking. One can only see the actual results of success on average and in the long run.

In Colombia the phenomenon of internal trafficking is manifested by minors working as forced sex workers, child soldiers in forced warfare or paramilitary groups and women working in armed groups.

Myths and realities of trafficking

Interests of power and the international market and trafficking in persons

The developed countries of the North have a large demand for inexpensive human labour. As UN special rapporteur the author has been able to observe and listen directly to high public officials say that they need to produce commodities at lower costs in order to be competitive in the global market, which is why they need "cheap labour" – referring, of course, to undocumented migrants coming from countries of the South. Paradoxically, these interests contradict their own restrictive laws on migration from Southern countries.

The dominant paradigm with which the problem of trafficking in persons can be addressed is not effective if it only refers to legal actions and does not specify attention to the victims. Gender inequity and the myths concerning the role of women ignore the physical, psychological and economic reality of the victim. The patriarchal society with difficulty considers the processes of rehabilitation and integral attention to the trafficked victim within national programmes. Moreover, functionaries have the responsibility for planning and implementing programmes, yet they confuse the problem of trafficking in persons with trafficking of *blancas* (white slavery); that is to say only trafficking of prostitutes.

It is necessary to promote a culture of solidarity and rights, with a deep knowledge of the different aspects of trafficking in persons; for example, the submission by debt in which not only the victim remains bonded/tied, but also their family in the country of origin. It is essential to take into account that many domestic workers are forced into slavery-like work, without time limits, which converts them into a clear example of trafficked victims.

In the same way, the "recruiting agencies" for international employment offer deceitful contracts and misleading promises, a trap into which women and young people in need of employment easily fall. One must not forget that through these contracts many persons obtain a legal visa to enter the country of destination, but upon arrival they realize that their work contract is in reality fraudulent. The deceits can be manifested in many ways: involuntary prostitution/sex slaves, slavery-like labour, donation of organs and debts, among others.

National legislation and international commitments as compared to trafficking in persons

The national legislation in most countries does not take into account the levels of impunity from which networks of criminals benefit, in the specific case of trafficking in persons and generally in the context of international migration.

Even though there are international instruments that define transnational organized crime in general, and typify the offence of trafficking in persons in particular, the reality is far removed from what these instruments establish. It is of little use for a state to declare that it subscribes to the contents of the Convention on Human Rights if it does not respect them in practice.

The author has frequently observed women in jail or migrant detention centres in European and North American countries who are in actuality trafficked victims and are in a condition of high vulnerability, with a dread of being deported. Victims are not granted temporary or permanent residence status and are often immediately deported to their country of origin. In the Latin American countries of origin of these victims, the majority have immense debts, and if returned to their country of origin will be revictimized by the abusive lenders who facilitated them with money to leave the country in an illegal manner in the first place.

Overall, the topic has not been conceptualized at the national sphere and the generalized lack of information has been converted into detonative principles of a wrongful/erroneous approach/discharge of the offence and its victims on the part of governments in general and society in particular. The efficiency of actions of protection for trafficked victims tries to use the lens of gender equality, starting from their country of origin. It is important to break the vicious cycle which uses power to abuse and disempower the female gender, especially when found in the host society: with a new opportunity it is important not to reproduce the same discourses of power. In fact, things often become even worse for women. They are victims of double inequality and discrimination, namely gender, cultural membership and (irregular) immigrant status.

The mass media and human trafficking

In this globalized world information is disseminated in an almost immediate manner and is easily accessible. Without doubt this has advantages, and the new technologies of communication can be used as a means to protect the human rights of migrants. But regrettably the mass media, including the internet, can serve as a means to disseminate racist and xenophobic propaganda. As an example, some countries offer tourism programmes that include sex tourism through travel agencies; it is also observed that numerous marriage offers are made through the internet.

For the most part the mass media do not collaborate in serious campaigns against human trafficking. In several South American countries, for example, the media present victims and their abusers in sensationalist ways; and do not fulfil the promise made to victims who decide to give a testimony that their identity and faces will be concealed. It has been possible to observe how trafficked victims are put in danger when they make their testimonies public.

The phenomenon of trafficking tied to the process of migration is not taken on adequately by the mass media: trafficking is countermanded/

displaced by the fact of migrant status, thus the victim is foreign and is in the territory through irregular means. These sensationalist, contemptuous and discriminatory views reflect, for the most part, the lack of knowledge on the part of the mass media, which fail to project the problem of trafficking as an offence.

HIV/AIDS and trafficked victims

In a like manner, the return programmes for trafficked victims, starting from the countries where they were abused, do not always count on the consent of the victims to make a voluntary repatriation. What awaits the trafficked victims upon returning to their countries? Unfortunately, in most cases they face a future of guilt and social sanction. In the area of health there are many prejudices against trafficked victims, and it is thought/believed that all or most of them are carriers of HIV/AIDS. Their children also suffer the stigmatization of the mother. When trafficked victims are deported or returned to their countries of origin, the stigmatization they suffer is much greater if they have been involved with prostitution and are carriers of HIV. Trafficked victims who have been forced into prostitution are often not allowed to use appropriate protection, thus they run the risk of contracting sexually transmitted diseases.

An approach to human trafficking from the point of view of empowering victims

The offence of trafficking targets mostly women, children and adolescents, but men are not excluded from this offence. The great problem with the recording of trafficked victims in Latin America is that in many countries national legislation (pending amendment) does not typify the offence as such, except in cases of trafficking *blancas*.

Among the damages that victims of criminal organizations suffer, in addition to the abuses due to the migration process, are sexual and occupational exploitation, violation of their basic human rights, lost contact with their families, physical harm, addictions, imprisonment, etc.

In a the same way in which nation-states ought to reinforce and continue their efforts to prosecute the agents of human trafficking, ensuring that crimes committed do not remain unpunished, it is important that victims should not be punished and protection mechanisms should be established for this.

It is fundamental to propose and implement projects and/or programmes that empower victims and possible victims. Concretely, it is nec-

essary to inform the potential migrant population of the myths and realities of the entire migratory process: how to migrate by regular means,
how to avoid networks smuggling migrants and human traffickers and
who to contact in order to denounce these offences.

However, few specialized programmes for the rehabilitation of victims
have been observed. For example, in Colombia there are programmes of
recovery for victims when they have been deported and received in that
country; but in Peru victims suffer from stigmatization on the part of the
mass media. In Latin America the development of programmes for the
empowerment of trafficked victims has been recent.

The problem is that victims dread saying what exactly happened to
them and try to conceal their true identity. In countries such as Ecuador,
Peru and the Dominican Republic, among others, there is no culture of
communicating such problems. Latin American culture is not accustomed
to people making public their "private" problems. To publicize or verbal-
ize these problems is considered harmful to the victim's family honour
and contradicts the values of families and small communities.

The patriarchal culture is still very present across Latin America: the
police and certain government institutions collaborate little with trafficked victims, to the extent that these victims are considered guilty of
having sought sexual work. This results, for example, in trafficked victims
ending up being forced into domestic work under conditions of slavery.
In Latin America many domestic workers are highly abused in their
hours of work, free time and freedom of movement and expression.

One must take into account that victims arrive in their countries of origin ashamed, humiliated and indebted, and they dread returning to their
nuclear families. There are few known social support programmes in
place at this time, with the exception of a few not-for-profit organizations. The programmes that have begun to visualize the topic in the entire region are incipient.

The destination countries of trafficked victims who travel from Latin
America should collaborate and assume their responsibility for being the
countries in which the offences occurred; in the case of international migration, they should also be very responsible in controlling the criminal
networks.

North America, Europe and some Asian countries have a high demand
for the sex trade market, child pornography, slavery-like work and forced
prostitution; and it is within their borders that these offences are committed. The author has observed in visits to Europe and North America
numerous trafficked victims of Colombian, Peruvian, Ecuadorian and
Dominican nationalities, among others, in jails, soon to be deported.
This is not the type of action which promotes the full and real empowerment of the victims. Instead, it is important to indicate that the return

to the country of origin of the trafficked victim ought to be absolutely voluntary – it cannot be induced.

Without doubt, the lack of adequate information is an aspect which contributes to the vulnerability of possible victims of human trafficking. This means that access to information is vital for victims to make digni-fied decisions.

In a similar vein, it is transcendental that governments direct their training efforts toward the entities and organizations that deal with the institutional treatment of the offence. Traffickers as well as their victims should be included. As an example, the network should cover the system of safety (police), advocates of the inhabitants (office of the ombuds-man), migration offices and ministries of foreign relations, health, work, women, etc.

Conclusion: A critical discourse on trafficking

The governments of source countries have obligations with respect to their nationals abroad. They ought to monitor the application of the rights of their nationals in all stages of the migrant process: assuring an exit under safe conditions which protect persons from risks of illicit traffic and human trafficking; guaranteeing access to effective consular protec-tion and assistance, especially to persons who are found confined in de-tention centres and subject to expulsion; and always demanding a digni-fied return.

Ever since the beginning of the mandate, the special rapporteur has established as a priority of her activities and studies the issue of the illicit traffic of immigrants and humans, underlining that solely through the concerted efforts of states is it possible to prevent the risks to which vic-tims are exposed, which are yet more serious in the case of women and unaccompanied minors. To prevent and combat these forms of crime ef-fectively requires a wide and international approach covering coopera-tion, the exchange of information and the adoption of other appropriate measures, including those of a socio-economic nature, in the national, re-gional and international spheres.

Notes

1. The author has undertaken official visits as special rapporteur on the human rights of mi-grants to Canada, the Philippines, Ecuador, Mexico, the Mexico-United States border, Morocco, Iran, Italy, Peru and Spain. In addition to these official visits she has partici-pated in various formal reunions, seminars and forums in the capacity of special rappor-

teur to countries such as Colombia, Chile, Guatemala, El Salvador, Nicaragua, Honduras and of course Costa Rica. This has given her an integrated vision of the migratory phenomena in Latin America countries in particular, especially from the standpoint of irregular migration.

2. Numbers of the different applicable resolutions of the UN Human Rights Commission: 54-2000, 58-2000, 59-2000, 62-2000, 46-2003, 48-2003.

3. Latin American countries that have ratified the two protocols are Argentina, Brazil, Costa Rica, Ecuador, El Salvador, Guatemala, Mexico, Panama, Peru and Venezuela, available at www.unodc.org/unodc/en/crime_cicp_signatures.html.

4. E/CN.4/2003/85, December 2002, p. 13.

5. Commission on Human Rights, 61st session, "Specific Groups and Individuals: Migrant Workers", Report of the Special Rapporteur on the human rights of migrants, Gabriela Rodríguez Pizarro (Addendum), 13 January 2005, available at http://daccessdds.un.org/doc/UNDOC/GEN/G05/109/07/PDF/G0510907.pdf?OpenElement.

6. E/CN.4/2004/76, January 2004, p. 12.

10

Human trafficking in South Asia: A focus on Nepal

Renu Rajbhandari

Over the last decade trafficking in women and children in South Asia, particularly in Nepal, has been discussed at length in both national and international arenas. Poverty, illiteracy, unemployment and discrimination against women and children have been raised as probable causes, and several national anti-trafficking programmes have been developed and implemented within government and NGO sectors. A great deal of progress has been achieved. Initiatives undertaken by the government and non-governmental sectors have facilitated greater conceptual clarity on the issue. This has contributed to a shift from the anti-trafficking movement's central focus on women, their mobility and sex work to a more mature view which includes trafficking of men and children and trafficking for various purposes. Consistent advocacy has led to the development and adaptation of a regional convention against trafficking in women and children for commercial sexual exploitation, commonly known as the South Asian Alliance for Regional Cooperation (SAARC) Convention against Trafficking. There has been growing recognition of the issue as being of concern by almost all states of South Asia, and identification of particular ministries or persons within certain ministries to work on this issue. In addition, Nepal and Bangladesh have developed national plans of action against trafficking in women and children for commercial sexual exploitation.

Simultaneous to the anti-trafficking movement's commendable achievements, there have been several limitations which have severely affected the rights of women. These should be considered as lessons learnt and

Trafficking in humans: Social, cultural and political dimensions, Cameron and Newman (eds), United Nations University Press, 2007, ISBN 978-92-808-1146-9

discussed at length to prevent further stigmatization and marginalization of trafficked persons. Anti-trafficking activities in Nepal began with a focus on the prevention of HIV/AIDS, and consequently regional anti-trafficking debates and programmes were dominated by the issue of trafficking in women and children for prostitution. This association meant trafficked women were portrayed as women who indulged in sex work and were carriers of HIV/AIDS and potential spreaders of the disease to the general population. This approach has stigmatized trafficking survivors, making their return to their own communities almost impossible. The equation of trafficking with prostitution and the mobility of women saw the development of stringent laws and policies restricting women's mobility. Trafficking for other purposes was largely undiscussed and unexplored.

Trafficking in human beings is affected by cross-border issues. It has been clearly observed that the socio-economic and political relationship of Nepal with neighbouring countries, particularly India, has a significant effect on trafficking in human beings from Nepal. India's migration, employment and labour policies affect the rights and situation of Nepali migrant workers, with conditions at sites of work largely being determined by the Indian market. Unfortunately this vital area is not being addressed by anti-trafficking activities.

Several studies have been conducted to analyse the root causes of trafficking in the region, but these have focused on poverty, illiteracy and lack of awareness, and have largely failed to raise issues of poor governance, discrimination based on class, caste and gender, widespread corruption, non-compliance with international commitments by national and international actors, international trade, labour and migration policies and other structural factors. Similarly, the strong patriarchal and semi-feudal social and political system, double standards about women's and men's sexuality, existing means of production and landowner relationships and other pauperization issues have not been adequately discussed or analysed.

This chapter presents practical examples, experiences and case studies, with a view to deepening the understanding of the social, economic, gendered and political contexts of human trafficking in Nepal. It is based on the grassroots experiences of staff at the Women's Rehabilitation Centre (WOREC) and other NGOs working in Nepal at the grassroots level. Relevant literature has also been reviewed and incorporated. The chapter does not provide a complete range of fully articulated answers, largely because of the current limited status of analysis being applied to trafficking rather than basic confusion on the part of this author. WOREC has worked to provide training and skills development to multiple players to facilitate a rights-based approach. Even so, work is frequently challenged by social and moral values and the existence of strong patriarchal, discriminatory, socio-economic and political values and policies at society, state and international political levels. The international commitment to fight poverty, injustice and discrimination at policy level is not always reflected at the practical level, and at times is implemented in a way which widens the existing gap.

The case of Nepal

Nepal is a land-locked South Asian country with a population of 23 million people. It borders India in the east, west and south, and China in the north. Nepal is a semi-feudal country although, in the words of Govinda Neupane,[1] the old types of feudal relationship are breaking down. Change has been influenced by a number of significant factors: a slow but steady process of capitalist development, starting in the mid-1930s; the impact of the 1964 land reform programme in land ownership and control; and the revolutionary change that has occurred in science and technology. In addition there is the diversity of labour demand created by the massive expansion in trade and commerce, including opportunities outside agriculture. Although there is only limited demand for labour in the industrial sector in Nepal, the labour market and service sector occupations have been rapidly expanding.[2] This demand has extended to neighbouring countries like India. Now, with increasing globalization and the government's liberal trade and economic policies, Nepal is supplying labour for similar demands in the service and informal sectors in countries such as those of the Gulf and Malaysia.

The failure to create and implement a coherent overall development strategy mobilizing all of Nepal's resources, including effective education, training and planning for human resource development, has led to low rates of growth and high levels of unemployment and underemployment. It remains a largely subsistence economy based on agriculture, handicrafts and the service sector, with around 40 per cent of the population living below the poverty line – hence the massive upsurge in migration from rural areas to cities and other countries. The implications of this situation are far-reaching for Nepal as a whole, for the structure and dynamics of regional and local economies and society and (perhaps most of all) for households and individuals all over the country, both those directly involved in foreign labour migration and those left behind.

Although Nepal has never been colonized by a foreign country, it has always operated as a semi-colonial state. Nepali people have had to live under authoritarian regimes since unification of the several small kingdoms of Nepal. Throughout modern history Nepali people have struggled against dictatorship: for a century against the Rana autocracy (1846–

1950); against the inadequate multiparty system which was very much controlled by Rana and people near the king (1950–1959); and against the Panchayat no-party system (1960–1990) imposed by King Mahendra, which resulted in most party leaders fleeing to India. In 1990 the people's movement succeeded in overthrowing the Panchayat regime. A new democratic constitution was drafted, making the king the constitutional monarch and people the source of sovereign authority, but the state remained the same. An aristocracy continued to hold control of national politics and state affairs,[3] failing to address socio-economic disparity among various groups. On 1 February 2005 the king took power by arresting all leaders of political parties and seizing all means of communication. He formed a new government under his leadership for three years, replacing all democratic norms and institutions. People continue to struggle for social justice and their democratic rights.

In short, Nepal has a long history of political unrest. The political system has never defended the needs and rights of the poor, landless and women. The dominant Hindu culture discriminates against people on the basis of class, caste and sex. Untouchability was created and supported by rulers; bonded labour was practised; and the labour of the working class was subject to landowners controlling land and means of production. Women's production and reproduction were controlled by men. These phenomena have provided the grounds for crimes against humanity, including trafficking, to grow.

Although human trafficking is not a new phenomenon in Nepal, it began to be discussed only after 1990. Women's groups raised the issue of trafficked women in the sex industry, which was later supported by human rights groups. There are several reports[4] which outline that for hundreds of years Nepalis have been deceived, kidnapped and kept as bonded labourers and sexual slaves by those in power. Similarly, the culture of gifting human beings to powerful persons has been commonly practised. Historical evidence suggests that this phenomenon has not been confined to Nepal's borders but extended to neighbouring countries; for example, the "gifting" of Nepali women or strong men to neighbouring rulers.

Migration from one place or region to another within the country and across borders also has a long history in Nepal. Labour migration across the border, mainly into India, started before the recruitment of the first Nepalese to the British Gurkhas in 1815. Much of the early migration occurred as the result of push factors, like the difficulty of shouldering the excessive taxes imposed by the state, exploitative situations and political instability.

Although even in the early days there were a few sporadic reports that migrant populations were being deceived, coerced and forced to work under slavery-like conditions, they did not capture the attention of the people or the state compared to the evident socio-economic gains of many who returned. The majority of those who migrated succeeded in finding work and were able to sustain a livelihood and contribute towards the socio-economic uplifting of their families, society and the state. Consequently, they have enjoyed relatively high social status.

In recent years the harsh reality of poverty and violent political conflict within Nepal has significantly increased the number of migrants seeking work abroad. Rapidly increasing unemployment, poverty and insecurity at home, weak governance and corruption are some of the factors pushing people to migrate. Youths have migrated to 108 different countries.[5] In 2001, according to the country's Census, 762,181 Nepalese lived and worked abroad and more than 1 million people were estimated to be working in different cities of India. The migrants had remitted 123 billion rupees, contributing a significant 25 per cent of the total GDP of Nepal.[6] Many pieces of research have identified that groups are vulnerable at many stages of the migration process. Vulnerabilities arise from a lack of information about safe migration and (sometimes) the legal provisions guaranteed by the first Foreign Employment Act 1985. The victimization of rural youth is very frequent.[7]

Due to the absence of sex-disaggregated data, it is not possible to state the exact number of migrant women working abroad, or the remittances generated by them. Strong patriarchal and moralistic values about women's mobility and work mean women are forced to remain either silent or underground, making estimations difficult. It is, however, very clear that women constitute a significant percentage of Nepalese migrants. Due to the clandestine acts they are forced to undertake to migrate, it can be speculated that substantial number of these women are trafficked or forced to work under slavery-like practices. The data on the number of those trafficked vary considerably. The most common figure found in various documents is 5,000–7,000 a year.[8] Due to fear of being judged on the basis of their work and mode of migration, women remain silent. They face a double challenge: first, that of being a migrant worker, and second, that of being women. Stigmatization is increased if they have either worked under slavery-like conditions in the sex trade or have been sexually exploited in other sites of work, particularly in the private sphere where there is increased likelihood of tolerating abuse. Until recently individual cases of trafficking were considered neither a human rights issue nor discussed under the broad umbrella of human trafficking. These women were morally judged.

In spite of the implementation of a national plan of action against trafficking, during the last six years the government has not succeeded in bringing about major changes in patterns of trafficking in women or in providing support to those trafficked. NGOs are the major actors.

Factors responsible for trafficking

A number of social, economic and geopolitical factors are responsible for trafficking in South Asia. These include the adoption of free market policies and growing fundamentalism (both common in South Asia), moralistic values of states and strong patriarchal control over women's bodies and work.

In the case of Nepal, the feudal structure of the state and strong discrimination on the basis of class, caste and geographic location must be considered. Growing political instability causing food insecurity and concerns about physical safety has increased vulnerability. These values intersect with the prevailing feudal structure of society and the state's treatment of women and people from lower classes and castes as commodities – with body and labour available for exploitation by those in power. Trafficking and entrapment under slavery-like conditions are an outcome of the desire to maximize profit by exploiting people's bodies and labour. This phenomenon is amplified in circumstances where competition in the market is strong. Market forces push people to engage in activities that produce profit from little investment. Trafficking in persons for various forms of labour is a perfect fit, with profits from human trafficking now exceeding profits from the illegal trade of arms and drugs.[9] As market forces are influenced by national and international politics, the magnitude and pattern of trafficking change.

Pull factors

There have been few studies on the pull or demand factors for human trafficking. Some relevant factors are international migration policies; demand for cheap labour in different sectors, including domestic and sex work; demand for children as entertainers and for needlework; developmental strategies of nation-states, which are influenced by international developmental strategies; and patriarchal attitudes.

In the present globalized economic regime, countries have moved towards a free market and the integration of their local economy with the world economy. This movement is reflected in the reduction and removal of trade barriers, assistance and encouragement for the free movement of capital and goods around the world and the privatization of economics. Development strategies, and their dependence on the new economic regime, have frequently facilitated demand. The globalized free market has had both positive and negative effects that are particularly evident in smaller economies. Positive effects include the free flow of capital, which has created employment. Negative effects include increased competition for the production of cheap goods, which has created a global demand for cheap labour. This demand in various sectors has thrived on the dis-integration of the lives of rural communities and marginalized people.

The informalization of labour and the weakening trade union move-ments due to the introduction of contract work, home-based work sys-tems and other types of informal work are some of the methods being used to make labour cheaper to cater to the demand for increased profit with little investment in the contemporary competitive market. They allow producers to control workers, and control becomes much easier if labour is sourced from outside the country or from other parts of the country. Migrant workers fit this criterion.

Push factors

Supply or push factors mainly operate at the place of origin. Families and communities that experience gross discrimination based on class, caste, ethnicity or gender are vulnerable to trafficking. In Nepalese Hindu-dominated patriarchal societies, women and children are perceived as physiologically and psychologically weak. Despite bearing a double work-load at household and farm level, women can legally own neither land nor parental property on equal terms with their male counterparts.[10]

Caste-based discrimination results in people being looked down upon with scorn. The treatment of people as outcasts leaves deep scars on their minds and behaviour. The situation is worsened when coupled with eco-nomic factors. The experience of organizations working with trafficking survivors reveals that the majority come from families which are dysfunc-tional due to economic reasons such as joblessness, landlessness and not having any means of survival, and discriminated against on the basis of class and ethnicity and their place of residence. Similarly, a large percent-age of survivors come from families requiring immediate health care for a relative which they are unable to provide.[11] Traffickers lure their victims by giving an assurance that they will be able to support those heath care needs. Similarly, the sudden death of a working family member can throw a family into crisis and leave a person vulnerable to the assurances of traffickers.

Structural variables

Social factors

No single factor is the root cause of trafficking in Nepal.[12] Factors vary from one country to another, from one location to another, one ethnic group to another, one family to another, one girl to another, etc. The root causes, however, are more or less the same. Discrimination based on class, caste and gender is manifested in forms such as denial of the right to general education or specialized skill training, health education and service, restricted access to the resources necessary for survival, restricted mobility and control over the physical body and decisions by others. In Nepal the strong patriarchal value-based legal system includes denial of citizenship and access to passports to women without the endorsement of a male family member, considered the head of the family, and limited rights over parental property. These practices infantilize women, making them dependent upon others and vulnerable.

Similarly discriminatory practices towards ethnic groups residing in and around the Kathmandu Valley make them vulnerable to trafficking. Discrimination based on class and caste denies citizenship to thousands of people, particularly those from the Dalit community, despite having their names on electoral lists or evidence supporting generations-long residence in Nepal. Discrimination and the division of work based on caste forces people (particularly those from lower castes) to work in limited spheres. There are various case studies to support the argument that women have had to use clandestine means of migration to work in the sex sector just to avoid the extreme humiliation of their own and their family's caste-based situation. There are examples where women have changed their surnames and taken surnames of higher classes after coming to India to work in the domestic sector. Women say they do so because of the fear that someone from their particular village or area will recognize them and tell others. They prefer to travel to India and change their surname and work.[13] Similarly, the discriminatory practices faced by ethnic minority groups residing in and around the Kathmandu Valley make them vulnerable to trafficking.

For centuries Nepalese rulers brought girls from these communities to serve them in their palaces, including domestic chores, child care and even sexual service.[14] The labour and sexuality of these girls was exploited by the rulers, while they were regarded as loose women who could be used by people with power and property:[15] a situation which has stereotyped women from these communities. Social values in these communities mean that women have to be silent about their exploitation because the exploiter never gets punished and the girls bear the stigma.

There are certain communities whose main occupation has long been to provide entertainment. Work among men and women of these communities was divided. Men usually made musical instruments and organized programmes. Women sang and danced. There were cases where women were also forced to provide sexual services to men from the upper class and castes, but providing such services was not their primary area of work. With the modernization of the entertainment sector and globalization of the media, traditional musical instruments have been replaced by modern factory-made instruments, and other methods of entertainment such as film halls and television have become available in villages. These phenomena have eroded the traditional entertainers' livelihood options – a situation which has been exploited by people in power to obtain sexual services from women from this community. Those with power decide how much to pay. They live a double standard: maintaining relationships with these women while preaching moral values and labelling the women as bad women, which then increases their power to exploit them. This stigma forces the women to remain silent against the exploitation of their work and bodies. They are vulnerable to being trafficked. The situation is being further aggravated by increasing fundamentalism and the consequent moralistic debate on sex work. This debate has enabled different groups to become active and push for an "end" to prostitution without analysing its consequences and livelihood destruction for women. This phenomenon was particularly evident in the Badi community, where social groups demanding an end to prostitution threw out hundreds of Badi women and their families from the places where they had lived and worked for hundreds of years. Their actions have created a vulnerable pool of displaced women and children.[16]

There are cases of rape and gang rape happening, particularly in Dalit communities, as revenge against a range of issues: the upper class or caste do not like the way an issue was handled by lower class or caste people; to give a lesson to a family of lower economic stratum or caste for not behaving properly, for example by taking control of their own life or labour; or to get families to flee a particular area that a landlord would like to redevelop.[17] These evicted women and children can be easily controlled, exploited and trafficked.

Strong patriarchal norms and gender discrimination

In broad terms, Nepalese society has very strong patriarchal values and norms. Women's oppression is firmly rooted in state-level policies and the dominant Hindu religion.[18] Women are considered family property. They are daughters until they marry (controlled by their fathers), wives after they marry (controlled and taken care of by their husbands) and then mothers (controlled and taken care of by their sons). Within families, girl children are considered a burden and boys are a means of livelihood. Girls are routinely denied even basic necessities such as food, education and clothing. Their right to self-respect, social dignity and self-determination is completely at odds with their lived reality. Boys are forced to earn for their family members, and their identities are based on how much they earn.

Strong social values about boys and girls of certain ages and social position force parents to follow societal practices. For example, in Makwanpur district (about 80 kilometres from Kathmandu) in Padampokahri, Basamadi and adjoining village development committees there is a practice of sending daughters to join the circus in India. These children are given to middlemen who come to the villages to recruit children as young as five years of age. These children are trafficked, but the way they are handed to recruiters by their parents poses certain questions. Why do parents give their daughters to circus recruiters at such a young age, and who exactly is responsible? The answer is that their actions are motivated by strong societal values which consider girls as family assets to be controlled by their fathers and used to make a living as needed. Society supports parents sending young girls away. When the state fails to protect fundamental rights to food, education and health care, and the right to grow up in a loving and caring environment (according to the state commitment to the Convention on the Rights of the Child), these cases becomes common.

According to a recent IIDS/UNIFEM report on trafficking within Nepal,[19] an overwhelming majority of survivors (92 per cent) reported social factors as the cause of their trafficking. Family relationships, violence, marriage, innocence and ignorance, illiteracy and discrimination stood as immediate causes that pushed them into the hands of traffickers. The same report reveals that economic vulnerability is the second most important factor to have pushed people (65 per cent of respondents) into the hands of traffickers.[20] Landlessness, the lack of local paid work, low wages and the lack of alternative economic opportunities pushed them to migrate without having proper information about their work situation.

Information relating to the trafficking of boys is scarce except for a single piece of research by WOREC/ILO in 2002, which suggests that economic factors seem to dominate (66 per cent) the trafficking of boys.[21] This indicates that the push factors for trafficking may vary according to gender roles and relations.

Research demonstrates that social exclusion based on gender is a major factor contributing to the risk of trafficking. In all South Asian countries, gender-based discrimination is perpetuated and institutionalized in the family, community and political spheres. In almost all countries women are socialized from childhood to be submissive, servile and obedient to men. Women are associated with "inside", i.e. the home. Men belong "outside", where livelihood is earned and political and economic power is exercised. These prevailing attitudes make it difficult for women to make independent decisions and take control of their lives.[22]

Gender-based discrimination is perpetuated and institutionalized in the family and community. In many Nepalese communities gender stereotypes are used to reinforce women's low status. Women and children are commodities that can be sold and resold in the market. Women are expected to accept their position without complaint. These stereotypes reinforce in young women a sense of helplessness and of being unprotected without a man, which facilitates traffickers taking control of women. A woman or girl is stigmatized if she loses her virginity or if her husband or parents abandon her. Similarly, when a girl or woman is physically tortured, raped or experiences incest, she loses her dignity and self-respect in the family and community. This forces girls and women either to keep silent and tolerate the situation or to run away from home. There is a clear need for support, counselling and places of refuge, but few places are available. A few NGOs run counselling centres in a few areas and homes in urban settings. Infrastructure for support is virtually absent. Consequently, the first person with whom a woman in crisis comes into contact becomes very important. That person is able to lure them by offering emotional and other forms of support. Traffickers usually look for such situations and will then act as "rescuers" of women and girls.

A similar scenario applies to boys, who may be continuously tormented or abused by their family and broader society for being idle or not being able to fulfil the needs of their family members. Boys in this situation will look for a mechanism to provide them with opportunities. Traffickers act as rescuers.

Geopolitical factors

Although Nepal has never been formally colonized, its politics have always been influenced by neighbouring countries, and this has impacted on people's migration. Nepal's politics have been affected by India-Chinese, India-Pakistan and India-US relationships, and were previously affected by the India-Soviet Union relationship. Nepal's struggle for independence was intertwined with Indian independence, and Nepal's long and ongoing political turmoil has been influenced by India ever since. India has made it clear that it supports the constitutional monarchy and multiparty democracy as two pillars for stability in Nepal. This approach has meant that theoretically the monarchy is not separable from democracy. Presently the king, who portrays himself as a symbol of national unity, has complete power.

Under various regimes the rights of women, the economically poor and ethnic minorities have been ignored and justice has been unavailable. Discriminatory provisions are entrenched in state legislation. Power has been given to privileged groups, those from high classes and castes, allowing them to exploit, abuse and control others. People's life situations have not changed and their aspirations have not been met. Conflict between groups has deepened, which has created a favourable environment for radical groups like the Maoists to grow. This has slowly converted into violent political conflict, which has had a tremendous impact on people's lives, security and livelihood. Dialogue between rebel groups and government failed twice, which became the king's rationale for taking power.

The current political unrest and armed conflict have created a population of displaced persons who are vulnerable to trafficking despite the efforts of several anti-trafficking programmes. In fact, ongoing violent conflict in Nepal has created a large group of internally displaced people in search of livelihood and security. Their situation places them at risk of becoming controlled by traffickers acting as "rescuers", for example in the guise of employment providers. Young people, particularly, fit this category.

The long-term political conflict that has violently surfaced during the last decade has affected people in different ways. People face the risk of being forced through threat of death to join the rebels or provide them with support. They also face the risk of being interrogated, tortured, "disappeared" or killed by security personnel without having done anything wrong. State security personnel deployed in different regions of the country interrogate young people on suspicion of their being rebel group allies. They can be humiliated, tortured, disappeared or killed by security personnel merely on suspicion of providing food or shelter to the rebels.[23] In some cases, villagers do provide food and shelter to the rebels because they are forced to.

The majority of people in this vulnerable situation belong to ethnic, Dalit or other marginalized groups.[24] Feeling trapped, people run away from their communities in search of a livelihood in nearby cities or the capital, where they face further discrimination: people will not rent them anywhere to live; and employers, suspecting they may belong to a rebel group, will not employ them. They may also face harassment, interrogation or torture by security personnel.

This situation worsened after the 11 September attack on the World Trade Center, when suddenly all rebels were labelled "terrorist" by the state. The situation of those residing in conflict-hit areas worsened. Interrogation, humiliation, abuse and coercion became a daily reality, especially for youths. Trapped in this multilayered discrimination and marginalization, people are forced either to leave rural areas or to take any kind of illegal, underground work to keep them away from the eyes of security forces. Their situation is exploited by those who want to profit from their sexuality and labour.

The following is a recent case study of two girls (aged 16/17 and 19) from the mid-western region of Nepal. For the purposes of the case study they have been given the names Rama and Sita.[25]

> We were studying at a school near our village. Our brothers, cousins and others from our community had joined the Maoist group. We liked the way they gave speeches, particularly that they were very supportive of the poor. We wanted to help them in whatever way we could so we began singing and dancing in their people's shows which they used to educate people about their ideology. We liked that. After some time they asked us to join the Maoist army. We refused. Later, several security personnel came to our village in their search for Maoists. They looked for people who were supportive of the Maoists and interrogated them. They found us. In their opinion, we were Maoist because we used to sing and dance in their program. We were taken by these security personnel to their barracks. We were severely tortured by them. We don't know why but after some time they released us and sent us home. Maoists came to our houses and asked what we had told the army personnel. They were suspicious of us and psychologically tortured us. Their pressure to join the army became more severe. Since we didn't want to join them, we decided to run away from our village and go to India to work. Unfortunately, we were intercepted by an organization at the border saying we were being trafficked. After a few months, we were sent back home with the help of police but our lives became a living hell. People started to look down on us. We were interrogated by both parties quite frequently. The psychological torture became severe. We wanted to escape from our situation so we started looking for an opportunity to get out. We met with a person who promised to arrange everything so we could leave our village and find work for us in India. We agreed with his conditions and ran away. Somehow we managed to reach India and landed here doing sex work. We never wanted this but what can we do? We neither wanted to be tortured nor could survive in the village.

The government's attitude towards those from conflict-prone areas – that they are all insurgents – has kept people silent. There are hundreds of cases of young Nepalis who have left for Mumbai on their way to the Middle East to work as migrant labourers. Recently there have been many reports of significant numbers of people working under slavery-like practices in Malaysia and Gulf countries. WOREC in Nepal interviewed 500 boys who were on their way to Gulf countries. They asked them whether they knew what their status, type of work and living conditions would be. The answer was "no". One attitude was common: "We know that we can be cheated and forced to work under slavery-like practices but there is also a chance that this will not happen as well." Similarly, they said, "We are absolutely suffering here, but there is a possibility of making a good life as well."[26] At present thousands of girls and boys (the majority are boys) are desperately looking for options to leave to find any work. They take loans with heavy interest to pay the brokers who promise to organize their work in other countries, particularly Malaysia and the Middle East. They are so desperate that they are not interested in advice about possible risks associated with this kind of migration. People even take the risk of travelling to countries where labour has been restricted by the state due to security fears, e.g. Iraq.

Economic factors

The common economic factors which make women and children vulnerable to trafficking are both push factors – research shows traffickers lure victims when they are at their most socially and economically vulnerable[27] – and pull factors – trafficking requires a demand for cheap labour across various sectors.

Tourism (a major source of income) has declined due to the present armed conflict, resulting in the closure of big hotels and restaurants. As a means of survival, the tourism sector has refocused itself on internal tourism. Rapid urbanization has seen a demand for dance clubs, bars and the services of sex workers. As the people using these services have a low capacity to pay, these venues have to be both attractive and cheap. To cater to these needs, desperate adolescent girls have been lured from conflict-hit areas. As sex work is illegal in Nepal, these girls are officially hired as waitresses and then forced to work as sex workers. Strong moral values informed by patriarchal notions of purity and impurity have then forced the girls to remain in exploitation without complaint or demand. Thus the culture of silence has developed.[28]

Proximate variables

Governance

As described above, Nepal is a county where the rule of law has largely been abandoned by those in power. The élite party, non-party politicians and bureaucrats control almost all productive means and politics. Corruption, strongly allied to the state machinery, has resulted in poor law enforcement and marginalization of, and denial of justice to, the poor. Even after the formation of a multiparty system and democratic government 12 years ago, governance has changed little, resulting in Nepal's present political situation. One significant change that did occur was the capacity for people to make things publicly known. Following the 2005 takeover by the royal family, that progress has been lost.

The Nepalese government has totally failed to protect the rights of its people. Social and economic rights have been violated, resulting in few employment options and increased insecurity. Although the new constitution of Nepal (written after the popular democratic movement of 1990) recognizes people as the source of sovereign authority and guarantees basic human rights to every citizen, the rights of women, children and Dalits are still far from realization. Although the constitution guarantees rule of law through a competent judiciary system, women are subjected to discrimination due to prevailing discriminatory laws against women, which were drafted during the autocratic Panchayati era and were not changed even after the restoration of democracy.

The government is continuously cutting its development budget in the name of security and peacebuilding. Billions of rupees have already been spent on security, and the unintended consequence is that people face economic misery and feel forced to migrate. Despite the huge expenditure on security, more than 12,000 people have been killed, thousands have disappeared and hundreds of thousands are displaced.[29] At the same time the government policy of trade liberalization has driven many domestic industries and products out of the competition, leaving behind a significant chunk of the population looking for employment opportunities abroad. Obviously, this is the group of people who are vulnerable to trafficking.

Being a significant source of foreign exchange, national income and employment, tourism is a powerful industry in Nepal. To date the government has neither properly regulated to prevent the exploitation of people involved in the tourism sector nor exhibited capacity to implement existing laws and policies. This is partly a consequence of the widespread practice of corruption in the governmental sector. Improper and inadequate governance practices have resulted in the commercial exploitation of children, abuse of domestic workers, sex tourism and other forms of abuses or slavery-like practices.

There is little protection from criminal acts of trafficking. Very few cases of missing girls are registered with the police compared to the number of girls actually missing. Cases are not reported for many reasons, several of which are associated with poor governance.[30]

Government-funded social and development services are not effectively targeting the most vulnerable groups. Women and occupational castes rarely have access to decision-making. Child protection measures have low priority. Since November 2001 existing development programmes have been almost abandoned as a result of budget cuts following the declaration of the state of emergency, which worsened after 1 February 2005.

Lack of government support mechanisms during natural calamities like flood, drought, famine and failed harvests leading to loss of livelihood has forced people to move away from their villages into uncertain circumstances. The erosion of livelihood options due to the international fluctuation of market prices in major cereal and cash crops like paddy and jute has deepened the economic crisis at the grassroots and national levels. Due to poor regulation of informal sectors of work operated by the private sector, abuses and exploitation are quite common, which creates an environment for trafficking to flourish. Women and children are the hardest hit by this situation. The heavy migration of people to brick factories, stone quarries and/or to work as contract wage labourers in the construction sector has had a huge impact on crop production in Nepal.

Poor compliance with UN conventions and treaties may also be considered a push factor for trafficking. Although Nepal is signatory to a range of UN conventions, their implementation is very weak. At least 100 laws require amendment, but despite advocacy programmes from civil society groups they are far from being amended. The law enforcement agency is free from neither corruption nor strong patriarchal values, and is not accountable.

Pressure from market forces and financial groups supporting the free flow of capital has overcome the relatively weak power of states, forcing government(s) to adopt weak labour policies resulting in the easy exploitation of labour. The increasing demand for cheap labour to maximize profit under this "competitive" economic regime has created demand for cheap workers. Women, children and people from marginalized communities fit this category.[31] The shrinking availability of legal work within the formal sector has pushed many to look for non-legal options, compromising their rights and making them vulnerable. Similarly, the lack of appropriate child labour prevention laws and strategies has resulted in children being forced into underground exploitative employment. These children are usually from the countryside. Banning girls from the garment industry has seen increased forced prostitution in Bangladesh.[32] The eviction of children from carpet factories has forced them to take more exploitative work. Making child work punishable in India has resulted in an increase in the exploitative conditions of that work for children. Research on cross-border trafficking of boys[33] revealed that due to the stringent policies against child labour, children have had to work in worse conditions in Mumbai. Children were trafficked from Nepal to work in Mumbai and kept under exploitative conditions with confined movement and lack of services. These children were in a situation of non-communication: due to their fear of police, they were kept in such a way that no one could have access to them. This situation made them more vulnerable to high levels of exploitation.

Increasing feminization of poverty

Due to discriminatory laws and practices in Nepal, women are marginalized. They do not have an identity in Nepalese society without the support of a male family member. The lack of a viable economic option, compounded by jobs (if any) being offered in the service sector at household or farm level at low pay, impacts more severely on women than men. In the family, women have to perform the role of service provider to family members and take care of children. If they do not fulfil this role they face continuous physical and psychological harassment, including sexual harassment, abuse and social stigma.

The adoption of a liberal economic policy by the state has meant an increasing shift of cropping patterns from cereals (the staple food crops) to cash crops. As women do not have access to the market or control of the income generated by cash crops, an increasing number of families are facing food insecurity at the household level. Women are responsible for feeding the family and, according to the intra-household level food distribution pattern survey, Nepali women are the last in their families to get food. The consequences are dire when combined with food insecurity, and have resulted in the feminization of starvation in Nepal.

Due to limited livelihood options, men are migrating, leaving women to take care of their families and farming. Contrary to the old practice of men sending money to their families, men are now taking out loans to go in search of work but are not able to repay the loans. Feeling guilty that they have encumbered their family with a large loan or sold their land, many men avoid contact with their families. Women are then pressured to repay the loans, which forces them to search for work.

Due to armed conflict, men and boys are either migrating or joining the armed forces, leaving women behind to take care of the family. Women are burdened by the responsibility for feeding and taking care of family members injured or orphaned in the conflict. Many women are genuinely vulnerable, desperate and looking for work in a market that offers employment only in the informal, illegal service sector. The market has an interest in keeping these sectors illegal as it creates an increased capacity to control desperate women labourers and maximize profit. Traffickers and the "market" win. Women and migrant workers, forced into slavery-like practices, suffer and remain silent, which in turn creates grounds for further exploitation of these and other people.

Human rights instruments and Nepal's commitment

Trafficking has gained attention because it is an issue of national and international concern. Given the nature of trafficking, combating it must combine international, national and regional efforts. International treaties and conventions are designed to strengthen or enforce legal frameworks. These instruments, which set out globally accepted standards and norms, can also be used to increase governments' accountability and improve programming. Within the last 12 years several international and regional legal instruments have been made public to assure states' commitment to fighting this crime. But these policy commitments have neither prevented trafficking nor held governments accountable for it. It is necessary to work on implementation mechanisms and to be committed to implementation of these policies and programmes in a real sense.

Nepal is a state party to 18 international human rights treaties and 4 Geneva Conventions, including the ILO Convention (No. 182) on the Worst Forms of Child Labour. Major conventions ratified or acceded to are as follows.

- Slavery Convention – acceded 7 January 1963.
- International Covenant on the Elimination of All Forms of Racial Discrimination – acceded 30 January 1971.
- International Covenant on Civil and Political Rights 1966 – ratified 14 May 1994.
- International Covenant on Economic, Social and Cultural Rights 1966 – acceded 14 May 1991.
- Convention on the Elimination of All Forms of Discrimination against Women (CEDAW) 1979 – ratified 22 April 1991.
- Convention against Torture and Other Cruel, Inhumane and Degrading Treatment and Punishment 1984 – acceded 14 May 1991.
- Convention on the Rights of the Child 1989 – ratified 14 September 1990.
- Optional Protocol to the Convention on the Rights of the Child on the Sale of Children, Child Prostitution and Child Pornography 2000 – signed 8 September 2000.
- Convention on the Suppression of Immoral Trafficking Protocol – acceded 27 December 1995.
- SAARC Convention on Preventing and Combating Trafficking in Women and Children for Prostitution 2002 – acceded 26 September 1997.

ILO conventions signed by Nepal are as follows.

- The Discrimination (Employment and Occupation) Convention 1958 (No. 111) – ratified 19 September 1974.
- The Minimum Wage Fixing Convention 1970 (No. 131) – acceded 19 September 1974.
- The Equal Remuneration Convention 1951 (No. 100) – ratified 10 June 1976.
- Convention on the Worst Forms of Child Labour 1999 (No. 182) – ratified 3 January 2002.
- The Weekly Rest Convention (No. 14) – acceded 10 December 1986.

- The Tripartite Consultation (International Labour Standards) Convention 1976 (No. 144) – ratified 21 March 1995.
- Convention Concerning Minimum Age for Employment 1973 (No. 138) – ratified 13 May 1997.
- Convention Concerning the Application of the Principles of the Right to Organize and Bargain Collectively 1949 (No. 98) – ratified 11 November 1996.
- Forced Labour Convention 1930 (No. 29) – ratified 3 January 2002.

Being a party to these treaties, Nepal is bound by its reporting obligations. Article 9 of the Treaty Act of 1991, ratified by the Nepalese parliament, recognizes all international human rights mechanisms to which Nepal is a state party as national law. Despite the ratification of the Convention on the Elimination of all Forms of Discrimination against Women (CEDAW) without reservation, recognition of the concept of land and resource rights for women, granting them a separate legal status or degree of autonomy, is far from reality. Discrimination against women continues, which makes them vulnerable to trafficking. There are more than 100 discriminatory laws which need to be immediately amended to satisfy international commitments.[34]

SAARC Convention on Preventing and Combating Trafficking in Women and Children for Prostitution 2002

The SAARC Convention is a regional document acceded to by all governments of the region. In 1997, at the ninth SAARC summit, human trafficking was officially recognized as a heinous crime. During the 1998 tenth SAARC summit a draft convention specifying a proposed legal mechanism for the prevention and remedy of trafficking activities was prepared, providing hope for positive changes. The eleventh SAARC summit held in Kathmandu in January 2002 ratified the SAARC Convention on Preventing and Combating Trafficking in Women and Children for Prostitution. Signing of this convention by the heads of state was a positive step, but there are many areas that need to be addressed and improved without delay. Due to the absence of a parliament, Nepal has not yet ratified the convention.

Besides this convention, the Indo-Nepal Friendship and Peace Treaty guarantees to citizens of each country equal treatment, including the same privileges in the matter of residence, participation in trade and commerce, movement and privileges of a similar nature. However, it is not being applied during the process of repatriating trafficking survivors. They are forced to return to their country of origin without the assessment of risks to their lives. Importantly, the SAARC Convention has not been enforced due to it not being ratified by the Nepalese government. Citizenship and other political issues cannot be resolved without having a bilateral agreement between the states, which seems very unlikely at this stage.

Trafficking myths

There are several myths related to trafficking in Nepal. These myths dominate analysis as well as intervention strategies planned and implemented so far – one of the reasons why anti-trafficking activities have been relatively ineffective.

- *All girls working as sex workers have been trafficked.* The reality is different. There are a large number of girls working as sex workers who migrated knowing where they where going and what they would be doing.
- *The majority of girls working in brothels in India are minors.* While it cannot be denied that there are many girls who are minors and forced to work as prostitutes, there are a large number of adult women who engage in sex work out of choice. Similarly there are some girls who were minors when they were brought to India but are now adult, working as sex workers and not wanting to be rescued.
- *All girls in brothels want to be rescued and go back to Nepal.* The reality is that the majority of girls do not want to be rescued, and of those who want to be rescued the majority do not want to return to Nepal. They give various reasons for this, including fear of stigmatization. Many would like to settle in India.
- *All trafficked girls end up as prostitutes.* There are various sites of work where trafficked girls are kept under slavery-like conditions.
- *All rural/uneducated/poor/migrant girls are trafficked girls.* With the changing lifestyles and opportunities available to women in different sectors, a lot of women are choosing to migrate with an aspiration of better livelihood options.
- *Only girls are trafficked.* Boys and men are also trafficked in large numbers from Nepal into various labour markets.
- *Trafficking can be prevented by intercepting girls at borders.* The interception of girls prevents them from crossing borders only for a very short time. The majority of these girls eventually migrate. This act only violates their right to free mobility, stigmatizes them and forces them to be clandestine in their movements, putting them at increased risk of trafficking.
- *All women working as sex workers are being exploited.* There are thousands of women who undertake sex work as an employment option and want their rights to be protected.

- *By curbing poverty and illiteracy, trafficking can be stopped.* There are various factors responsible for trafficking. While it is necessary to make major changes to reduce poverty and consequent illiteracy, curbing poverty and illiteracy might reduce trafficking for a short time but it would not be sustainable.
- *Women and children are similar, and need to be protected otherwise they may be trafficked.* These patriarchal values lump women and children together, whereas in fact they face different realities. Particularly, adult women have the right to make their own decisions.
- *Stringent laws can prevent trafficking.* It is questionable whether stringent laws prevent crime. In reality, stringent laws result in lower reporting of crimes, which makes underground criminal networks stronger and more effective.

Responses to trafficking

As a result of pressure from civil society groups and international communities, the governments of South Asia have officially recognized human trafficking. Almost all states have demonstrated their commitment at national and international levels. Countries like Nepal and Bangladesh, which are considered source countries, have taken greater responsibility for the elimination of trafficking. India, as a country of transit and destination, has also initiated various programmes to combat the problem. All three governments have included three major components within their anti-trafficking strategies.

Prevention

Presently the major focus of anti-trafficking programmes is on preventive activities. For the last 12 years programmes including awareness-raising, school education and women's literacy have been common. The majority of these have focused on women, with a hypothesis that if women get information they will be less vulnerable to being trafficked.[35] Similarly, in Nepal some organizations started working with district taskforces formed by the government, including different government agencies functioning at the district level. District women's development officers were appointed as secretaries and district development committee chairpersons were appointed as chair. This approach proved sustainable and effective.[36] Unfortunately, these district taskforces are no longer functioning well due to the dissolution of democratic institutions by the government in 2002, with the exception of Morang, Sunsari and Dhanusha districts where district taskforces are strong due to effective government/ NGO partnerships.

   Preventive activities are currently dominated by two ideologies: prohibitionist and rights-based.

• Prohibitionist programmes mainly focus on trafficking for prostitution. All their activities are geared towards the abolition of prostitution as a means to prevent trafficking in women and children. Surveillance or vigilance committees operate with the rationale that women can be trafficked during their migration. To prevent them from being trafficked, it is argued that it is necessary to restrict their movement. These village-level surveillance committees watch for women who run away or move. They advocate that all women should be registered before leaving their place of residence.

• Rights-based programmes focus on trafficking in various sites of work and maintain a woman's free right of movement. Information and legal and social support are key areas of intervention. This approach recognizes that trafficking and prostitution are separate issues and includes activities to secure the human rights of every person as a means to prevent trafficking. Several programmes are focused on safe migration, safeguarding the right to mobility and the empowerment of women. Women's groups are formed and their rights explained. Education about workers' rights is also carried out.[37] Community-based poverty reduction programmes fit within this approach, being based on the rationale that improved economic opportunities in rural areas will prevent women and girls from needing to migrate and being trafficked.[38]

Interception

Interception is a strategy used mainly by groups with a prohibitionist approach, particularly at cross-border trafficking areas, i.e. between Nepal and India and between India and Bangladesh. This approach advocates prevention of a person's movements during trafficking, including return of trafficked persons, border rescue, internal rescue from exploitative conditions and dealing with the trafficked person during and after trafficking. Brothel-based raids and rescues in destination countries fall within this approach. Similarly, programmes like community-based surveillance and interception at borders have been developed and implemented. These programmes are heavily loaded with patriarchal values and incorporate the concept that women and girls cannot move alone. They also presume that all girls in the sex trade are trafficked, by ignoring the complexity of circumstances under which girls are trafficked and to which they are "returned". This approach also mainly focuses on the trafficking of women for prostitution. Trafficking of boys and men is usually not considered.[39]

Rehabilitation/reintegration

Anti-trafficking programmes are being implemented using two approaches by different groups: welfare and rights-based approaches.

The welfare approach has been applied by all South Asian states and some of the major NGOs in the region. This approach is driven by the ideology that all girls in the sex trade are trafficked and need to be rescued and rehabilitated. This notion presumes that the girls' and women's behaviours need to be changed, i.e. they need to learn to become a "good" girl/woman. Stereotyping is intrinsic to this approach, which does not recognize the rights of a person to have control over her body, decisions and livelihood. It tends to ignore that once a trafficked female is rescued she faces different challenges, which must also be addressed.

The rights-based approach argues that women (those over the age of 18) who have been affected by trafficking have the right to make decisions concerning their personal circumstances. It is up to them whether or not they want to be "rescued" from the situation where they are currently working. If they want to be rescued then support must be provided and different options discussed according to their need. Organizations working within this approach focus their activities on the process of empowerment. Examples include facilitating the formation of self-help groups and survivors' organizations, and planning and implementing support programmes through survivors' groups.[40]

Although Nepal's anti-trafficking national plan of action has mentioned reintegration as a programme component, unfortunately there are no programmes or projects to reintegrate trafficked persons. The Nepalese government does not have a reintegration policy; only NGOs are active. It has been widely observed that activities adopting a rights-based approach have proven more sustainable and empowering than traditional rehabilitation methods, which have not resulted in sustainable social integration of trafficked persons.[41] Unfortunately, due to the centuries-long practice of the welfare approach and society's strong paternalistic values through which people enjoy offering something to others and giving charity, the welfare approach is continuing, despite the fact that these practices actually increase the stigma of trafficked victims and their dependence.

Difficulties, dilemmas and discussion

It is widely recognized by international communities that trafficking is a gross violation of human rights. Initially, in almost all South Asian countries, trafficking was mainly recognized as a problem of forced migration of women and children for prostitution. Particularly in Nepal, trafficking was considered a problem of law and order, and was also associated with AIDS. That understanding was reflected in government and NGO programmes. Women's rights and human rights were never prioritized. This is still true of many programmes and of proposed amendments to the law. There is a strong move towards the criminalization of prostitution, as can be seen in regional documents like the SAARC Convention. Another issue, which has been associated and in some cases become synonymous with trafficking, is the migration of women. In a country with strong patriarchal values and moral judgements about issues related to the mobility of women, all anti-trafficking efforts have been geared towards the restriction of women's mobility. As a result, various policies such as prohibiting single, unmarried women from travelling to Gulf countries and monitoring the movements of girls from villages have been formulated and put into action. Both Nepal and Bangladesh have had a policy to prevent the movement of women, which was amended following continuous pressure and opposition from women's rights groups; as a result of education and discussion about the agreed definition of trafficking under the Trafficking Protocol, migration and trafficking have emerged as separate issues. Unfortunately, this understanding is not universally shared and misguided policy has been developed. There remains a focus on three issues.

- *Curbing migration to prevent trafficking.*
- *Stigmatizing migrating women.* Due to the equation of trafficking with migration, all statistics count migrated women as "trafficked" women. Resulting policy focuses on curbing the mobility of women to reduce the number of trafficked persons.[42]
- *Equating trafficking with prostitution.* In most South Asian countries there is a tendency to equate trafficking with prostitution. This equation has resulted in the forced eviction of sex workers and the closure of brothels in countries of transit and destination.[43] This attitude is being witnessed all over South Asia and particularly in Nepal, with stringent laws to criminalize prostitution and in some cases the clients of prostitutes.

The following two case studies reveal a number of weaknesses in the current responses to individual cases of trafficking, and their lack of effectiveness in addressing the broad factors that make people vulnerable to trafficking. These broad issues need to be answered before interventions and strategies can succeed.

Manorama

Manorama is a 17-year-old girl from Makwanpur district. When she was five a middleman took her from her parents to work in a circus in India. Her parents were given 1,000 rupees by the middleman and told they would receive 1,000 rupees per month after a one-year training period. In her first days in the circus she cried a lot and wanted to return to her family but did not know what she could do. After a few years she became a trained circus worker, and according to her she was well paid and did not feel abused. She used to go home once every two years and bring money to her parents. She said she was satisfied with that.

Last year when she was returning to India after visiting her parents, a guard at the India/Nepal border intercepted her. She was brought to a transit home and kept for some time. She was repeatedly asked by the manager of the transit centre to learn stitching, which could be useful for her future. According to Manorama, she does not like stitching. The transit centre offered her three months' stay, after which she had to return to her home to earn her living. She feels very insecure because she does not want to stay at home and she has no skills except circus skills. She says she does not mind being in Nepal but she wants work to support herself and her family.

Some of her friends have faced similar situations. They are now at home after spending time in the transit centre, and are facing difficulties because everyone knows their status and presumes they are HIV-positive because they were intercepted at the border. Previously, girls used to return from the circus and were able to get married and settle back into their communities easily. Now, with the work on trafficking and its association with HIV/AIDS, it is becoming difficult for all of them.

Manorama asks, "Why is this happening?" According to her, she was not forced to do any sex work and nor was she sexually abused, so why do people presume she is HIV-positive? Her main questions are: what wrong has she done; where should she move to from here; and what can she do in the future?

Halil

Halil is a seven-year-old boy from a rural district of Nepal who belongs to a minority Muslim community. He was on his way to Mumbai to work in a Jari factory (of which he was unaware) and was accompanied by his uncle. He was happy for some time and was enjoying his surroundings when, after a few hours, he thought of his mother and started to cry. At this stage he was about board a train and leave for Mumbai. An NGO activist who was working in a nearby migration information booth suspected what was happening and intervened. After discussing the situation with fellow travellers, she discovered that Halil was about to be trafficked with 20 other children aged 5 to 13 years. She asked for help from nearby authorities and got their support (which is most unusual). The people travelling with the children left immediately.

The activist took the children to the police station and, with great difficulty, convinced the authorities that the children were about to be trafficked. All the children were under 14 years of age and consequently are the responsibility of the state. The activist pointed out to the district magistrate that, being a signatory to the Convention on the Rights of the Child, it is the government's obligation to support these children.

It took almost the whole night for the activist to register the complaint at the local police station. Under pressure from people from various sectors, particularly from human rights and civil society groups, the case was registered and the children were taken back to their district. After their arrival at the district police office, the parents of the children were informed. When they arrived at the police station they were angry because, according to them, the children were going to work so the authorities had no right to intervene and bring them back. The parents were convinced with great difficulty and sent home with their children. With continuous pressure from the human rights group and women's rights group, the traffickers were arrested and jailed.

After a year, researchers learned that all the children involved had later taken another route to Mumbai because their parents needed money for a bribe to police and other authorities, as well as for the families' survival. The traffickers were released. Although this was not a remote district, there was not a single school in the huge area nor any development programme or means of livelihood. The village was neglected because all residents belonged to a minority group.

After a long conversation with community members, it became clear that people knew the children would be exploited, but sent them because they felt they had no other choice. Community members face harassment from all sectors, including authorities, and feel humiliated. According to some, they do not want their children around to experience that humiliation, and prefer to send their children away where they can earn an income and survive with some dignity.

Conclusion

There are thousands of cases like Manorama's and Halil's. What interventions can address such deep-seated vulnerabilities and how can the government be made responsible for fulfilling its obligations? These are difficult questions for which the author does not yet have answers. There is agreement among all the actors involved in anti-trafficking programmes that trafficking is a clear violation of human rights. Yet even while human trafficking is a crime that carries heavy punishment, there is little hope that it will end any time soon.

Human trafficking is based on the strong drive to profit from using and exploiting the human body and labour. In this economically competitive world, everyone wants cheap products and services and maximum profit. This can happen only if labour is cheap; thus exploitation is almost inevitable unless a balance is struck between profit and the fair treatment of workers. Structural changes need to be made. People in power need to stand up in support of the protection and promotion of rights of those whose rights are being violated and who are being treated as second-class citizens. This requires strong political will. In the absence of that, it may appear that human trafficking is being reduced, but that is just another myth.

Notes

1. Govinda Neupane, "The Maoist Movement in Nepal: A Class Perspective", in Arjun Karki and David Seddon, eds, *The People's War in Nepal: Left Perspectives*, New Delhi: Adroit Publishers, 2003, pp. 291–314.
2. David Seddon, Jagannath Adhikari and Ganesh Gurung, *Foreign Labour Migration and the Remittance Economy of Nepal: A Report to DFID, Kathmandu*, Norwich: Overseas Development Group, University of East Anglia, 2000.
3. Arjun Karki, "A Radical Reform Agenda for Conflict Resolution in Nepal", in Arjun Karki and David Seddon, eds, *The People's War in Nepal: Left Perspectives*, New Delhi: Adroit Publishers, 2003.
4. IIDS/UNIFEM, *Status and Dimensions of Trafficking Within Nepalese Context*, Kathmandu: IIDS/UNIFEM, 2004.
5. Simone Wyss, *Organisation and Finance of International Labour Migration in Nepal*, Kathmandu: NIDS, 2004.
6. Nepal Rastra Bank, 2005, author's source.
7. NIDS, "Concept Paper for Safe Migration Policy", paper developed for SARIQ.NIDS, Kathmandu, 2005.
8. IIDS/UNIFEM, note 4 above.
9. UNODC, "Trafficking in Persons: Global Patterns", UNODC Report, April 2006.
10. Comrade Parbati, "Women's Participation in People's War", in Arjun Karki and David Seddon, eds, *The People's War in Nepal: Left Perspectives*, New Delhi: Adroit Publishers, 2003, pp. 165–182.
11. IIDS/UNIFEM, note 4 above.
12. WOREC/ILO/IPEC, *Cross Border Trafficking of Boys*, Kathmandu: WOREC/ILO/IPEC, 2002.
13. Personal interviews with women working in domestic sector in New Delhi, India, 2005.
14. Renu Rajbhandari and Binayak P. Rajbhandari, *Girls Trafficking: The Hidden Grief in Himalayas*, Kathmandu: WOREC, 1997.
15. As documented in numerous historical reports of Nepal. Similarly, it appears in different reports produced by activists working against trafficking.
16. In Nepalgunj, in mid-western Nepal, Badi women lived and worked with their families in an area called Gagangunj. This area was targeted by local groups who decided to get rid of sex workers and "clean" the area by throwing them out on the street. In this process, centuries-old communities of women were thrown out of their houses. These women organized together and gained the attention of the state. They visited the home

minister in Kathmandu, with the support of women's organizations like WOREC and the Forum for Women, Law and Development. The home minister assured them of his support, but this was not forthcoming. The women were forced to move to other places and many were exploited.

17. WOREC, "Rape Cases in Morang Sunsari", WOREC, 2003, unpublished.
18. Nepal is considered a Hindu country. According to this religion, the king is an incarnation of Vishnu (a god worshipped by Hindu practitioners).
19. IIDS/UNIFEM, note 4 above.
20. Ibid.
21. WOREC/ILO/IPEC, note 12 above.
22. G. K. Siwakoti, "Country Paper on Nepal", A5948, Kathmandu: ADB/RETA, 2004.
23. INSEC, *Human Rights Year Book*, Kathmandu: Informal Sector Service Centre, 2003.
24. WOREC, *Human Rights Situation in Nepal – Survey Report*, Kathmandu: WOREC, 2003.
25. From the author's personal interview with girls at GB Road, New Delhi, 2005.
26. Information collected at safe migration booths operated by WOREC in five different districts of Nepal, WOREC, 2005, unpublished programme reports.
27. Rajbhandari and Rajbhandari, note 14 above.
28. WOREC, *Situation of Migrant Women Working in Informal Sector of Work in Kathmandu*, Kathmandu: WOREC, 2004.
29. ACHR, *100 Days of Tyranny in Nepal*, Kathmandu: Asian Centre for Human Rights, 2005.
30. Ibid.
31. Jyoti Sanghera, *Strategic Frame Work*, New York: UNICEF, February 2002.
32. Ibid.
33. WOREC/ILO/IPEC, note 12 above.
34. Siwakoti, note 22 above.
35. District taskforces are district-level structures formed by government. Each taskforce is headed by the chair of the district development committee, who is generally an elected person. The women's development officer, who is a government employee with a mandate to work as a gender focal point for that particular district, works on the committee as a member secretary. Besides these two members, other government employees from the education office, agriculture office, police and others constitute the composition of each taskforce.
36. PLAN/Nepal, *Program Evaluation of the Project Prevention of Trafficking and Commercial Exploitation of Children*, Kathmandu: PLAN/Nepal, 2003.
37. WOREC, *Program Evaluation Report of WOREC 2003*, Kathmandu: WOREC, 2003.
38. Siwakoti, note 23 above.
39. WOREC, *Annual Report*, Kathmandu: WOREC, 2002. Twenty-five boys were rescued from the Dhanusha-Indo-Nepal border with the help of WOREC in 2001.
40. WOREC, *Annual Report*, Kathmandu: WOREC, 2004. Formation of Shakti Samuha (an organization of survivors) is an outcome example of this approach.
41. Renu Rajbhandari, *Chelibeti bechbikhanko serophero* (a collection of articles against trafficking), Kathmandu: WOREC, 2004.
42. Jyoti Sanghera, "In the Belly of the Beast: Sex Trade, Prostitution and Globalization", in *Moving the Whore Stigma: Report on the Asia Pacific Regional Consultation on Prostitution*, Bangkok: GAATW, 1997.
43. Jyoti Sanghera, "Enabling and Empowering Mobile Women and Girls", paper presented at Seminar on Promoting Gender Equality to Combat Trafficking in Women and Children, Bangkok, 7–9 October 2002, unpublished.

11

Trafficking in persons in the South Caucasus – Armenia, Azerbaijan and Georgia: New challenges for transitional democracies

Gulnara Shahinian

It is paradoxical that in an age of celebration of human genius and considerable advancement in human rights, there are countries where slavery was only recently officially abolished and in others it remains in its diverse and appalling forms. According to UNICEF, there are 246 million children engaged in child labour, and we are witnessing an increase in the disgraceful phenomenon of human trafficking, which treats people as "disposable" commodities to be used, reused and thrown away.[1] While trafficking in humans is a very old phenomenon, it has been modernized to suit the new world. It remains cruel and inhuman but is extremely dynamic in nature, adapting to the specific combination of local factors that influences demand and enhances the vulnerability of its victims. Trafficking in persons as a global transnational criminal business usually exploits the extreme situations of poverty, despair, crisis, war, human insecurity, cultural and religious traditions, transformation of traditional labour migration patterns and other factors specific to certain geographic areas.[2]

New tactics of ethnic strife and modern wars, inefficient economic and social policies, constant turbulence and sharp political transformations, structural corruption and weak law enforcement have created new dimensions of vulnerability that force people to leave their homes in search of stability and security. More and more people see migration as their only option. Yet while new technologies and global markets accelerate the movement of money and goods across borders, it seems a new "iron curtain" has been created for those who make these goods.

Trafficking in humans: Social, cultural and political dimensions, Cameron and Newman (eds), United Nations University Press, 2007, ISBN 978-92-808-1146-9

Trafficking in humans is not confined to one region. The trafficking web covers the entire world: rich and poor areas of origin, transit and destination. Supply and demand factors have become increasingly integrated and globalized.[3] There is no longer a clear division between origin, transit and destination countries, with a growing number of countries combining all vectors. New expressions of human trafficking include trafficking in organs, trafficking in children for adoption, begging and slavery in armies and the recruitment and use of victims by peacekeeping forces involved in clandestine criminal activities.

The Protocol to Prevent, Suppress and Punish Trafficking in Persons, Especially Women and Children (the UN Anti-trafficking Protocol), supplementing the UN Convention against Transnational Organized Crime, has been ratified by many countries and is now in force. Although the most important and advanced tool defining the phenomenon and combating trafficking, it provides insufficient mechanisms to protect victims. A new Council of Europe Convention against Trafficking in Human Beings, launched by the Council of Europe's Ad Hoc Committee on Actions against Trafficking in Humans (CAHTEH), puts special focus on the human rights of victims of trafficking and presents a framework for the protection of victims and witnesses. It also takes gender equality aspects into consideration. This convention, which has already been signed by many member countries, has also developed effective monitoring mechanisms.

South Caucasus: A new state of affairs – Unknown realities

> If national boundaries should not be obstacles to the trade – we call it globalisation – should they also not be obstacles to compassion, generosity.
> Howard Zinn, *My Country: The World*

The trafficking of human beings from the countries of the newly independent states (NIS) and Eastern Europe has been recognized as a major intensive wave of trafficking during the past decade. Transitional transformations following the disintegration of the Soviet bloc have been raised as a significant factor increasing the vulnerability of people to trafficking, but it must be acknowledged that trafficking in human beings is not a new phenomenon for these countries. The Soviet system by definition employed a repressive policy of control, doing whatever was considered "necessary and sufficient". This created a perfect environment for the exploitation of its population, with numerous instances of exploitation satisfying the definition of "trafficking" under the UN Anti-trafficking Protocol. For example, during *perestroika* there was significant media

coverage of criminal cases against clandestine cotton factories in Uzbekistan and Middle Asia. Brezhnev's reign included situations of people
working in conditions of extreme exploitation, receiving almost nothing
for their work while being denied the right to leave. The situation in the
cotton industry remains exploitative, although the industry is not alone.[4]

In the South Caucasus the issue of trafficking did not enter mainstream
awareness until the year 2000. The first systematic research on trafficking
in persons in the countries of the South Caucasus was published by the
International Organization for Migration (IOM) in 2000–2002.[5] To those
based in the region, the research findings were shocking – an alarming
outside view of the "invisible" processes that were occurring in societies
which prided themselves on having strong traditional value systems, community ties and an inherited philosophy of great national character.
People could not understand how, while they had been busy with daily
survival, such values had corroded, resulting in shocking instances of
trafficking – for example, people trafficking their own neighbours' children, or someone's aunt becoming the victim of a man specifically hired
to pretend to be in love with her.[6]

The IOM's research revealed much in common about the *modus operandi* of criminals and crime partners, the profile of victims and the countries of destination, which are predominantly Turkey, the United Arab
Emirates and Russia, and to a lesser extent Greece and other EU countries, the United States and Israel. Men, women and underage girls are
trafficked for different purposes: labour, sex, begging, transplantation of
organs and adoption. As well as all three Caucasian countries being prin-
cipally countries of origin and transit, there were reports and media coverage that they may also be countries of destination. There has been
some evidence in police reports and the media that Armenia and Georgia
have been "targeted as destination countries ... though the extent is un-
known" for women from Russia and Uzbekistan.[7]

There are many different methods of recruitment, although the majority of victims are recruited through friends, neighbours, tour agencies and
ads in newspapers. There is scarce information on organizers and recruiters, but there is significant evidence of the organized character of
the trafficking chain.

There are no exact statistics on the number of victims from the countries of the Caucasus. The IOM Armenian report gives approximate
data only on the annual number of women who travel to Dubai, but
does not include figures on trafficked victims.[8] The IOM report on Azerbaijan states:

> According to official data, women from Russia and Ukraine were most fre-
> quently detained in the UAE in 2000 and 2001, followed by women from Azer-

baijan and Uzbekistan. About 900 Azerbaijani women were detained on suspicion of involvement in prostitution in 2001 and the first months of 2002.[9]

The IOM suggests that not all those detained with Azeri passports may have been Azeri nationals, as sometimes traffickers use Azerbaijan as a transit country and obtain Azerbaijan passports. Also some of the deported victims re-entered Dubai using other names and documents.[10]

In recent times the necessity for more comprehensive research on the impact of current policies and programmes has been raised. Some research, addressing specific areas such as the impact of awareness-raising campaigns and forced labour of children, is under way in the region.

The human dimensions of post-Soviet transformation in the South Caucasus

Within the last century the Soviet Union, which included a huge geographical space and numerous nationalities in 15 republics, was created and disbanded. Little more than a decade ago the Soviet system of political control, economic planning and predictability collapsed for millions of people newly "located" in independent countries. *Perestroika* was born – meaning the transformation of the entire philosophy of relationships between citizens and the state, and the introduction of transitional social, political and economic arrangements. While these new systems have the long-term goal of developing modern democracies, they are still in the process of building the foundations, which in these fragile and turbulent times is no mean feat.

Hopes of a swift move to a democratic and prosperous future were frustrated. Many of the expected reforms have turned into a chronic process of problem-solving exacerbated by the disappearance of public sector employment, the loss of agricultural competitiveness and state-subsidized health care and education, the erosion of the social protection system and the hyperinflation which wiped out the savings people had accumulated though years of hard work under socialism.

Armenia, Azerbaijan and Georgia share much common history yet differ in many historical, cultural and religious ways. Riddled with the difficulties of building new societies and adapting to neo-liberal markets, these countries have also suffered internal conflicts and natural disasters.

Even by rough estimates, the number of migrants from the CIS has risen to alarming heights. In 1990 the population of Georgia was approximately 5.4 million. According to Georgian data the unofficial number of people who left between 1990 and 1998 is between 800,000 and 1 million.[11] In 1990 the population of Armenia was 3.7 million.[12] It is commonly acknowledged by most scholars that since 1991 at least half a million, or possibly as many as 1 million, have left.[13] Some have joined relatives and/or gained employment through official channels, but pressing conditions and limited official opportunities for migration made many turn to smugglers.

Unemployment, poverty and economic decline

Some assessments place the number of those living below the poverty line in the NIS at around 10 per cent of the world's poor.[14] According to official statistics, the registered unemployment rate is 14.9 per cent in Georgia, 20 per cent in Armenia and 20 per cent in Azerbaijan.[15] In reality the number is much higher. Official data reflect registered cases of unemployment. Many people do not register simply because unemployment benefit is extremely low and registration does not lead to employment. Those employed short term are counted as employed. The unemployment rate of women is much higher than that of men. For example, in Armenia women comprise 66 per cent of all registered unemployed.[16]

The lack of employment opportunities, and corresponding livelihood, is a strong incentive for migration, particularly for those with labour skills. This was particularly the case with early migration. People hoped to find somewhere abroad where their education and knowledge were still in demand. Their belief in their chances of success was based on unrealistic expectations developed as a result of their isolation (the result of information censorship under Soviet rule). Their confidence was bolstered by having achieved high educational levels, but their isolation meant they were ill-informed about the requirements of modern Western labour markets.

At first success stories seeped through of intellectuals who had been oppressed under Soviet rule but had become well known in the West following their emigration. Later, some years after independence, when tragic stories of (some famous) émigrés emerged, the flow did not stop. With the decline in living standards, people found themselves ready to take any job abroad if it was paid and it could help their families survive. No effective labour migration policy has been developed in Armenia, Azerbaijan or Georgia, reflecting a gross mismanagement of human potential. Even with limited foreign investment, the governments of the Caucasus demonstrated an inability to use the benefits of globalization and assist their nationals to meet new market requirements – to protect their labour force and create jobs.

According to UN data, the poverty rate in Armenia is 42 per cent of people living below the national poverty line, with 17 per cent extremely poor. The reality is much higher. In Azerbaijan 68 per cent and in Georgia 23 per cent live in poverty.[17] In 1990, after Armenia's economic decline had already started, it ranked forty-seventh in the UNDP's Human Development Index (HDI) but was still considered a "developed" country. In 2002, 10 years after independence, Armenia was ranked seventy-sixth of 173 counties in the HDI, and was listed in the "medium human development" category.[18]

The general level of accessibility of health care has declined significantly from the Soviet period. Armenia is now third among NIS countries regarding maternal mortality, Azerbaijan eleventh and Georgia twelfth. The drop in the quality of medical services and the introduction of paid medical services, combined with the rise of poverty and other negative phenomena, have caused a fall in population.

The difficulty of adapting to these new conditions is exacerbated by the fact that this population, especially the middle class, had known a middle-class lifestyle and good social protection. There is great frustration and cynicism, because on the one hand people have skills, knowledge, energy and the potential to work, while on the other there is absolutely no place to apply these. People experienced great psychological distress as they became "unwanted" in their own societies. For many, dignity and rights are closely connected with being able to participate in the labour market and being appropriately rewarded. While the provision of international humanitarian assistance was highly appreciated by the states because it enabled survival strategies to be developed, the use of human skills and potential came late. Those with rich, industrious capabilities became passive consumers, with no other option but to wait and receive assistance or to migrate.

Man-made and natural disasters

> The contemporary situation of armed conflicts or internal disturbance ... leads to trafficking. And women and children are disproportionately targeted during such situations and constitute the majority of victims.[19]

For the former republics, independence was accepted as a new political condition offering the opportunity to restore justice to the many issues and territories in dispute. Territories had been identified and "given" to different republics without close attention to their histories and the ethnicity of their citizens, on the whim of whichever Soviet leader had power at the time. This process and the resulting "distribution" of territories created tensions between republics, while also giving Soviet leaders a useful tool to keep the republics under control. Similar to other countries of the former Soviet Union, Armenia, Azerbaijan and Georgia experience political and military conflicts that remain unresolved. The independence declared by Nagorno Karabach as an autonomous republic turned into full-scale war between Azerbajan and Armenia. Internal conflicts in Georgia over the status of Abkhasia and South Osetia created a mass of internally displaced persons (IDPs) within the country. The consequent destruction has had a heavy impact on regional economic development by influencing investment activities and budget distribution and hampering the region's integration into European and international structures.

In addition to the damage created by conflict, the situation in Armenia was aggravated by the 1988 earthquake that affected almost 20 per cent of the territory and, according to official statistics, resulted in the death of around 50,000 people and the destruction of houses and infrastructures of many hundreds of thousands of families.

Insecurity and alarm

The collapse of communism brought about many positive changes relating to freedom and democracy. Apart from guaranteeing security for the state and its population as a whole, a comprehensive concept of security has increasingly included the notion of security for the individual and the protection of human rights. Security, especially external security, is no longer viewed in military dimensions only, as it was during the Cold War, although new areas likely to pose physical security risks are gaining importance. There is now a close connection between internal and external security problems. Apart from defence, these include foreign and domestic affairs, economic policy, education, information and communication and the environment. The significance of each individual aspect is subject to swift change given the dynamic development and mutual interdependence of these areas.

Unfortunately the transitional social, economic and political structures resulting from the fall of communism effectively resulted in lower social and economic indexes, higher unemployment, growing poverty and a broadly held perception that the state had left individuals unprotected. "Frozen or forgotten conflicts" also created uncertainty about long-held expectations of stability.[20] Although the rapidity and nature of changes had a mixed impact on people, many experienced them with alarm and fear; people felt a sense of alienation. Weakening social cohesion, even at the level of family, had a strong impact. People lost their sense of "home", which influenced their decision to look for opportunities abroad.

Unequal status of women

The transformations that took place in the Caucasus have disproportionately impacted on women. Women are among the majority of unemployed and poor, and the representation of women in decision-making positions is insignificant. Existing inequalities have been exacerbated by new social policies that have resulted in the closure of childcare centres and a reduction in pensions and social welfare packages. Traditional ideology limiting women's roles to familial responsibility seems to have been strengthened, making local employment impossible, so pressing poverty and a sense of duty towards children and family have forced women to look for work abroad.

Research demonstrates that the majority of women who have chosen migration have done so as the only means of survival for themselves and their families. The situation at home is often dire for single women or single heads of households whose husbands have died or migrated in search of jobs, leaving women to take care of children or their extended family alone. These women include single women, widows whose husbands died during recent wars and local and refugee women whose husbands migrated and failed to assist their families or started new families in their country of migration.[21]

According to ILO estimates, the feminization of international migration is the most pronounced social and economic phenomenon of migration.[22] If single men or families are predominantly smuggled, single women are mostly trafficked. Gender plays an important role in influencing whether migrants end up smuggled or as victims of trafficking. Even upon return, women and men are accepted differently by society, with women judged mercilessly.

For women, traditional stereotypes and discriminatory labour and career policies in countries of origin are exacerbated by discriminatory labour policies and narrow opportunities in countries of migration, limiting women's employment mostly to the informal sector: domestic households, entertainment venues, hotels, restaurants and sales and manufacturing, which traffickers tend to control.

The demand for Armenian women's labour, in particular, has increased in recent years as more and more diaspora women, along with female emigrants from the former Soviet Union, are now living in the United States. Armine Ishkhanian writes that many such women are working and/or have become affluent.[23] These women either need or want domestic workers to care for their children or parents and to keep house for them as they pursue their careers or recreational activities. While "employing" Caucasian women as domestics is extremely economical for the families, it places these women in a dependent and vulnerable position with little or no place for privacy or freedom. There are many stories of abuse and mistreatment of women in these situations.

Women have been the major victims of the negative effects of privatization and globalization, as a result of limited opportunities and restrictions on the labour market for women in their own countries coupled with the international labour market providing jobs for women primarily in unregulated markets such as domestic work and the sex industry. As mentioned by Patrick Taran and Gloria Moreno-Fontes, "restrictions on entry, admission and work affect men and women migrants differently".[24] For instance, most legal channels offer opportunities in male-dominated sectors (construction and agricultural work). The situation seems to marginalize female migrants even further and exposes them to the worst forms of abuse.

Traditional labour migration patterns exploited by criminal groups

The seasonal labour migration of men from the Caucasus for construction, agricultural work or trade has a long history and tradition. The traditional migration pattern to certain regions of Russia was facilitated by workers' knowledge of the language, the absence of borders and relationships with state agencies that provided work and supplied labour for seasonal work. That seasonal work was beneficial to both sides. Seasonal migrant workers from the South Caucasus were welcomed by village or regional administrations for construction, road-building and agricultural work. Local authorities legalized their stay and took care of workers.

With the dissolution of the Soviet Union, the introduction of privatization and the economic decline in Russia, labour relationships underwent a drastic change. State agencies that contracted labour migrants have been replaced by private agencies, some of which view migrants as a free labour force that will do their work for no or very limited investment. The new, very restrictive mechanism of immigrant registration and the bureaucracies connected with that process restrict the possibilities of legalizing the stay of migrant workers. Employers use workers' illegal immigration status and threaten reporting them to police. Some are never paid for their work. In some cases gangs act as labour recruiters, ostensibly recruiting for seasonal labour but actually recruiting those they can make work under conditions of severe exploitation and forced labour.

Unfortunately some factors, including turbulence in the Russian economy, appear to have exacerbated xenophobia towards Caucasians and there have been numerous registered cases of violence against workers and tradesmen of Caucasian origin.

Absence of comprehensive migration policies and monitoring

The majority of those who find themselves caught in the trafficking chain are looking for labour opportunities in foreign countries, as they could not find jobs that corresponded to their education and experience, or for that matter any jobs at all, in their own countries. Governments have made very few attempts to regulate labour migration or facilitate cooperation with those countries that have a demand for skilled professionals. In some CIS countries labour recruitment agencies no longer require licences to develop their activities, which gives them great freedom to manoeuvre. Simultaneously, the restrictive policies of destination countries increasingly view trafficking as a security issue, thus equating the status of trafficking victim to that of illegal migrant, with the applicable punishment and deportation.

Corruption of state officials and weak rule of law

The corruption of state officials has been stressed in all three South Caucasian countries in the US Department of State *Trafficking in Persons Report*.[25] Corruption and the absence of law enforcement effectively corrode the morals of society, resulting in the most unacceptable violation of human rights: the buying and selling of human beings. This business is not only lucrative for all operators in the entire trafficking chain, but each element of the chain is very much connected with the participation of state officials.

In some instances consular officials in destination country consulates carry out corrupt practices. For example, underage children must have notarized letters of permission from both parents before they can be granted appropriate travel visas; these are not always possible to get and traffickers use forged documents. Or the age of an underage girl may be increased in order to get permission to enter, for instance, an Arab country. These situations involve forgery of documents and/or the negligence of border control officials.

It is very difficult for "outsiders" to get a visa to countries of the Shengen Agreement (which allows people who are legally present in European countries that are party to the agreement to move about freely without having to show passports when crossing internal frontiers – the name comes from the village of Schengen in Luxembourg where the agreement was signed in 1985). Tour agencies that recruit and transport victims promise visas to the Shengen zone in their advertisements, making their services essential for those wishing to migrate for work. Some consular officers "collaborate" with criminal groups. Later, in the destination country, extending the visa only becomes possible because of corrupt local officials. These processes are possible because of weak law enforcement. Countries do not always apply the international instruments to which they are party, or the local legislation that has recently been introduced.

Attractive neighbours – Destinations

Research on trafficking from countries of the South Caucasus has identified the United Arab Emirates and Turkey as the primary countries of destination used by criminal groups, though the geography of criminal trade has tended to change, involving such countries as Israel, Spain and Greece.

Divided by conflicts, the countries of the South Caucasus have been united by criminal groups transporting victims through each other's territory. Georgia, being the closest neighbour to Turkey, has been used by criminal groups transporting victims from Azerbaijan and Armenia to Turkey. Reports and interviews with victims also mention that child victims from the South Caucasus are not transported directly from their country of origin to the United Arab Emirates but through transit countries, even when there are direct flights from source to destination countries.

United Arab Emirates

Dubai, one of the seven United Arab Emirates, has enjoyed enormous economic development primarily based on large oil and gas production. Development of a free economic zone combined with the favourable economic climate means Dubai has become one of the most prosperous countries in the Gulf, attracting foreign investment and migrant labour. Dubai's economy provides citizens with a high per capita income. The development of tourism and other sectors has increased the demand for labour in the services sector, such that foreign guest-workers comprise up to 98 per cent of the country's private sector workforce, with foreign nationals comprising about 85 per cent of the population. The local population's increase in living standards has facilitated increased demand for domestic servants. As well as the demand for labour, Dubai offers comparatively high salaries, which has attracted workers from India, Pakistan, the Philippines and other Arab states. Since the disintegration of the former Soviet Union (FSU) many workers from the Caucasus have also found jobs in the service and construction sectors in Dubai. Maids from the CIS have become popular in domestic service, as they are well educated and in many cases can combine different services, such as being a maid and also a music teacher for the household's children. Maids or domestic help may be obtained either through agencies in Dubai or directly from abroad. A simple procedure was established for recruitment of foreign domestic labour, allowing maids to be recruited either through an agency or by a resident of Dubai directly, but not by businesses. The maid can receive a working visa for one year. It is illegal to employ domestic help sponsored by another person. Transferring the sponsorship of a domestic helper to a new employer is not permitted unless a period of at least one year has elapsed from the date the helper last left the country.

Foreign investments and booming business have also increased demand in the entertainment sector. Although Dubai is a free economic zone, liberal labour recruitment laws and the market regulate the demands of all sectors of social life, including the entertainment industry. Prostitution is officially prohibited in Dubai, though it seems these laws have little impact on the operation of prostitution from disco bars and hotels, perhaps reflecting the inherent contradiction between the driving ideologies: the market-oriented economy and the "restrictions" of Islam. For example, the sale, purchase or consumption of alcoholic beverages outside hotels is not permitted. The majority of hotels belong to foreigners, and in them the use of alcohol and entertainment is allowed.

The United Arab Emirates is not only a country of destination for trafficked women from the Caucasus. In disco bars and hotels in Dubai one can see women from Russia, Moldova, Ukraine, India, the Philippines and Middle Asian republics of the FSU. According to the US *Trafficking in Persons Report*:

> women trafficked into domestic servitude come primarily from Sri Lanka, Indonesia, India, and the Philippines. Victims trafficked as domestic male servants, labourers, and unskilled workers in construction and agriculture come mainly from Pakistan, Afghanistan, India, and Bangladesh. Many low-skilled foreign workers have their passports withheld, contracts altered, and suffer partial, short-, or long-term non-payment of salaries. Women from Central Asia and Eastern Europe have reported being lured with the promise of legitimate jobs and then forced into commercial sexual exploitation. Boys from Pakistan and Bangladesh have been trafficked to the United Arab Emirates to be camel jockeys.[26]

The IOM's report on Azerbaijan raises the point that the majority of hotels where victims of trafficking are brought are expensive, prestigious hotels that are visited by rich Arabs and foreign businessmen. In one interview, a high-ranking immigration official blamed the policy of allowing the use of alcohol and the introduction of the entertainment business, as it has had an extremely negative impact on the value system of Arabs. "Opening the doors to globalisation and its benefits, we were not ready to accept its negative implications on the formation of the values and outlook of young Arabs."[27]

All reports underline that the key reasons for the intensive trafficking in humans to Dubai are the high market demand, the relatively high payment for services, simple transport through direct flights, the liberal visa regime and visa-extension mechanism and the absence of legislation punishing traffickers.

There are no exact statistics on the number of victims from the countries of the Caucasus, although women from Russia, Ukraine, Azerbaijan and Uzbekistan have been detained in the United Arab Emirates. However, the official data are not exact: as mentioned earlier, not all those detained with Azeri passports may have been Azeri nationals. Also, some of the victims had been deported and re-entered Dubai using false names and documents. The IOM's Armenian report gives approximate data only on the annual number of women who travelled to Dubai, but does not provide figures on trafficked victims.

Turkey

Since the 1960s Turkey has pursued a pro-tourism policy as a means to enhance its foreign currency reserves. Although traditionally a country of labour export, nowadays Turkey is a country of transit to other European countries, particularly Greece, for women and girls trafficked for sexual exploitation, and a destination for persons trafficked for the purposes of sexual and labour exploitation. Most victims come from countries of the FSU, including Azerbaijan, Georgia, Armenia, Russia, Ukraine, Moldova and Romania. A number of factors make Turkey attractive to migrants from those countries:

- there is the possibility of getting short-term employment in the shadow tourism industry and the informal market
- there is a simple visa regime – the visa can be obtained at the border and is valid for up to one month
- it is close to the Caucasian countries and transportation is cheap and easy; for example, the bus travels every day from each capital city and there are comparably cheap and direct air links
- it provides an effective transit point to Greece and other EU countries
- there is a similarity of religion, language and culture for Azerbaijanians.

Many people travel to Turkey to do petty trade and earn money in the service sector. For those willing to work, the economy in Turkey, especially in Istanbul, offers the possibility of finding employment, even though it provides no social or economic security and migrants face deportation if caught working without a valid visa or work permit. There is some anecdotal evidence that fear of deportation or being put in a detention centre is used by criminal groups to threaten victims and coerce their acceptance of traffickers' exploitative work conditions. IOM research and articles in the media have identified frequent deception and exploitation after arrival, including being forced to work long hours, confiscation of passports, lack of freedom of movement and wages being either reduced or withheld altogether.[28]

Current responses in the South Caucasus

There has been significant progress from the governments of the South Caucasus since the year 2000, when the first reports of human trafficking were largely rejected as sensationalist information. Only a very short time has elapsed in which to understand the complexity of the phenomenon and develop policies and measures to counteract it. Pressure from international intergovernmental organizations and the US Department of State added incentive for the governments to acknowledge the need to develop policies to fight trafficking in persons.

All governments have moved forward. Almost simultaneously (2002 in Armenia and soon after in Azerbaijan and Georgia) all governments established interagency taskforces, composed of representatives of various ministries and NGOs, with responsibility for coordinating efforts to combat human trafficking. In Armenia the anti-trafficking commission is located in the Ministry of Foreign Affairs, in Georgia it is under the Security Council and in Azerbaijan under the Ministry of the Interior. Plans of action have been developed, outlining timetables and joint actions for states, international agencies and NGOs.

All three countries have signed the UN Convention against Transnational Organized Crime and its supplementary protocols. Armenia and Azerbaijan have ratified the umbrella convention and protocols, while the Georgian government is in the process of ratification. The countries are all signatories to the Convention on the Elimination of All Forms of Discrimination against Women (CEDAW) and the UN Convention on the Rights of the Child. Some countries have signed the new Council of Europe Convention on Actions against Trafficking in Human Beings.

Significant changes have been made to legislation. For example, in all three countries child trafficking attracts a severe penalty and trafficking has been criminalized. Additional to the development of separate articles in their criminal codes, all three countries have also been developing separate, comprehensive laws to combat trafficking in human beings. For example, in Georgia and Azerbaijan anti-trafficking laws have been developed and adopted by the National Assembly. In Armenia discussions are in process. All three countries perceive punishment of traffickers as their primary goal. Mechanisms for the protection of victims remain insufficient or are only beginning to be addressed.

All three governments have signed agreements on legal assistance and information exchange on a wide range of issues with transit countries and some countries of destination. Armenia has signed an agreement on extradition with the United Arab Emirates. Azerbaijan and Georgia have signed agreements on legal assistance and extradition with Turkey.

The existing plans of action suffer some common shortcomings as a result of their conventional bureaucratic approach. Trafficking prevention is predominantly based on multilevel education and information strategies. Some are very creative, including posters, performances and films, but these strategies are only a partial remedy and need to be combined with a wider range of programmes addressing the very root causes of the problem: strategies to increase gender equity, provide greater social and economic empowerment and address labour migration, weak law enforcement and corruption. These areas are insufficiently covered.

The plans of action contain victim protection programmes that include a wide range of initiatives. Some are currently being implemented and have produced impressive results, such as running hotlines and shelters providing legal, medical and psychological assistance and accommodation for victims. While this emergency assistance is commendable, medium- and longer-term support is required, particularly assistance to facilitate reintegration into victims' home communities. This would include provision of vocational training, support finding employment and housing for the victims and education and sensitizing of home communities. A complex project of victim identification, assistance, community sensitization and information is being successfully implemented by a joint project of the government, the UNDP and UMCOR in Armenia. A number of other programmes have been initiated in all three countries to assist victims of trafficking, including providing information on assistance through media campaigns and hotline services and information programmes targeting the entire population on the risks of being trafficked. State-based interagency commissions, while important mechanisms for coordinating and developing anti-trafficking policies, commonly lack sufficient human and financial resources to be truly effective. Armenia, Azerbaijan and Georgia have recently introduced special units to deal institutionally with the fight against trafficking. This fight requires the participation of many actors, government and NGO, drawing on their particular areas of expertise. It is also vital that state agencies, including law enforcement, recognize the importance of civil society in the process of policy development and the implementation of those policies. The development of common goals and collaboration between state agencies and civil society are innovative processes for CIS countries and begin to transform power relationships. Significant achievements are reported by these countries in this area.

The need to facilitate cooperation and complementary policies is vital but extremely difficult in the South Caucasus, as it remains divided by conflicts. A number of international agencies have acted as facilitators, establishing regional cooperation. For example, the Council of Europe conducted a seminar in Tbilisi (Georgia), with participants from Georgia, Armenia, Azerbaijan, Turkey, Ukraine and Russia, with the aim of establishing cooperation and an exchange of experiences and ideas. The Organization for Security and Cooperation in Europe (OSCE) and the American Bar Association Central and Eastern European Law Initiative (ABACEELI) organized regional activities at state and NGO levels. These strategies mark the beginning of anti-trafficking methods that need to be systematic and coordinated, envisioning long-term strategic and creative approaches.

Migration policies in the countries of destination

The main destination countries for victims from the South Caucasus have also been active in introducing policies and programmes to combat trafficking in humans.

United Arab Emirates

Over the last few years the government of Dubai has demonstrated greater interest in developing policies to combat human trafficking, with measures including stronger border screening and identification of illegal entries. The Department of Naturalization and Residency (under the Ministry of the Interior) established a central operations room to track the arrival and departure of individuals in the Emirates. The government instituted the use of retinal scanning to add biometrics identification information to its databases as a means to combat document fraud.[29] According to information from border police, a watchlist has been introduced identifying agencies and individuals who have been active in illegal activities. Computerized data identify companies that have operated illegally in the past and reject "invitations" to migrant workers sent by those companies. Trained women border guards now intervene to interview female migrants in cases of suspected trafficking.

In 1999 the government limited the number of female migrants coming unaccompanied from CIS countries. National authorities banned single NIS women under 35 years of age from entering the United Arab Emirates without an accompanying male relative, or if coming for business purposes they must have special documents confirming the purpose of their visit. The *Gulf News* recently stated that the government is planning to raise the age threshold to 41 for single women entering Dubai alone. The government has also recently criminalized the use of child camel jockeys and will now conduct DNA and medical tests to investigate "parents" of camel jockeys.

According to the US *Trafficking in Persons Report*, the Dubai Police Human Rights Department has delivered a number of outreach programmes.[31] The Dubai Tourist Security Department operates a 24-hour hotline to assist visitors with enquiries or problems. Information about the hotline is distributed to tourists identified as potential trafficking victims at points of entry. The Ministry of Labour and Social Affairs distributes an information booklet to foreign workers outlining their rights under labour law, describing how to pursue labour disputes and providing contact information for assistance. Victims' assistance coordinator positions have been created at each police station, with coordinators receiving special training in victims' assistance and protection.

The penal code specifically prohibits trafficking, although cases of trafficking can also be prosecuted under other statutes. Law enforcement actively investigates trafficking cases and complaints of abuse. The Ministry of Health requires annual physical examinations of foreign employees by medical personnel with specialized training to look for signs of abuse.[30]

According to the IOM, the Ministry of the Interior and national security bodies take necessary measures to detect illegal migrants and publicize monthly reports on arresting illegal aliens.[31] They also do police raids in places where female migrants often congregate and detain them for three main offences: involvement in prostitution, possessing alcoholic beverages in their flats (where, if they are prostitutes, they accept clients) and not having proper documents. Dubai police have also documented many cases of murder of women from the NIS. The US *Trafficking in Persons Report* mentions that there have been special programmes targeting protection of victims of trafficking:

> They are not detained, jailed or deported. The Ministry of Health maintains social workers and counselors in all public hospitals to which medical personnel refer patients when abuse is suspected. Counseling services are available in

public hospitals. It has also been mentioned that police departments have special shelters for victims that are separate from jails, though it would be more desirable if these shelters were operated by NGO or Ministry of Social Protection. Victims are not prosecuted for violations of other laws, such as immigration or prostitution.[32]

Irrespective of the above statement, there are still cases of immediate deportation of victims of trafficking, though fewer than before. The United Arab Emirates has ratified the UN Anti-trafficking Protocol and the Convention on the Rights of the Child, but is not party to the Convention on the Rights of Migrant Workers and has not ratified CEDAW.

Turkey

The government of Turkey has initiated significant legislative and institutional reforms in response to human trafficking. Programmes have been developed jointly by government agencies and NGOs. In August 2002 new laws were introduced: one covering issues related to smuggling, the other related to trafficking. According to one new law (No. 4817), work permits are now more restrictive, with the aim of limiting the number of illegal migrants entering the country. Limitations have also been introduced to citizenship laws to curb the acquisition of residency permits through marriage.

The new penal code, amended in 2002, includes a definition of trafficking and determines heavy penalties for it. While voluntary individual prostitution is legal in Turkey, incitement to prostitution and trafficking in human beings are crimes and are punishable under the penal code and the Law on Combating Benefit-Oriented Criminal Organizations.

In Turkey the Ministry of Foreign Affairs chairs the National Task Force on Combating Trafficking in Human Beings, which is comprised of representatives of different ministries. The Directorate General of the Status and Problems of Women facilitates cooperation and coordination with NGOs. In accordance with the national action plan, NGOs active in the protection of foreign victims of trafficking are encouraged and supported "by the best means possible".[33] The director-general of consular affairs in the Ministry of Foreign Affairs is the designated focal point for general international contacts on anti-trafficking efforts. The Ministry of Interior has also appointed national contact points to cooperate with the Stability Pact Task Force in areas of awareness-raising, exchange of expert information, law enforcement and victim protection. The contact point within the Ministry of Justice has assumed coordination of legal reform. A new Department for Children's Affairs has been established within the Ministry of Interior to address the specific needs of children.

The Ministry of Labour and Social Security is the agency responsible for providing foreign workers with work permits.

Turkey has signed a bilateral agreement to combat trafficking and organized crime with Azerbaijan and is expected to ratify it soon. According to a Turkish government report, a special budget allocation has been made to assist victims of trafficking with health care and accommodation.[34] These activities are being implemented by the government in cooperation with NGOs. Governors have been authorized by the Ministry of the Interior to issue humanitarian visas and temporary residence permits to victims if necessary for rehabilitation.

Turkey is party to the Convention on the Rights of the Child and adopted the optional protocol to the convention; and in 2003 it ratified the UN Anti-trafficking Protocol. Turkey has signed an agreement on legal assistance in criminal matters with Azerbaijan, as well as an agreement on extradition.

Combating trafficking in human beings: Looking forward

Though they differ in history, culture, religion, modern political situation, economic structure and their relationships with each other, the five countries of Armenia, Azerbaijan, Georgia, the United Arab Emirates and Turkey have been united by criminal groups using them for their modern-day slave trade. No conflicts, "hot" or "frozen", no issues related to past history and no ideologies divide the criminals who operate there.

As described above, significant work is being done in these countries to fight human trafficking. The advancements are obvious, but are these efforts enough to lessen trafficking and protect the majority of victims? Of course not. There is still much to understand and to do. Many victims are treated as criminals. Many are deported. Having experienced trafficking's horrors, they are sent by governments to their home countries where they have no support or, if they are lucky, the limited support of temporary shelter before being left on their own as no comprehensive reintegration programmes exist. They face increased vulnerability and are prime targets for retrafficking.

The histories of all these countries strongly impact on the relationship between state security, human security and human rights. Adding to the current complicated regional situation, international events appear to be strengthening society's expectations of protection from the state, which in turn means the prioritization of state security over human security. Alongside the threat of terrorism and trafficking in drugs and weapons, human trafficking is considered a challenge to state security. This may partly explain why new legislation has predominantly been repressive in nature: only determining punishments for traffickers, while offering very limited protection for victims. We are witnessing increased limitations on legal entry to destination countries and their labour markets.

This restrictive attitude is also reflected in the work and composition of the South Caucasian counter-trafficking taskforces. Governments control the agenda by ensuring representation from national security, justice, border police, federal police and immigration ministries, while representation from labour and employment, social protection, health and education ministries and NGOs, which play a tremendously important role in trafficking-prevention programmes and victim assistance, is limited. This approach is supported by many donor agencies that fund capacity-building programmes for law enforcement agencies. It goes without saying that this is an important component of counter-trafficking policies, but as the root causes of trafficking are unemployment and social insecurity, trafficking policies are unbalanced and do not address the core issues. There have been very few programmes in the Caucasus addressing the training and capacity-building needs of labour and social protection agency employees.

In recent times the knowledge, experience and collected data in these countries have gradually brought an important shift and a broader conceptualization of the trafficking phenomenon. Trafficking is not only realized as an issue of the sexual exploitation of women and children but also as an issue of the labour exploitation of men, women and children. It is the search for employment opportunities that drives these hard-working and skilled Caucasians out of their homes, and in many instances into trafficked situations, as the legal avenues for employment become increasingly limited.

As the fight against trafficking is a partnership between many actors, states, international agencies and NGOs, each has different areas of mandate and expertise. It is important that these roles are clearly defined, with no governments dominating the entire sphere, international agencies replacing governments or NGO programmes or NGOs taking on the enormity of all the activities required.

The success of counter-trafficking policies lies in the establishment of effective prevention programmes, broadening the scope of victim protection programmes, cooperation between different counter-trafficking partners within countries and cooperation between countries. The provision of assistance to victims of trafficking should be unconditional, irrespective of country "budget limitations". The key dimensions of vulnerability must be addressed in anti-trafficking action plans in all three Caucasian countries, with prioritizing the development of new labour and migration policies that address the modern realities of the labour market, the provision of complex measures of social protection and strategies to fight against corruption. Legislation, policy and programmes to address the vulnerability of children must be developed in the best interest of the child. These must include measures to address the conditions of children in special institutions and street children. Though almost all countries have ratified the Convention on the Rights of the Child and have local legislation on this issue, careful analysis is necessary to identify all aspects of children's vulnerability. Areas requiring close attention include systems of registration of birth, adoption mechanisms and child slavery.

Central to the development of anti-trafficking policy must be a clear and broad understanding of the phenomenon so that all interconnected elements may be effectively designed and synchronized. The fight against trafficking in human beings requires broad vision and supra-political interests: the main interest being the protection of those who need help. Cooperation between countries of origin and destination is of vital importance, as both parties in the process surely must be driven by common goals. In the existing political situation, with frozen conflicts and the absence of diplomatic relations in the region, international agencies can act to facilitate these programmes with NGOs, which have proven dynamic and important partners for building relationships and working on joint and mutually beneficial projects. There is increased understanding of the benefits of cooperation over isolation in anti-trafficking work, and meetings and other cooperative measures are being reported between representatives of various levels of government and representatives of different agencies. The fight against trafficking is the perfect arena for cooperation and mutual understanding, as, irrespective of each state's differences, the goals are the same: the protection of human beings.

Notes

1. UNICEF, "Child Labour", Fact sheet, 2004, available at www.unicef.org/protection/ files/child_labour.pdf. The term "disposable people" is used by Kevin Bales, *The Disposable People. New Slavery in the Global Economy*, Berkeley: University of California Press, 2004, p. 11.01.
2. UN Office on Drugs and Crime, *Trafficking in Women and Girls. Report of Expert Group Meeting*, Glen Cove, NY: UN Office on Drugs and Crime, Division for the Advancement of Women, November 2002.
3. Vitit Muntarborn, "Human Rights Versus Human Trafficking in the Face of Globalization", paper presented to Conference on Human Rights Challenge of Globalization in Asia-Pacific-US: Trafficking in Persons, Especially Women and Children, Globalization Research Center, Hawaii, November 2002, available at www.hawaii.edu/global/projects _activities/Trafficking/Vitit.pdf, p. 4.
4. International Crisis Group, "The Curse of Cotton: Central Asia's Destructive Monoculture", Asia Report No. 93, Bishkek/Brussels: ICG, 28 February 2005, p. 1.

5. IOM, "Trafficking in Women and Children from the Republic of Armenia. A Study", Yerevan: IOM, 2001, p. 4; IOM, "Shattered Dreams. Report on Trafficking in Persons in Azerbaijan", Geneva: IOM, 2002, p. 17; IOM, "Hardship Abroad or Hunger at Home: A Study on Irregular Migration in Georgia", Georgia: IOM , 2001, p. 10.

6. Nana Nazarova, "Problem of Trafficking in Humans in Georgia", Trafficking in Humans, Resource Book, Democracy Today, Yerevan 2003, p. 46.

7. International Organization for Migration, "Analysis of Institutional and Legal Framework and Overview of Cooperation Patterns in the Field of Counter Trafficking in Eastern Europe and Central Asia", Research Report, IOM, Geneva, November, p. 3.

8. IOM Armenia, note 5 above, p. 10.

9. IOM Azerbaijan, note 5 above, p. 6.

10. Ibid.

11. Available at www.protectionproject.org/projects.htm.

12. Victoria Ter-Nikoghosyan, "Armenia Human Development Report 1996", UNDP, 1996, available at www.undp.am/docs/publications/publicationsarchive/nhdr96/.

13. Armine Ishkhanian, "Mobile Motherhood: Armenian Women's Labour Migration in the Post Soviet Period", *Diaspora* 11(3), 2002, p. 19.

14. Boris Vasilevsky, Yelena Panina and Tatyana Kucher, "Poverty in NIS", *Eco Pravo-Kiiv*, 2003, available at www.ecopravo.kiev.ua/epk/docs/povertyof_nis.pdf, p. 3.

15. Available at www.protectionproject.org/projects.htm.

16. Ishkhanian, note 13 above, p. 18.

17. Ibid., p. 7.

18. UNDP, *Human Development Report 2002*, New York: UNDP, 2002.

19. UN Office on Drugs and Crime, note 2 above, p. 4.

20. Ceslav Ciobanu, *Frozen and Forgotten Conflicts in Post Soviet States*, US Institute for Peace, Senior Fellow Project, Jennings Randolf Program, available at www.usip.org/newsmedia/contacts/emailform/html, p. 1.

21. IOM Armenia, note 5 above, p. 11.

22. Patrick A. Taran and Gloria Moreno-Fontes Chammartin, "Getting at the Roots, Stopping Exploitation of Migrant Workers by Organized Crime", paper presented at International Symposium on UN Convention against Transnational Organized Crime, Turin, 22–23 February 2002, available at www.ilo.org/public/english/protection/migrant/download/pom/pom1e.pdf, p. 2.

23. Ishkhanian, note 13 above, p. 17.

24. Taran and Moreno-Fontes, note 22 above.

25. US Department of State, *Trafficking in Persons Report 2005*, Washington, D.C.: US Department of State, 2005.

26. US State Department, *Trafficking in Persons Report 2003*, Washington, D.C.: US State Department, June 2003, p. 156.

27. IOM Azerbaijan, note 5 above, p. 30.

28. International Organization for Migration, *Irregular Migration and Trafficking in Women. The Case of Turkey*, Geneva: IOM, November, p. 17.

29. US Department of State, *Trafficking in Persons Report*, Washington, D.C.: US Department of State, 2004.

30. Interview conducted by author with IOM Official, Dubai, January 2001.

31. Ibid.

32. US State Department, note 26 above.

33. IOM Azerbaijan, note 5 above, p. 36.

34. Ministry of Foreign Affairs of Turkey, "Turkey on Trafficking in Human Beings", updated country report, 25 June 2004, available at www.mfa.gov.tr/MFA_tr/.

Index

274